Bali and the Tourist Industry

ALSO BY DAVID SHAVIT
AND FROM MCFARLAND

*Hunger for the Printed Word:
Books and Libraries in the Jewish Ghettos
of Nazi-Occupied Europe* (1997)

Bali and the Tourist Industry

A History, 1906–1942

by DAVID SHAVIT

McFarland & Company, Inc., Publishers
Jefferson, North Carolina, and London

LIBRARY OF CONGRESS CATALOGUING-IN-PUBLICATION DATA

Shavit, David, 1936–
    Bali and the tourist industry : a history, 1906–1942 / by David Shavit.
       p.   cm.
    Includes bibliographical references and index.

    ISBN 0-7864-1572-X (softcover : 50# alkaline paper) ∞

    1. Bali (Indonesia : Province)—History—20th century.
    2. Tourism—Indonesia—Bali (Province)—History—20th century.
    3. Bali (Indonesia : Province)—Description and travel.   I. Title.
DS647.B2S53   2003
338.4'7915986—dc21   2003011420

British Library cataloguing data are available

©2003 David Shavit. All rights reserved

No part of this book may be reproduced or transmitted in any form or by any means, electronic or mechanical, including photocopying or recording, or by any information storage and retrieval system, without permission in writing from the publisher.

Cover photograph from the Koninklijk Instituut voor Taal-, Land- en Vokenkunde, Leiden, The Netherlands; background ©2000 Artville.

Manufactured in the United States of America

McFarland & Company, Inc., Publishers
  Box 611, Jefferson, North Carolina 28640
    www.mcfarlandpub.com

Acknowledgments

I wish to acknowledge the assistance I have received from several individuals and institutions. They have provided me with material and information that was helpful in the research and writing of this book. I particularly thank Elisabeth Edson Nordman of Palo Alto, California, for making "Katherine Philips Edson Remembered" available to me; Renée Roosevelt Denis of San Dimas, California; Alva Moore Stevenson, UCLA Oral History Program, University of California at Los Angeles; Anne Holliday, Stowitts Museum and Library, Pacific Grove, California; Harold L. Miller, State Historical Society of Wisconsin, Madison; C. L. Stroud and Renee Braden, National Geographic Society, Washington, D.C.; Deta S. Davis, Music Division, Library of Congress; Susan Boone and Susan Barker, Smith College Libraries, Northampton, Massachusetts, and Andrew L. Thomas, Smithsonian American Art Museum. The staff of the Information Delivery Service at Northern Illinois University Libraries, especially Ron Barshinger, Cherie Hauptman, and Amber Bates, have been, as always, very helpful.

Contents

Acknowledgments		v
Preface		1
Introduction		3
1.	The *Puputans*	5
2.	A New Vision of Paradise	14
3.	Paradise Gained	22
4.	*Dolce-Far-Niente*	49
5.	"Saint" Walter	73
6.	Last Paradise	83
7.	Goona-Goona	101
8.	Living Treasure	107
9.	Imaginary Museum	119
10.	Oh, Noble Breasts of Bali	132
11.	Little Grass Shacks on the Beach of Bali	135
12.	The Last Garden of Eden	146
13.	Belated Gauguins	165
14.	The Dark Side of Paradise	174
15.	Witch Hunt	180
16.	Paradise Lost	183
Chapter Notes		193
Bibliography		201
Index		211

Preface

While preparing a historical dictionary of the United States and Asia, I became aware of the activities and publications of several Americans who visited or lived in the island of Bali. Indeed, it was an American journalist who wrote a book about Bali, titled *The Last Paradise*, that inspired this book. The introduction to that book, by André Roosevelt, raised, for the first time, environmental issues regarding Bali. I have reviewed and read the contemporary travel narratives written by travelers and residents, as well as their memoirs and biographies.

The result of my reading and research is this book: a history of the development of tourism to Bali between World War I (after which Bali became a magnet to tourists) and the Japanese invasion of Bali during World War II.

My research raised many questions. Why did westerners go to the island of Bali, and why did some settle there as expatriates? What did they contribute to the development of Bali? How and why did the island of Bali become known as the "last paradise"? And was it indeed a paradise for the Balinese, or only for the American and European visitors and expatriates?

Stuart-Fox's bibliography of Bali, which covers the period from 1920 to 1990, provided the initial guide to the literature about Bali, but I have succeeded in finding several additional books and articles. In the last decade, several important biographies and general studies of Bali have appeared, which have been very useful. I also obtained access to some interesting unpublished material. Much of the material was available to me at the Don V. Hart Southeast Asian Collection at Northern Illinois University Libraries in DeKalb, Illinois, one of the major collections of Southeast Asian material in the United States.

Although a number of contemporary books have used initials or fictitious names to describe some of their contemporaries, I have succeeded in ascertaining the correct names for most of them, although not all.

Introduction

It is Bali's fate to have been officially declared a paradise.
—Allington Kinnard[1]

Bali is one of the islands of the Indonesian archipelago. Lying to the east of Java, it is the most westerly of the Lesser Sunda Islands. Bali is a small island, ninety miles at its widest and sixty miles from north to south. The mountain range which crosses the island from west to east includes four volcanoes. Bali also has four lakes and many splendid beaches. Beautiful natural scenery of luscious tropical vegetation and terraced rice fields dominate the landscape.

The Balinese managed to preserve their religious traditions and their cultural independence, against the advance of Islam. A unique form of Hinduism, on which Bali's culture was based, has been retained. Bali has magnificent temples and shrines, as well as colorful religious festivals and ceremonies. Traditional music, dance and theater, in various forms, expressing Balinese religion, play an important part in both secular and religious life, and provide an abundance of musical and dancing activities.

Declared a Dutch colony in 1908, Bali was controlled by the Dutch colonial authorities until 1942, when it was occupied by the Japanese army. Needing a source of revenue, the Dutch government soon realized that making Bali a tourist attraction was the best way to obtain the necessary funds. The image of Bali as the ultimate tourist destination was developed, and Bali began to be advertised as the "Jewel of the East," the "Island of the Gods," and the "Last Paradise." Tourist agencies were established and a regular shipping service to Bali was inaugurated in the early 1920s. The first hotel was opened in 1928.

The tourist propaganda emphasized the people of Bali and their singular culture. Bali was advertised as a "paradise island" in which noble, happy and spiritual men and women lived in innocence and in peace with nature and with each other. Sexuality was seen as a natural expression of their innocence. Tourist brochures, advertisements, and photographs, as well as a host of books and articles about the island, fueled this idyllic image of Bali. The island evolved into one of the most romantic stops on tourist itineraries, and Bali became a chic place to visit. Predominating in travel writing were sensual, often prurient, images of physically beautiful men and women coexisting in healthy, natural and erotic nudity, living simple lives on an enchanted isle, unspoiled by modernity. Stereotypical views of Bali sex life were perpetuated and exploited by the tourist industry. Photographs of bare-breasted Balinese women reinforced the image of Bali as an erotic paradise. Bali also acquired a reputation as a homosexual paradise.

The titled, the rich and the famous, as well as beachcombers, flocked to Bali during the 1930s. The Balinese became synonymous with artistic talent. Every Balinese was considered an artist. Scholars came to study the Balinese, their music and dance. Artists came to paint them. Some Europeans and Americans came as expatriates, living a comfortable life in inexpensive Bali.

The Balinese made little profit from out of the tourist traffic. They were the magnet that attracted the tourists, but the Dutch took all the profits. The western image of Bali as paradise had endured against all odds, but to the majority of the Balinese, the depression years were dark and dismal. As the war drew nearer, fewer tourists arrived, and, eventually, the "last paradise" which the tourists expected came to an end.

1

The *Puputans*

The soldiers of the Royal Netherlands Indies Army marched toward the royal palace of the rajah of Badung in south Bali in September 1906, to bring this rebellious independent kingdom of Bali under direct Dutch control. The heavily armed Dutch troops marched in orderly ranks along a long roadway that led to the royal palace in Denpasar, expecting the action to be more of a dress parade than a pitched battle.

The Rajah of Badung knew that his downfall was inevitable. Unwilling to face the humiliation of surrender, he chose the *puputan* ("ending"—the traditional sign of the ending of a kingdom) for himself and his entire court. As the Dutch troops drew closer to the palace, they observed flames and smoke rising over the palace and heard the wild beating of drums within its walls. Then a strange, silent procession emerged from the main gate of the palace. It was led by the rajah himself, seated in his gilded sedan chair, dressed in white ceremonial garments, splendidly bejeweled and armed with a magnificent *kriss*, and surrounded by his wives and children, his nobles, generals, ministers, courtiers, retainers, and other relatives. All were wearing white ceremonial dress, with flowers in their hair. They were richly ornamented and splendidly armed as if on their way to a temple feast. In spite of warnings, the procession continued to make its way toward the soldiers.

One hundred paces from the startled Dutch soldiers, the procession stopped. The rajah stepped down from the chair, gave a signal, and the ghastly ceremony began. A priest stabbed the rajah in his heart, and the others then began killing each other. Men, women, and boys attacked the Dutch troops with lances and spears, while some of the women mockingly threw jewels and gold coins at the stunned soldiers.

The Dutch troops reacted to the attack by firing their rifles into the surging crowd. A massacre ensued. The Balinese who were not shot down used their daggers to kill first the wounded around them and then themselves. As more and more persons kept emerging from the palace gate, the

The Puputan of the Rajah of Badung. From *Le Petit Journal*, Supplément Illustré, 14 October 1906.

mounds of hundreds of mangled and bloodied corpses rose higher and higher. The spectacle of looting was soon added to the scene of the carnage as Dutch soldiers stripped the valuables from the corpses and then began sacking the palace ruins.

Another *puputan* happened two years later in Klungkung. Dressed in white, the rajah of Klungkung led a procession toward the Dutch guns. Pausing at the center of the crossroad, he raised his sacred *kriss*, the most revered and magical of all his heirlooms, and stabbed it fiercely into the ground. According to prophecy, this dramatic act would have gouged a chasm deep enough to swallow all the kingdom's enemies. Unfortunately, a new era had overtaken Bali and the power of the rajah's *kriss* had waned. A Dutch bullet caught him in the knee and as he fell, another entered his heart. Amidst the roar of field guns, his six senior wives knelt beside him and plunged their own *krisses* into their breasts. It was the signal for the rest of the family and retainers, children included, to follow suit. The already burning palace was then systematically razed.

The last royal houses of Bali had chosen a glorious end rather than capitulate to the foreign invaders. The military conquest of Bali by the Dutch was finally completed. The whole island of Bali was now forcibly put under the direct rule of the Dutch colonial government.[1]

The *puputans* were not well received in the Netherlands. They were regarded as shameful affairs. The reports of the massacres and the looting deeply disturbed private citizens, religious groups, and even official agencies in Batavia and The Hague. The shock waves spread to London and Paris, and even to New York. Protests poured into the Dutch colonial office. The Dutch, who were under pressure, resolved to make amends. The protests raised over the military's brutality were a source of international embarrassment to the Dutch government, which attempted to atone for the bloodbath by displaying an image based on the preservation of Balinese culture and its promotion as a tourist attraction. The Dutch did everything to cover up the precise number of Balinese killed, writing off the violent outburst as a cultural curiosity of Bali. The affair could not be denied, but given some time it could be comfortably hushed up. And hushed up it was. The scar on the liberal imagination of the Netherlands produced by the massacres had to be healed, and preservation of Balinese culture, in combination with tourism, was the most effective balm for the healing process.

The Dutch government tried to obliterate the memory of its brutal intervention and the spectacular self-sacrifice of the Balinese nobility by developing a worthier image of its colonial policy in Bali. Seeking to renovate their image, the Dutch turned their efforts toward the two forces that would play a major role in molding Bali in the years to come: tradition and tourism.

The Dutch civil servants developed a scholarly description of Balinese society: Bali was incomparable and unique; Balinese people were prosperous, happy, independent, autonomous, and they were all artists; and the Dutch have done no harm to Bali. The Dutch tried to ease their conscience, and the Dutch government was eager for the world to think of Bali positively, and tourism was the best way to present positive images. The bloodbath had to be forgotten quickly, and it was soon forgotten, because for the next years Bali was to enjoy the *Pax Neerlandica*, an imposed peace that was soon considered to be an essential characteristic of Balinese culture.

Dutch Orientalists, employed by the government, held that Bali was a "living museum" of the Indo-Javanese civilization, the depository of the Hindu heritage that had been swept from Java by the arrival of Islam. In their view, the Hindu religion was the foundation of Balinese society, the guardian of its cultural integrity, and the inspiration of its artistic works. To the Dutch, Bali was a sanctuary, a world apart, fragile and unique, to be protected by the enlightened paternalism of colonial guardianship against pernicious foreign influences and the traumatizing impact of modernity. The Dutch scholar Gerrit Pieter Rouffaer, one-time director of the Bali Instituut, summarized in 1915 the prevailing position of the colonial administration:

> Let the Balinese live their own beautiful native life as undisturbed as possible! Their agriculture, their village-life, their own forms of worship, their religious art, and their own literature—all bear witness to an autonomous native civilization or rare versatility and richness. No railroads on Bali; no western coffee plantations; and especially no sugar factories! But also no proselytizing, neither by Mohammedan, nor Protestant, nor Roman Catholic. Let the colonial administration, with the strong backing of the Netherlands (home) government, treat the island as a rare jewel that we must protect and whose virginity must remain intact.[2]

Vicki Baum wrote later in the preface to her novel *A Tale from Bali*, "I would like to believe that the self-sacrifice of so many Balinese at that time had a deep significance, since it impressed upon the Dutch the need of ruling this proud and gentle island people as considerately as they have, and so kept Bali the paradise it is today."

The Dutch, however, began to present a more positive image of their colonial policy based on the preservation of Balinese culture and the development of tourism for a very pragmatic reason. Bali was regarded as "unspoiled," but it offered few commercial opportunities. There were no spices, and the island lacked lands suitable for commercial crops. Tourism seemed to be one of the few viable industries. The Dutch policy of making Bali the showcase of enlightened colonization earned the Dutch government its greatest claim to glory, although it profoundly disturbed Balinese society. The Dutch benevolence was also self-serving. It deliberately cultivated Balinese culture as a safeguard of the colonial policy of "peace and order."[3]

The Dutch succeeded in turning Balinese culture into an object that was repackaged as something that could be sold. By advertising Bali as a "paradise island," where happy peasants lived in quiet rural villages in harmony with nature, where a great Hindu civilization still respected its ancestors, gods, and kings, and where wise, proud priests preserved ancient traditions against the onslaught of modernity, the Dutch were able to both erase their problematic part in shaping Bali's history and increase their revenues by luring curious tourists to the island. The Western image of Bali became one of a noble, spiritual people living in peace with their environment and each other, and, most importantly, extending a warm welcome to their foreign guests. Lured by this vision of a tropical paradise on earth, a new European and American colony began to invade Bali.

The Dutch began to paternalistically promote Bali's positive attributes, and to create "the prettiest little exhibit in the whole of the Indies of Dutch efficiency and enlightenment." A growing number of concerned individuals began to celebrate the island's charms and idyllic qualities. Given the fragmented condition of Bali's society, the Dutch also strictly and paternalistically regulated the comings, goings, and many varied schemes being promoted by the many and assorted entrepreneurs, missionaries, and outright scam artists who invariably flocked to such places for an easy life and quick money. Extremely strict travel restrictions were imposed on such outsiders, making it difficult for all but the most enterprising of their ilk to visit—and cash in—on this new Eden.

The Dutch government claimed to protect the island from Christian missionaries in order to preserve "authentic" Balinese culture for posterity in all its artistic glory. The island would be an open-air exhibit featuring expensively restored temples and special "Hindu-Bali schools," which would teach children Balinese dance, gamelan music, drawing, and Hindu religion and philosophy. The attempt to safeguard "authentic" Balinese culture and society by conserving it in a pristine bell jar surrendered the island to the anthropological imagination and erotic fantasies of a large contingent of North Americans and Europeans.

The Dutch came to regard Bali as the cornerstone of their effort to contain the spread of Islamic radicalism and various nationalist and com-

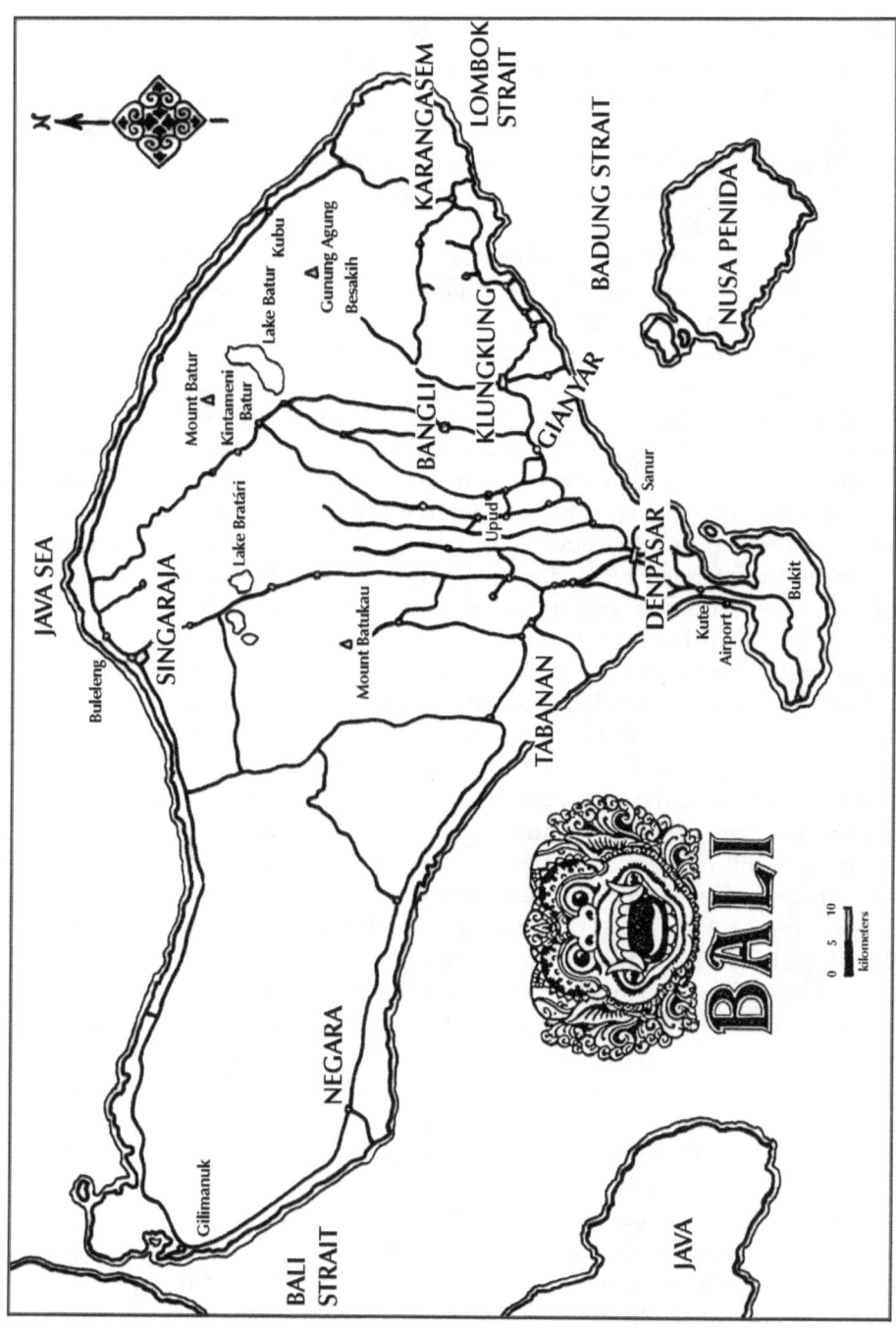

munist movements. As it turned out, it was not only against nationalism, communism, and Islam that Bali had to be protected, but against Christianity as well. Missionaries were encouraged neither by the Dutch nor by the Balinese. The Dutch Orientalists opposed missionary activities on the ground that religion and social order formed an inseparable whole in Bali. Therefore, by deliberately attacking the religion of the Balinese, missionary work would bring the collapse of their entire culture.

Bali was certainly not the place where missionaries could improve in any way the moral and physical standards of the people and it was hard to believe that they would succeed, opined Miguel Covarrubias, author of the book *Island of Bali*. Religion was to the Balinese more than spectacular ceremonies with music, dancing, and a touch of drama for virility. It was their law, the force that held them together. It was the greatest stimulus of their lives because it gave them their ethics, culture, wisdom, and joy of living by providing the exuberant festivity they loved. It was difficult to imagine that it would ever be supplanted by a bleak escapist faith devoid of beautiful and dramatic ritual.[4]

The missionaries decried the "despicable greed" of the Dutch government, which would not let them into Bali for fear that the missionaries might ruin a delightful native custom—the exposed upper half of the Balinese women—and thus lessen Bali's attraction for tourists. Missionaries complained that the Dutch attitude toward them was influenced entirely by commercial considerations. The Dutch public was highly amused by what they called "The Great War" between the government, and the tourism industry forces, and the missionaries who were supported furtively by the textile industry. As Ruth Masters Rickover, a student of international law, noted: "At issue was the exposed upper half of the Balinese women which the government and KPM wished to keep that way in the interest of the tourist trade."[5]

The occupying Dutch, however, were not entirely altruistic. If there was money to be made on the island of Bali, the Dutch made it, even if the product that was going to be sold for profit was of dubious nature. The greatest source of Dutch income on Bali during the decade following the *puputan* was opium. Although the Dutch knew well how dangerous this drug was to any society, they decided to make the most of what, by then was a well-addicted and captive Balinese opium market. Instead of out-

Opposite: Map of Bali. From Willard A. Hanna, *Bali Profile: People, Events, Circumstances (1001–1976)* (New York: American Universities Field Staff, 1976). Published with permission of the Institute of Current World Affairs, Inc., Hanover, New Hampshire.

lawing the drug, they opted to regulate it. The opium monopoly on Bali proved to be extremely profitable. But little of the money made in this nefarious way ever trickled down to the Balinese.[6]

Holland's official hands-off policy was often credited with preserving what was left of things Balinese, and with encouraging a renaissance of culture on the island. The Dutch endeavored to make Bali conform to their image. Not only was Balinese culture to be saved for tourists, but the Balinese people were to be taught by their new masters how to keep on being more authentically Balinese.

The Dutch soon found it difficult to keep a bureaucratic lid on this fantasyland called Bali. Soon after political matters had settled down, reports began filtering back to Europe and the Americas that the newly "discovered" and accessible island of Bali, not Hawaii, Tahiti, or the Virgin Islands, was the Last Paradise on Earth and the chic place to visit in this part of the world. Westerners could thus enshrine Bali as a romantic paradise and concoct fantastic stories about the essence of "The Balinese Character," about ancient village democracies, and the happy and harmonious integration of art and religion in daily life. These fairy tales, however, often degenerated into horror stories with pornographic overtones. Depicting a "natural" Bali that resembled the erstwhile Tahiti of Paul Gauguin, such seductive narratives portrayed a world uncontaminated by stultifying Victorian mores. It was an Arcadian landscape in which Western voyeurs could feast on nubile bodies and bare breasts, rejoice in the gorgeous physicality of Balinese men and disclose their residual homoerotic desires, and presumably take part in an uninhibited sexuality. The Dutch colonial regime, meanwhile, congratulated itself for having created tranquility and order in one of the most densely populated places in the entire world, where social tensions and desperate poverty were perceptible, and diseases such as tuberculosis and syphilis were endemic.

The tourists, artists, and scholars who sojourned in Bali between the two world wars were instrumental in popularizing the extravagant artistry of Balinese ceremonial pageants. The writings, paintings, photographs, and films brought back from the island forged a sensational image of Bali—an image that the promotional services of the emerging tourism industry quickly exploited. Not only did western visitors and their works certify and disseminate to the West the image of Bali as paradise, but also they identified Balinese society by its culture, which they saw mostly in terms of its artistic and religious activities.

The Western romance with Bali was largely composed of images of a tropical Eden where men and women—all prodigiously creative artists—lived in innocence, uncorrupted by Western acquisitiveness, and closely in touch with nature, of which the gods were a loving and protective expression. The Balinese were seen as happy, healthy, and even wealthy and free to do as their "naturally creative" impulses directed. Sexuality was seen as a natural expression of their innocence. These perceptions have been, in many cases, quite false, and the imagery they produced varied, but the central themes remained remarkably constant. Predominant in travel writing were sensual, often prurient, images of physically beautiful men and women coexisting in healthy, harmonious natural and erotic nudity, living simple lives on an enchanted isle that was unspoiled by modernity.

2
A New Vision of Paradise

"The name of Maurice Sterne is neither romantic nor glamorous. Yet it belongs to one of America's most important modern artists, one whose career trails the pervasive loveliness of the particular isle of Bali. It is the name of the man who discovered Bali for the Western world."[1]

Sterne was born in Libau, Russia, and spent his early youth in Moscow. When he was eleven or twelve, he and his widowed mother emigrated to the United States. Winning a traveling scholarship, he went to Europe and lived a bohemian life in Paris. He then started his travels, which took him to Egypt and Greece. A series of accidents took Sterne to India, Java, and Bali. He planned to go to Borneo, but he had forgotten his father's watch in the hotel in Surabaya, Java, went back to fetch it just before he was to sail away, and missed his boat. With a number of days to wait for the next boat, he asked the agent where he should go since he could not go at once to Borneo. The agent suggested Bali, so Sterne decided to make the excursion, "before the world tourists began to invade that island of romance." He got a ticket good enough for a one-month stay. The year was 1912.[2]

He went to northern Bali and did not like it at all. But one day in the bazaar he saw the group of strangers—beautifully formed men and women almost nude. He was amazed; they looked like ancient Greeks. He asked the Dutch official who they were. The official said, "They are South Balinese." Sterne asked, "Are there any more people like that in south Bali?" The Dutch official answered, "Oh, yes! They are all crazy in south Bali; they all go around like that." So Sterne went to south Bali. As he crossed the volcanic mountains to the southern part of Bali, the landscape became more beautiful hour by hour. On the south coast, he found an old bamboo hut near the river, and there he lived, settling down for a period of two years.[3]

Sterne's stay in Bali had a strong influence on his life and art. Out of that "exotic sojourn" came some of Sterne's best paintings. In Bali, he absorbed the artistic trends of the natives and borrowed their knowledge of the use of color, which served to enhance work already dignified by a sense of form and design. For various reasons it was a dark time in his life, and this darkness was projected in many of his drawings and paintings of the period. During his stay in Bali, he produced several thousand studies and drawings in various degree of completion, mostly on rice paper.

He was carried away by the beauty of the people. The men and women were, against a background of fantastically beautiful landscape, bare to the waist, presenting perfect brown-skinned models for his brush. He continued to work from his sketches, painting fantasy pictures of Balinese figures for all the remaining years of his life.

"Bali was a completely satisfying artistic experience," Sterne later told an interviewer. "The landscape, the beauty of the people, their exquisite aesthetic sense contributed to a greater whole, a completeness that one finds only in the greatest art. From the very beginning I found in South Bali beauty that moved my soul."

From the start, Sterne thought he had found the peace of the Garden of Eden on Bali. Geographically and culturally remote and only recently colonized by the Dutch, the island was scarcely tainted by contact with the West. Astonished by the paradisiacal lushness of the landscape, Sterne was even more enthralled by the physical beauty and grace of the Balinese people. On Bali, Sterne could satisfy his artist's appetite to study the human body as it was created. Like Gauguin he went native, adopting the dress—or undress—and the manners of the villagers.

There were two or three white people in Denpasar, the nearest town, but he did not go to the town. At first the Balinese resented his going into the temples, but when they saw that he respected their religion, they became kind and would tell him when anything interesting was to take place. Bali was a completely satisfying artistic experience for him. For two years he lived an enchanted, sensual dream, vowing repeatedly never to leave the island. Sterne was especially drawn to the hypnotic Balinese music and dance. Many of his drawings and paintings depict dancers at the elaborate religious festivals that were so much a part of Balinese life. Though often swooning in a trance, the dancers moved with exquisite grace to the intricate rhythms of the gamelan orchestra. Their dances reenacted legends of gods and heroes, conjuring a magic unity between past and present, myth and reality. The timeless character of Balinese dance represented for Sterne the "static ideal of the East." His paintings celebrated this ideal.[4]

In Bali, Sterne could not stop working. He felt it was a crime to sleep. But in spite of its surface harmony, Bali eventually became a place of enormous emotional strain for him. He could not seem to stop painting the singularly beautiful Balinese rituals. Many of the events took place at night, so that he seldom had enough sleep. He realized that he was an exile, surrounded by a way of life that would eventually destroy him. The silence, even the great, wandering eyes of the island women he made love to, seemed vacuous and unsatisfying.

When Sterne left Bali, he took with him hundreds of paintings and drawings, which were a "rare sensation" in New York City the next season. Sterne was vaulted into the vanguard of modern American artists. The review of the exhibit stated that, "Maurice Sterne has conventionalized and interpreted the spirit of Bali in a way like that in which Gauguin treated Tahiti."

Sterne never saw Bali again, but in his mind it remained a paradise although he knew that in later years it changed, becoming "westernized" in the worst sense of the word. The pure innocence of Balinese sexual freedom had been turned into exhibitionism by foreign exploiters. Even before he left there were warnings of the ugliness that would overwhelm the island. But the Bali he remembered made of every phase of daily life a ritual in which all the people participated. "Life was an undulating spectrum of colors which played against the most lush and fecund background, which moved to the constant, exotic pulsing of the Balinese music."[5]

Of the many image makers of Bali, two of the earliest were of particular importance: Wijnand Otto Jan (W. O. J.) Nieuwenkamp and Gregor Krause. It is to Neiuwenkamp—a Dutch explorer, adventurer, ethnologist, artist, art collector, and writer who made several visits to Bali in the early years of the twentieth century—that we owe the first albums, abundantly illustrated with drawings by the author, describing for the general public the island of Bali, the daily life of the people, and their artistic traditions. Above all, it was he who first called the attention of his compatriots to the beauty of the island that they had just conquered.

Nieuwenkamp, a multifaceted self-taught artist whose motto was *Vagando Acquiro*, "Wandering I Acquire," was the first European artist to visit Bali. He came not only to make his own art but to learn Balinese traditional painting as well. He first set foot on Bali in 1904, and felt as if he entered paradise. "I am now in Bali," he wrote to his wife, "and it suits me perfectly. What a heavenly place, always beautiful weather, always sunny, very artistic, beautiful trees, mountains, beaches, temples and pleasant people—in short a fantastic place, a small paradise."[6]

He explored the northern part of the island by bicycle to the amusement of the Balinese people, who had never seen such a thing. A stone relief immortalizing Nieuwenkamp riding his bike, which can still be seen in a little North Balinese village of Kubutambahan, shows how deeply the Balinese were impressed by the novelty.

2. A New Vision of Paradise

The Man on the Bicycle. The first man to bring a bicycle to Bali, Nieuwenkamp was immortalized in a stone relief at the Meduwekarang Temple in Kubutambahan. When the relief was repaired after an earthquake, the wheels of the bicycle were transformed into lotus and infinite knot. Courtesy of J. F. K. Kits Nieuwenkamp, The Stichting Nieuwenkamp, St Vleuten, Holland.

He returned two years later to purchase Balinese objects for several Dutch scientific institutions, and was witness of the invasion of the Dutch troops at Sanur, and the *puputan* of the rajah of Badung and his followers. He was totally impressed with the Balinese people and utterly shocked by the despicable behavior of the Dutch occupying forces. He visited Bali again in 1917, and although he later settled in Italy, he returned to Bali again in 1925 and finally in 1937. He systematically crossed the island six times from north to south, visiting areas no European had ever visited before, and was the first European to climb the sacred Mount Batur. He authored the most important early book on the island, *Bali en Lombok* (1906–1910). His greatest accomplishment was the completion of more than one thousand drawings, etchings, lithographs, and paintings, many of Bali. Upon his return to the Netherlands, he started encouraging his colleagues to share the Bali experience with him. He played a critical role in creating the myth of Bali, most importantly through his support of the German doctor and amateur photographer Gregor Krause. Together in Amsterdam in 1918, they held the first exhibition of Balinese art that had firmly rooted the Bali myth in Europe.

Gregor Krause, a German physician who had been commissioned as a temporary medical officer in the Royal Netherlands Indies Army, was posted to Bali in 1912. He was sent to Bangli, a highland village in central Bali. He remained there for eighteen months, attending to more than ten thousand patients. A keen and sensitive amateur photographer, he traveled throughout Bali during his spare time, equipped with the world's earliest portable camera, a 35 mm Leica, and took more than four thousand photos of Balinese people, places, and objects. He was the first photographer to document the island systematically. "I took the photographs with a small camera," he wrote, "in such a way that nobody even noticed that I was taking them, and sought out neither the most beautiful nor the most ugly ... but there was a tendency toward the beautiful because the Balinese are inconceivably beautiful."[7]

In 1920, four hundred of Krause's photographs, accompanied by his own text, were published in two volumes in Hagen in Westfalen, Germany. The book was such a publishing success that its first printing was sold out within six months. A second edition appeared in 1922, and a revised edition was published in 1926 in Munich. A French translation appeared in Paris in 1930, and English translations appeared in 1988 and 2000.

The book was the decisive first step in the tourist promotion of Bali. The success of this book, as its subsequent editions attest, was related to the great care with which the author emphasized the physical beauty of Balinese bodies and to his enthusiasm for the photographic theme of Balinese women at their bath. Krause's sensual photographs of Balinese people firmly established Bali as a paradisiacal land unlike no other on earth. This "inconceivable beauty" Bali owed primarily to its women. The breasts of Balinese women constituted a major attraction to the island during that time, but the text accompanying Krause's photographs gave a better idea of the European perception of Bali when the first tourists were beginning to arrive. Twenty-six of the 176 photographs in Krause's 1922 edition of

Bali featured nude bathers. These images ignited a worldwide obsession with the Balinese body and particularly the bare-breasted female.

The photographs and textual narrative of Gregor Krause were instrumental in focusing global attention on Bali's picturesque and cultural features. The publications were pivotal in attracting a larger public to Bali by fueling a passion for the exotic among wanderers and artists. The popularity of his publications in Europe and elsewhere, and the frequency with which subsequent visitors to Bali cited the inspiration of his photographs, attested to the pivotal role photography played in establishing Bali's fame.

"The inhabitants of Bali were beautiful and, incredibly as it may seem, inconceivably beautiful," Krause wrote. "Anyone at all in Bali, seated by the side of the road or elsewhere, who bothered to simply look at what passes before him, will begin to doubt the reality of what he sees. Everything is beautiful, the bodies, the clothing, the gait, each pose, each movement. The Balinese women are beautiful, as beautiful as one can imagine, with a physiologically simple and dignified beauty, full of Eastern nobility and natural chastity. For these happy people, life on earth seems to be an almost uninterrupted festival, an ecstasy of overflowing joy in life and of gratitude and devotion to the Gods."[8] Krause was furious with God that he was not born in Bali.

The book struck a chord in a Europe newly emerging from four years of world war and still struggling through the hard and troubled years in its wake. The effect of the photographs on Europe was dramatic. Here were pictures of a hallowed land of love, peace, and beauty—everything that Europe would have liked to be. The poetic testimony to Bali's remarkable landscape, people, and culture left a deep impression on those who saw it. Bali must have seemed to offer answers to many of the problems afflicting the industrial nations. The publication also coincided with an era of fascination with the beauty of the unclothed human body, and the images of healthy, near-naked Balinese possessed an appeal they may not have had at other times.

The book was significant in telling the world about the then little-known island and its extraordinary culture, and it helped persuade more writers and photographers to follow him. It found a readership eager to believe that the photographs depicted an earthly perfection. It appealed to visitors seeking an unsullied paradise far away from the despoliation of Europe.

Krause, as one of the most important image creators of Bali, became celebrated as the man whose photographs gave Europe "a new vision of paradise." His photographs portrayed Bali as a weird and wonderful place, a society at one with nature, where mud-walled villages and rice terraces eventually gave way to the ever present jungle. It was a feudal world in which princes sat cross-legged dispensing justice, and the gods were placated with sacrificial gifts. Men attempted to stab themselves in frenzied dances while the women brought more and more offerings, and fantastic pillars of flowers and fruit filled temple forecourts with color. The scantily clad bodies of the men and women exuded an air of vitality as they wove their way through the rice fields or posed handsomely beside traditional dwellings.

The German author, Vicki Baum, later wrote: "It must, I think, have been in 1916, and hardly anybody had heard of the existence of a little island called Bali, that I came by chance into the possession of some very beautiful photographs. One of my friends had got them from an acquaintance—a doctor who lived in Bali. The pictures made such an impression on me that I coaxed my friend into giving them to me. To these men and animals and landscapes, I turned again and again, whenever the discomforts to which my generation was exposed—war, revolution, inflation, emigration became unbearable. It was not until 1935 that I could afford to make a voyage to Bali. My first visit was the realization of a lifelong wish without a hint of disillusionment."[9]

The pervasive influence of Krause's book is indicated by references made to it on numerous occasions by later visitors, including Walter Spies and Miguel Covarrubias. Time and again those who saw the remarkable photos would decide that they must visit this island. The result was a generation of idealistic visitors, many of whom would stay and create a "golden age."

The beauty of the Balinese women was important in the blooming fame of Bali as the "Island of the Bare Breasts." Images of a pristine island populated by a seemingly innocent people with no shame about nudity, combined with their exotic sensuality, contrasted strongly with the inhibited modesty of European society. Krause's role in the creation of the myth of "Bali Paradise" cannot be overestimated. It would not be an exaggeration to say that his book of photographs had the single greatest impact on the spread of Bali's fame until the publication of Covarrubias's *Island of Bali*.

Krause's book had everything needed to entice those dreaming of an Eden outside the despoiled and decadent Europe. Unquestioning in his dedication to the cause of colonialism, Krause reduced the *puputan* to the level of timeless tourist exotica, having no fundamental effect on Balinese society. His chapter on the passing of the last princes of Bali concludes with the words of Balinese peasant farmers working the fields while their princes were being killed: "It is the will of the Gods."[10] In his treatment of the massacre as an unreal event with no meaning for the majority of Balinese, Krause's book was a blatant apology for colonialism. The photographs in his book, however, said more than the text. So strong were these images that they acted as a magnet for future generations of tourists and travelers.

The first travel guide to Bali in English appeared in 1914. Because transportation and lodgings for travelers were in a stage of development and a little primitive, the Official Tourist Bureau did not recommend Bali to tourists who wanted comfort. But those who did not mind roughing it a little would never regret making the trip because, "so many interesting and beautiful things will be encountered there."[11]

A most delightful trip to the island of Bali was recommended for tourists whose time was not too limited. The great drawback to this trip was that Bali did not possess any hotels at all, compelling the travelers to stay in the government rest houses, which had a limited number of rooms. The rest houses provided good meals, drinks, and good beds with sheets, but they did not provide blankets or towels. The rate at Denpasar's rest house was five guilders (about two dollars) a day. Parties larger than three could not visit Bali at one time. Travel on the island was done by trap and in some places just by horseback. The guidebook concluded that Bali was undoubtedly one of the most interesting and beautiful islands, and the "beauty stop par excellence."

3
Paradise Gained

> What was it that brought tourists in their thousands half-way across the world to Bali from America and Europe? Not altogether, perhaps, the play of lights and shadows on the rice fields, nor yet the slopes of the volcano. What was this dream that passed with such regrettable swiftness—often in so short a time, indeed, as thirty-six hours. To spend which in the island cruising Britishers and Americans were willing to spend hundreds of pounds and weeks at sea? These lures were certainly potent enough in their way, but there was something else which the shipping company did not have to express in print. Their brochure's cover picture of a native girl in two colors, brown and red, told the story better than words. A feature of Bali's lure that could not be lightly dismissed was nothing more nor less than the human mammary gland.
>
> Cedric Belfrage[1]

The need for new sources of revenue, the policy of being seen to be preserving "native" culture, and perhaps some guilt, combined to produce a Dutch colonial policy of making Bali a tourist destination. The tourist vocation of Bali, turning the island into an object of curiosity for westerners in search of the exotic, was the result of deliberate decisions made by the Dutch. The Dutch decided to establish the island as a living museum of Indo-Javanese civilization. Bali was not allowed to be modern; it was not supposed to be touched by new ideas. Although the Dutch administration understood little of the society on which it had imposed its authority, it had some idea about what that society should look like and it endeavored to conform Bali to that image. It was not enough that Balinese cultural heritage be rescued from the onslaught of modernization. The Balinese people had to be taught by their new overlords how to remain authentically Balinese—such was the aim of the cultural policy known as the "Balinization"

Opposite: The front cover of *Bali*, a travel brochure, published in 1930 by the Officieele Vereeniging voor Toeristenverkeer in Nederlandsche-Indie in Batavia, Netherlands East Indies.

3. Paradise Gained

of Bali. Once restored to its pristine splendor, Balinese culture could then be presented to the appreciation of the outside world. But part of the "Balinization" of Bali was also the intrusion of the colonial government into the sexual life of the Balinese.[2]

Bali conformed well to the age. It offered dazed westerners the harmony and satisfaction which had been replaced in Europe by the slaughter of World War I. Bali became a popular destination due to tourists who spread the island's fame, but were wishing to keep the paradise they had discovered for themselves.

Robert Koke, proprietor of the Kuta Beach Hotel in the 1930s, stated: "Everybody in Bali was an expert whether they had been here for a week or ten years. It was like some fanciful dream where every person claimed to have been the first to have discovered this or done that. For the most part most of the island had been explored long before any of us came."[3] Job De Jong, wife of the head of Denpasar's electricity department, was a remarkable woman with a sharp tongue and a deep insight into Balinese ways and culture. She loved the island and its people as few westerners did. Once, when asked to write a text for a KPM (short for Koninklijk Pakestvaart Maatschappij, or Royal Packet Navigation Company) tourist book, her rather characteristic reply was that if she had been asked three weeks after her arrival, she would have agreed without hesitation, but having lived on the island for nine years she had come to realize only too well how little she really understood Balinese culture.[4]

Despite all the exaggerations and layers of tourist propaganda, the island, its people, and their culture were genuinely singular. If any one place deserved such appellations as the "Island of the Gods" and the "Dawn of Paradise" then it was Bali. One important aspect of the myth was the obvious need of the western psyche to project this image of paradise on another people without asking their permission—even if in many ways the reputation was deserved. This was the stuff that dreams were made of.

The Association for Tourist Traffic in Netherlands India was founded in Batavia in 1908 by representatives of commercial banks and rail, insurance, and shipping companies. The KPM, which had a monopoly on shipping in the Indonesian archipelago, was a member of the association. In the same year, this government-subsidized association opened an Official Tourist Bureau in Batavia which established relations with the principal tour operators of the time and installed representatives abroad. Its field of action was extended in 1914 to Bali, when is was deemed that the pacification of the island was complete, and the government replaced the occupying army with a civil authority. Travel in Bali was considered safe, and

3. Paradise Gained

Bali was christened in the KPM's brochures as the "Gem of the Lesser Sunda Isles."

Bali had to be made accessible. Realizing the tourist potential of Bali, the Dutch authorities made an economic decision to try to fill the berths of the empty KPM boats, which were returning from Singapore after delivering their loads of pigs, with European travelers. It was "a decision the Balinese have been trying ever since to recover from!"

Realizing the advantages of the island, the KPM issued tourist brochures that featured images of Bali and followed them with a series of advertisements in English, all rhapsodizing about Bali as an enchanted Garden of Eden. For example:

> TO BALI
> Oh! Linger a while
> In this wonderful Isle
> Enjoy your trips
> On "all-white" ships
> By K.P.M.[5]

and

> BALI
> You leave this
> Island with a
> Sigh of regret
> And as long
> As you live
> You can never
> Forget this Garden of Eden.[6]

"Do not fail to visit Bali, the enchanting island with its interesting population, ever so full of joy—the land of peculiar customs and magnificent temples. Nobody has ever regretted a tour through Bali."[7]

Thilly Weissenborn, the first major female photographer of the Netherlands Indies, "brought the romantic qualities ... to bear on the mountains, temples, women and princes of the island of Bali," and had great impact with her best-known photograph of a young dancing girl seated before a gong, which captured all the lure of Bali, and which became a recurrent image of Bali.

> It has the quality of an invitation, the girl's hand raised as if she is beckoning us to come to Bali, but at the same time she does not look directly into the camera. Her eyes turn mysteriously, as if she has the

BALI

The Official Tourist Bureau has been instrumental in inducing hundreds of tourists to visit Bali and so far as we are aware not one has ever regretted the decision.

Bali is easily reached by steamer from Sourabaya—an over-night trip. Motor cars are available for tours throughout the island, and comfortable, if not luxurious, accommodation may be had at the Government *pasanggrahans*.

No visitor to the Dutch East Indies should fail to include Bali in his itinerary. The additional cost is negligible — the experience cannot be duplicated anywhere else in the world, regardless of cost.

Descriptive literature will be sent gratis upon request

OFFICIAL TOURIST BUREAU

"Travel Talks Concerning the Netherlands East Indies." Advertisement for Bali by the Official Tourist Bureau, Weltevreden, Java. From *Inter-Ocean*, January 1927.

inscrutability of the whole of Asia under her gorgeously carved and elaborate headdress. Her costume and appearance do not show the kind of fresh and natural sexuality evinced by the women photographed topless in the street. Instead her charm comes partly from the sexual distance implied by her youth, as if she not only held the promise of hidden pleasures and fecundity, but maintained the remoteness of an ancient yet young civilization. The flower she holds, like the gold flowers in her head dress, speak of the natural lushness of the island, and the decoration of her dress implies that this natural lushness is closely linked to cultural riches. It is no accident that this photograph was so frequently chosen by the tourist authority for reproduction in the tourist pamphlets.[8]

The KPM and the other lines also sponsored a number of early tourist pamphlets and publications, the most lavish of which was the journal *Sluyter's Monthly*, the first tourist magazine of the Netherlands Indies. It was published in Batavia by an insurance and shipping company, and was later renamed *Inter-Ocean: A Netherlands East Indian Magazine Devoted to Malaysia and Australasia*. In this journal appeared the first effusive reports in English, such as the articles by Myron Zobel. A host of other books and articles on the island fed the romantic image of Bali and evolved the island into one of the most romantic stops on the tourist itinerary.

Bali was then accessible by boat from Surabaya, Java, and travelers could get around the island by horse or by automobile and—space permitting—stay overnight in the government rest houses used by Dutch officials on their inspection tours around the island. But tourists did not begin to visit Bali in earnest until 1924. In that year, the KPM introduced a weekly steamship service between Singapore, Batavia, Semarang, and Surabaya in Java, to Buleleng in Bali, and to Makassar in the Celebes, when it decided to carry passengers on the boats it sent to Buleleng to pick up loads of copra, coffee, and pigs. This line, called the Bali Express, soon earned the unflattering nickname, "Babi Express" (*babi* meaning "pig" in Malay).

The down trip of the "Pig Express" must have been far more pleasant then the return, for though the ship was kept scrupulously clean, a breeze from the direction of the afterdeck, where a couple of thousand pigs were penned in rattan crates, must have been "something requiring a bit of philosophy to cope with." Soon after, the KPM agent in Singaraja was appointed as the representative of the Official Tourist Bureau for Bali, on hand to help tourists hire a taxi with an English-speaking guide or reserve a room in the government rest house of their choice. The Tourist Bureau also published a short guidebook, the first dealing exclusively with Bali. It

The Bali Myth. A studio image by the Dutch photographer Thilly Weissenborn. This photograph was used in official tourist brochures of the 1920s and 1930s. Courtesy of the Photo and Print Collection of the Koninklijk Instituut voor Tall-, Land- en Volkenkunde (KITLV), Leiden, Holland.

did not take long before the dirty postcard industry had also reached the island, where some Balinese were willing models.

Bali began hosting a steady stream of wandering westerners who came to Bali to take refuge from the stresses and restrictions of the modern world. During those days, a westerner of even moderate financial means could live comfortably in Bali. It was only after World War I that Europeans and Americans started to visit the island by the hundreds; indeed, it became fashionable to do so. Among the early visitors to Bali were the French statesman Georges Clemenceau, the Indian poet Rabindranath Tagore, the English authors Somerset Maugham, H. G. Wells, and Violet Clifton, and Frank Hedges Butler, a British balloonist and pioneer of flying and one of the first persons in England to own an automobile. Since the turn of the century scores of foreign painters have visited or lived in Bali. "Some were good, some were great, and most have been forgotten." The Swedish artist Fröken Tyra de Kleen, who came to Bali to study its sacred dances, lived and worked there for almost ten years, and wrote the first article in English about Balinese dance, which appeared in *Sluyter's Monthly*. Other early visitors included the English artist and traveler Hilda May Gordon, who sketched a volcano in the act of eruption while in Bali, the Swedish artist John Sten, who rented a house in Karangasembut died a few months after arriving in Bali, and the American painter William Frederick Ritschel. The French artist Gabrielle Ferrand, traveled alone through Bali, an activity not without danger.

"Six o'clock in the morning," Ferrand wrote. "On the horizon Bali emerges from the Oriental dawn like a fairy pyramid of green. Its base as a nimbus of thin, transparent fog, above which rises a chain of mountains, as with a fur, with a luxuriant vegetation of palms, forest trees and shrubbery. We draw near the coast and the ship is at once surrounded by native boats which dance over the waves like so many cocoanut, and we go ashore upon this hospitable isle which appears as an Eden in the radiant daybreak. There is a joyousness in the air, in the glances which are directed at me, in the languid softness of the morning sky and in the gay laughter with which I am received. The novel atmosphere of the country is attributable as much to the half-naked natives whose skins are of bronze with golden high lights as to the villages, temples and palaces, constructed, the first of clay with thatches of rice straw, the others of lofty piles of pale gray stone, pricked out here and there with soft violet-rose bricks and invariably covered with moss about the base."[9]

The Dutch artist Willem Dooijewaard, who befriended in Bali a fellow impressionist painter, the Austrian Roland Strasser, left together for a trip to China, Tibet, Mongolia, Japan, and India, before returning to Bali.

"L'enthousiaste a Bali—Lovely!!" Cartoon by O. Fabrès. From *Aux Indies Neerlandaises* (Amsterdam: P. N. van Kampen & Zoon N. V., 1934).

Strasser, who stayed in Bali almost eighteen months, later recalled: "What I found in Bali was of quite a different character—the soothing inducement of a delightful language and charming people. Here the nights were ablaze with distant stars and always full of the syncopated music of the Gamelans which accompanied dance and drama. The love of the Balinese for elaborate religious ceremonies is universal. The people were shy and unaccustomed to being painted as they engaged in cock fighting, ritual dancing, or their professional ceremonies. It was truly fascinating to work and live among such graceful wealth of everyday life."[10]

Pieter Adriaan Jacobus (P. A. J.) Moojen, a multi talented Dutch architect and painter who later designed the much-praised Netherlands Indies Pavilion for the 1931 Paris Colonial Exposition and who accompanied the first Balinese dance troupe to visit Europe, was an avid collector of Balinese art and a student of Bali architecture. His book, *Bali Kunst*, has been the best book on Balinese architecture. He was also one of the main participants in the founding of the Bali Museum in Denpasar.

Violet Clifton, an Englishwoman who spent very little of her life in England and traveled abroad many years, reported that "the villages were gloomy, walled-in and dirty; lean dogs prowled about, dogs that none may kill, because, maybe, the soul of an ancestor dwells therein. No man may kill the dogs, but all men may kick them." "There goes somebody's father," said Talbot Clifton, Violet's husband, as an unhappy cur went screaming down a lane. Frank Clune estimated that there were one million dogs—all barkers, too—in Bali. The dogs live on the rats in the rice fields. "No dogs, no rice."[11]

Passengers on the KPM ships disembarked at Bulelang on Friday morning and departed on the same boat returning from Makassar on Sunday evening, giving them just enough time to make a quick trip around the island by automobile, via Denpasar and Lake Batur. The tourists would be off-loaded from the steamers in small boats that would take them through the surf, after which helpful Balinese would carry them onto dry land.

Up until the late 1920s, there were no hotels on the island, but the Netherlands Indies government made good use of the rest houses (known in Malay as *pasanggrahan*). To accommodate the growing inflow of tourists to Bali, the government allowed them to use those rest houses, originally designed to lodge Dutch officials on their periodic visits to the island. The Official Tourist Bureau reported that the accommodation in the government rest houses, little inns with three or four bedrooms, was comfortable if not luxurious, but visitors' opinions varied.

Myron Zobel, editor of the fan magazine *Screenland*, and author of several articles about Bali in *Inter-Ocean*, reported that in the little rest houses, run by a Balinese caretaker, there was peace, there were no crowded lobbies, noisy dining rooms, or hectic guests. "As long as the rest houses prevail, Bali will keep its charm. With the first hotel will come the rubberneck wagons and the huge tourist parties with all their 'alarums and excursions.'"

Zobel and his party lived in the rest house at Klungkung. During their stay they had the house completely to themselves and the staff were like their personal servants. They lived there for twelve dollars a day. Four dollars of this sum paid for the rental of a brand new Buick, including a chauffeur and his assistant. Of the other eight dollars, forty cents went for the chauffeur's board, twenty cents for garaging the car, and one dollar and forty cents covered the cost of bottled water, beer, wine, and ice. The remaining six dollars covered the cost of the double room and meals: early morning coffee, an excellent breakfast of eggs, toast, tea, jam, and fruit, an incomparable *rijstafel* ("Dutch housewife's gift to the colonies") for lunch, comprising about two dozen varied dishes from chicken to shrimp, afternoon tea and a thoroughly first rate dinner. Their private staff included a chauffeur, footman, butler, serving man, second maid, scullery maid, and cook. Considering their scale of living, twelve dollars a day did not strike Zobel as excessive.[12]

Oswald Hering described a resthouse: "The bungalows are comfortable....

The doors and windows are screened and a canopy of mosquito netting hangs on the beds. Each bed is provided with a Dutch wife. This is a cylindrical bolster about three feet long and a foot in diameter. It lies longitudinally in the center of the bed and you drape your arms and legs about it. It is designed to provide an air space between your limbs and is a most comfortable contrivance in a tropical climate. I soon found that I couldn't get to sleep without my Dutch wife."[13]

Templeton Crocker reported that the rest houses were "really small hotels, where, with a Dutch indifference to surroundings, a guest is as secluded as if he were living under a tree in the Avenue de l'Opera." In the evenings, the guests gathered in their open porch living rooms, which were lit by a single hanging electric bulb covered with a large pink silk shade. If one cared to do so, it was easy to see from the main street how everyone's time was occupied, what pajamas were worn, and what was eaten for breakfast.[14]

E. Alexander Powell, on the other hand, had a completely different experience. He "passed" the night in the small rest house at Denpasar. He wrote that he *passed* the night, refusing to toy with the truth to the extent of writing that he slept. Why they called it a rest house he could not imagine. Only in a zoo would he have found himself on such intimate terms with so many forms of animal life as he had in that rest house. Cockroaches nearly as large as mice, spiders, centipedes, ants, and beetles made his bedroom an entomologist's paradise. Some large-winged animal, presumably a fruit bat entered by the window and circled the room like an airplane. Judging from the sounds that came from beneath the bed, he gathered that the room also harbored a snake or a large rat, though he was not certain as he saw no reason to investigate. A family of lizards disported themselves on the ceiling, and when he menaced them with a stick they departed so hastily that one of them abandoned his tail, which dropped onto the wash stand. A squadron of mosquitoes—a sort of *escadrille de chasse*, as it were—kept him awake until daybreak, when they were relieved by a skirmishing party of *cimex lectulariae*, which are well known in America by the shorter and less polite name of 'bed bugs.' Fishes only were absent, but Powell was convinced that their neglect of him was due to ignorance of his presence; had they known of it, he felt certain that the climbing fish, which was one of the curiosities of those waters, would have flopped on to his pillow.[15]

The food served at the rest house was excellent. The *rijstafel*, called "the Dutch lunch which takes twenty-three men and a boy to serve!" took a long time to eat. According to Hering, there was plenty of good food on the island for everyone. Louis Couperus, Dutch novelist, essayist, short

3. *Paradise Gained* 33

"Rijstafel—the serpent one can see and taste." Cartoon by O. Fabrès. From *Aux Indies Neerlandaises* (Amsterdam: P. N. van Kampen & Zoon N. V., 1934).

story writer, and journalist, visited Bali as special correspondent of the *Haagsche Post*, and wrote: "Bali is an idyll. A strange Oriental idyll, wonderful in line and colour. We must not compare it to other idyll. Bali is itself. Bali is Bali and nothing else."[16]

Jan Poortenaar, a self-taught Dutch painter, visited Bali in 1921 and expressed enthusiasm for the island. He then wrote a book, illustrated with his own paintings and drawings.

> Bali, state the guide books, covers only one sixth of the area of the Netherlands, but they make no computation of the overwhelming proportion of dogs which it boasts. As soon as one leaves the main roads and essays a footpath, a yard, a temple-court, a dozen of these beasts are at one's heels, shrieking, barking, yelping, howling as only the dogs of Bali can. Against their unceasing din there is no hope of enjoying the sublime mood engendered by the stately waringin trees. Perhaps these innumerable beasts are a dispensation of Providence to put to the test the tourist's genuineness in his enthusiasm for the island, for they cause many visitors to stay in their automobiles and so leave the life of Bali, its arts and crafts intact. Which, for a country so threatened by the disaster of becoming a fashion, must be a real boon.
>
> Other factors combine to protect Bali and its arts from a plethora of popularity. There is hardly any accommodation for travelers and no comforts; hardly any motor cars, the *sine que non* of existence to the dilettante tourists of the East, without which nothing can be seen. To most tourists it will not sound inviting that the boys in a rest house not only use a serviette to clean the plates, but also use it for those functions where your European finds a handkerchief a valuable asset. The fastidious, therefore, will be advised to stay at home. Moreover, the roads are seldom used, and if here or there something goes wrong with your car no help is likely to be forthcoming.[17]

Like so many of those who followed him, Poortenaar was afraid of what tourism might do to Bali. His outrage was incited by the following advertisement:[18]

> BURNING OF THE DEAD
> Have you ever seen this ritual Buddhist Ceremony
> (in connection with the Popular Festivals) ? ? ? ? ?
> Come with us to Bali ! !
> Motor-car trips, Swimming, Rowing, Dancing.
> Riding. Visits to Temples and Museums. Lawn
> Tennis. Football, etc., etc.
> UNDER THE MANAGEMENT OF A THOROUGHLY
> RELIABLE COURIER

And Poortenaar concluded that two things constituted Bali's glory. The first was that the land was of a nature and structure that could be apprehended and therefore enjoyed. The second charm of Bali was that there were so few Europeans. "Should Bali become all the fashion then Bali shall soon be no more."[19]

The Dutch steamship line was almost scooped by the activities of an enterprising clique of friendly rivals. From the start, the KPM had to face the competition of several colorful characters, such as Jacob Minas, a Persian-Armenian entrepreneur who owned a traveling film house and operated, in partnership with André Roosevelt, an American adventurer, the Roosevelt-Minas Tourist Office, representing American Express and Thomas Cook on the island. And then there was "Princess" Patimah, a Balinese woman mentioned by many of the travelers. Thanks to the tourists, she became the richest businesswoman on the island, owner of a fleet of taxis, goldsmith workshops, and weaving studios.

Jacob Minas introduced motion pictures to the Balinese villages by traveling with a portable projector. He later established the first movie theatre in Buleleng. At first he cleaned up because all the Balinese had to see the miracle. But, not used to paying for entertainment, they soon grew bored with something they could not understand and the movies were a failure. It seemed to Helen Eva Yates as another proof that Bali would not be spoiled by foreign intentions. As soon as curiosity over a novelty was appeased, the Balinese would have no more of it. Realizing the tourist potential, Minas started picking up passengers off the KPM ships who had been put ashore by rowboat at Buleleng with little advice but an admonition to avoid Minas's attentions. Louis Couperus described Minas, who acted as his chauffeur and guide, as a person who possessed all the admirable qualities of his Armenian race. "Remember his name well, Reader!" Couperus admonished, and "turn to him with complete confidence should you be traveling to Bali!"

The British journalist Elinor Mordaunt also declared that Minas was Bali "in some queer way," who had "that mixture of extreme business ability and affability; that faculty for taking hold and keeping hold; of missing no possible opportunity of doing business with kindliness; that complete integrity; that imagination and appreciation; that power to grasp the needs of others, almost before they themselves have had time to realize them for themselves."[20]

Mordaunt, who stayed some time at the resthouse in Munduk village was one of the few visitors who had much critical to say about the Balinese. "What the people here call me it is best, judging from the faces, the rude gestures of the boys who shout after me, to leave to the imagination; for though the tourist guide books include the people of Bali among its beauties no word could be said for their manners."

> The women are in general the worst slatterns I have ever seen; wearing their masses of dark coarse hair ties in a sort of knot, like a

—— NOT TO SEE ——

BALI

THE

"GARDEN OF EDEN"

IS TO MISS

THE LOVELIEST AND MOST FASCINATING SPOT ON EARTH

THE

MINAS-ROOSEVELT TOURIST OFFICE
SINGARADJA — BALI

is entirely at your service to show you the only medieval country now existing in their new and comfortable **Fiat Cars**
We Personally Conduct our Parties

For Particulars see

AMERICAN EXPRESS Co.
ORIENT TOURING Co.
THOS. COOK & SON, RAYMOND & WHITCOMB

and all the reliable touristic firms —

Only 16 hours from Java —

horse's tail with the end hanging out, the whole thing slithering sideways. Their lips are reddened with betel-nut, slobbered over, or distorted round, a disfiguring wad of tobacco, which sticks for more than an inch out of their mouths.

These same guide books extol them for their habit of bathing; but it seems to me that it is only—if one may so express it—the torrid zone with which they concern themselves: sitting in the streams which run along either side of almost every road, with their feet and legs and upper portions of their bodies completely out of the water, scowling around them, as never before have I seen any women scowl; dropping their rags of clothes at the edge of the road and picking them up and putting them on to their still damp bodies without so much as a shake.[21]

Mah Patimah was a local notoriety about whom many legends were told. According to one story, when she was a little child she was seen by a rajah who made her one of his hundred wives and kept her in his palace where she, a queen, danced for him and answered his every want. Then the rajah sickened and died. His widows made ready to give themselves to the flames, but Patimah stole at midnight from the palace, fled across the island, and put herself under the protection of the Dutch. According to another story, she was a princess and one of the widows of the rajah of Klungkung who fell at the head of his household in the *puputan* of 1908. She was said to have taken part in the death charge and to have escaped. But fiction was more romantic than fact. The truth was that Patimah was neither a princess, nor was she a wife of the rajah. But she was a member of his household. She should have been in the *puputan*, but had gone over previously to the Dutch. She then converted to Islam, and married a Muslim. She was, nevertheless, the most remarkable woman in Bali.[22]

Patimah became a wealthy woman who made her money by trading in cloth and beaten silver. Barefooted, she drove a Buick. She had built up a profitable business in silver and an impressive fleet of taxis. She was rowed out to sea to meet all ships, armed with flowers and a bottle. She was never known to refuse "the cup that cheers" and had an exceptionally strong head for alcohol. She was a favorite of all, despite her keen business sense and shrewdness in bargaining. She tended at times to become a bit forgetful about business while dallying with the officers and the crew, so her personal fleet of a half dozen automobiles was generally available to KPM for hire, and she did a lively trade with the tourists in of Balinese arts and crafts.

Opposite: Advertisement for the Minas-Roosevelt Tourist Office. From Orient Touring Company, *Travel Through the Mystic Isles of Java, Sumatra and Bali* (n.p.: G. Kolff, 1925.)

Patimah ("you will be pleased, indeed, with Patimah") brought a bundle of native silks and brocades and a basketful of Balinese antiques to the veranda of the rest house and gently solicited the tourist patronage. Although Carl Shreve was the only passenger to land in Buleleng, he was not allowed to miss the welcome of Patimah. She was a "character," he wrote, and, as the captain of the Dutch ship introduced her, "not to know Patimah is not to know Bali!"[23]

Patimah was called the most interesting woman on the island—stately, middle-aged woman, silk clad, and a great lady turned businesswoman. The tourists spun about the island in her automnolies; her curios and the weavings of her looms filled their trunks when their stay in Bali was over.

Miguel Covarrubias recorded:

> Landing on a primitive wooden pier, we received the inevitable welcome of Patimah, a gay and dignified middle-aged Balinese "princess" from whom one rents a car to go to the south of the island.... She was a prosperous owner of a silver and brocade shop and a fleet of fine motorcars for hire. The traveler succumbs easily to her charm, her lively sense of humor, and her hospitality when she serves coffee on her veranda, and he seldom fails to buy a hammered silver bowl or a brocade scarf. But some Babbit has taught unsuspecting Patimah that typical American greeting is "Shake the bottle!" followed by a significant gesture of the hand. This is the only English she knows.[24]

André Roosevelt was described as a beachcomber and a renegade who did his best to live down the family name's association with "the strenuous life." André took his name for granted. He could have held important positions despite his lack of business sense, but he didn't give a damn about prestige. He was an adventurer. He traveled around the world, and wherever he found an exotic land with sensuous women, he stayed to become happily familiar with the country and its people. Hickman Powell described him as "a tall man, a bit stooped but still athletic, with twinkling eyes behind thick spectacles, which looked with pleasure on the world. A perennial playboy. A grandfather who never grown up." André's father, a first cousin of President Theodore Roosevelt, after founding the first telephone company in Europe, returned to Paris, wed, and enjoyed the fruits of his leisure. André "was incorrigibly irresponsible. He was invariably tardy. He was defiantly lazy." He was an "astoundingly gifted black sheep," who lived a life "as checkered as a paddy field." He was a bluff man of little patience, immense vitality, buoyant enthusiasm, and the endearing capacity for wonder and surprise that children and true explorers have.[25]

Born in Paris, he quaffed beer in Heidelberg with a student corps, sipped wine in Montparnasse, won championships as an athlete in both Europe and America, played water polo for the New York Athletic Club, and won a silver medal at the 1900 Olympics in Paris, playing soccer for a French club team. He also played tennis with his second cousin at Oyster Bay, and in general enjoyed his patrimony. He then grew rice without profit in Texas, engineered in Missouri, barnstormed for the Wright brothers with one of their first planes, managed production for a motion picture company, and did liaison work in the First World War. His proudest possession of the war was a friendly letter from his wartime colonel, which called him "the worst damned soldier in the American Army."[26]

For several years he received an allowance from his family and then came into his inheritance. Having no feeling for business, he was always surprised when his investments did not prosper and he had to find a job. He was, however, dynamic and charming, superb in public relations—particularly in promoting travel—and was in demand by the growing travel industry. But he rarely stayed long in one place.

In 1924, finding himself running out of money again, he accepted a job with Raymond & Whitcomb, traveling as program director on a posh cruise ship making a world tour. The ship broke down in Singapore. Faced with a three weeks' delay, he was not sure what to do with the passengers. André and a few of the more adventurous passengers took the smelly "Pig Express" to make the trip to Bali, stay three days, and return. One look was enough. André was enchanted by the island. "Bali was the tropical paradise, with coconut palms swaying over white sand beaches, forested mountains rising beyond terraces of rich green rice fields, beautiful temples and peaceful villages. Best of all were the most exquisite, exotic women André had ever seen." At the end of three days, André took his party back to Singapore, politely put his charges back on the boat, and shipped them home, saying, "I am so glad to have known you, but I am staying here in Bali." He returned to Bali. There would be a hand-to-mouth living in guiding tourists now and then and in selling them photographs. But he would be in Eden. He was very happy, with no possessions to worry him.[27]

Scientifically his imagination was piqued by Wallace's Line, which divided the adjacent islands of Bali and Lombok. Aesthetically he was lured by tales of the most beautiful scenery, temples, music, and dancing women in the world, and he was not disappointed. He spent five years on the island with little money, but he had a dream of sometime making a motion picture there. And eventually his daughter Leila and her husband, Armand Denis, came out to join him in the shoestring production of the film *Goona-Goona*.

Although André Roosevelt arrived with little money, he had good

Tourists in Bali in the late 1920s. Walter Spies is third from the right; André Roosevelt sits on the far left. Courtesy of Renée Roosevelt Denis, San Dimas, California.

connections. He joined with Jacob Minas and brought American Express and Thomas Cook patronage with him. The KPM experienced some discomfort but no serious damage from these activities. After Roosevelt's departure, the KPM wooed and won American Express and Thomas Cook patronage and, thereafter, dominated the tourist scene. Anthropologist Margaret Mead later contended that the KPM owned Bali more or less.

Roosevelt had a tolerably large European-style one story house with three bedrooms, a dark room, and a great three-sided room opening onto a courtyard, beyond which were the kitchen, bathroom, and servants' quarters. The place was somewhat furnished. If a person wanted to sit in another room, he carried a chair in there. The narrow beds were serviceable. After the first few nights, a person learned quite efficiently to arrange odd anatomical corners between the slabs.

Four years later, André came to the United States to make a promotional tour. He arrived in the middle of winter at a Brooklyn dock, in the snow and slush. He was miserable. He honored his tour engagements up to a point, but Chicago's icy winds were too much. He wired his daughter and son-in-law: "I have to get out of here! Let's go back to Bali and make a film." As André's granddaughter recalled, "It was just about as casual as that."

Leila, André's daughter, was only twenty-one at the time, but she already had three children. Her mother, divorced from André, traveled and indulged in her passion for art, and put Leila away in a Connecticut boarding school. When Leila was eighteen, she met Armand Denis, who was on a holiday trip to Long Island. Armand Denis, the son of a Belgian judge, went to England as a refugee from World War I, graduated from Oxford University, and then emigrated to the United States, working as a research chemist. They were married in the garden of Sagamore Hill, the Roosevelt estate at Oyster Bay, Long Island.

Leila was thrilled, and Armand and André liked each other immediately. The two men were remarkably alike. They were both adventurers and shared a passion for cinematography. Armand needed no persuasion to leave for Bali, and they were soon calculating what they needed: movie equipment, film, developing solutions, and heat-proof containers. Armand bought a pair of second hand wooden cameras from a shop off Broadway in New York. He later realized quite what antiques they were, even for those days. Good carpenters in the village in Bali built a darkroom, extra drying racks, and developing tanks—perfect copies—in teak.[28]

"If everything I heard of it was true," Denis wrote about Bali, "it was an earthly paradise. The scenery was spectacular, the climate perfect, and the people were said to be a carefree, spontaneous race with a unique art of their own. Several writers commented on their natural skills as actors, and when I read of their wealth of legends and folk stories, I decided that there was all the material a filmmaker could ever need."[29]

Armand, Leila, and their children, Renée, Armand, and David, along with a giant fifty-pound Galapagos tortoise named Jake, spent a year in Bali while making the film *Goona-Goona*. (When Denis wrote his memoirs, he eliminated everybody from his story of Bali—his father-in-law, his wife (who later divorced him) and his children. Only Jake the tortoise survived.) Their arrival in Bali was celebrated by a host of André's friends. The Denis family was treated to more than ordinary ceremony, because it was considered favored by the gods. Armand and David were twins, and that was a great blessing in Bali. More important than the twins, they also had a god with them. Most Balinese believed that the earth was resting on the back of a tortoise. Jake was worshipped and adorned daily with flowers (which he ate) and he almost exploded from the copious sacred offerings of fruit.

Roosevelt and Denis took advantage of the enthusiastic cooperation of the Balinese in making the film. Because exposed film had to be processed as quickly as possible before the image would fade, a room was built by the Balinese, who could not understand why people wanted a house completely sealed off from light. Despite careful control, the film density varied so much that some parts were too light and others too dark.

When he reached Bali, Denis found that none of the extravagant praise he had heard before he left had quite prepared him for the beauty and strangeness of the island. "Since then it has been developed and commercialized out of all recognition," he later wrote, "but in those days it was still practically untouched." He lived in one of the villages on the lower slopes of the spectacular Mount Batur and was enchanted with Balinese life from the moment he arrived. In the morning he would watch the ducks being herded through the village in great flocks by a man with a bamboo pole. But the greatest impression that Bali made on Denis was through its people. From his first contacts with them, he could see that all his preconceptions about them were entirely wrong. The Balinese were highly civilized, but their culture and their morality were utterly different from anything he had ever known before. Essentially, they were a race of artists. Bali itself was the most beautiful place on earth. Living was easy. "The people were as beautiful as the country and there seemed to be nothing to upset a way of life that had proceeded for centuries."[30]

Bali was Denis's first real contact with a tropical country, and the climate and way of life suited him so well that he was soon having to remind himself that he had come to make a film as well as to take a holiday. At first, he intended simply to film scenes from the lives of the Balinese people, but as he lived among them he began to learn something of the wealth of their legends and folktales. He decided to draw on these for the film, and one of their stories was easily adapted to form the plot of what finally became the film *Goona-Goona*.

When he made this decision it was "with all the rashness of the complete novice," but he was saved by the remarkable acting skill of the Balinese, who provided him with his stars, his extras, and his supporting cast. Denis found the Balinese to be warm, kind, and immensely tolerant, "but most of the passions and extremes of emotion and ambition which plague the Western man were totally incomprehensible to them." The Balinese excelled at fights and crowd scenes. But although the young Balinese who was playing the part of the unskilled laborer was a most accomplished natural actor, Denis found it impossible to make him register anger or jealousy against the prince. He would grimace in a half hearted fashion, but even though Denis rehearsed him several times, he was quite unconvincing. Denis soon realized that this was because the whole idea of jealousy in this situation was completely foreign to him and to the Balinese in general.

3. Paradise Gained

On one occasion Denis complained despairingly about his actors. "They're impossible! They're utterly indifferent! They act gloriously for no other reason than a mood. Why, this morning in the middle of a scene the whole crowd of them decided suddenly that they were going home. Bored, that's all. They've lost the mood. We offered them double their pay to remain, but they merely walked away saying that if we offered them five times as much they would not want it. Bored, simply bored. They're rich from years of exportation and don't have to work. They're impossible!"[31]

"But just think," Denis said to the Balinese actor, "you have a young wife whom you are very much in love with. You go away on a journey. You come back and you find out that she has deceived you with another man. What would you do?" The young Balinese stared blankly at Denis and shrugged his shoulders. "But you'd have to do something," Denis said, getting impatient. "You couldn't just accept a thing like that." By now the young man was clearly trying very hard to be helpful and thought for a minute or so before replying. "I know what I would do," he said. "I'd go and get myself another wife."[32]

Denis soon found that this summed up the attitude of the Balinese, not just about morality but about life in general. They were warm, they were kind, they were immensely tolerant, but most of the passions, extremes of emotion, and ambitions that plagued the Western man were totally incomprehensible to them. Denis admired this on the whole. It certainly made life easier and probably more enjoyable. But at the same time, he always felt that there was something missing in the Balinese. He felt that their characters lacked depth and mystery, and the idea of ever forming a lifelong friendship with a Balinese was impossible.

"Bali was the nearest I ever got to Paradise," concluded Denis. "I found the peace and beauty of the island growing on me, and I sometimes wonder whether I would ever left had the *Silver Prince* not called again to remind me that it was time to be getting back to America and reality." He left Jake on the island "where life was so good for a tortoise of such sanctity."

Denis was concerned that Balinese culture would degenerate into a caricature of their former civilization to amuse the tourists.

> It soon dawned on me that none of this richness of culture was going to last. Almost everything on the island I so admired—the carving, the music, the decoration—was already doomed. The signs were everywhere. Bali had survived untouched for as long as it had mainly because it possessed little to attract the traders who were drawn to Sumatra, Java and the other islands of the Dutch East Indies. Now, at last, the traders had arrived and were firmly installed. Already the Balinese were eagerly buying their first bicycles and cars. Corrugated iron

had begun to scar the villages. Machine-woven cotton goods from abroad had already made obsolete the old hand looms, and cheap Swiss dyes were being imported by the industrious Dutch to take the place of the rich batik dyes that had been made in Bali for centuries. The wealth of the island was beginning to drain abroad as the Balinese traded their gold that had remained in their families for years to pay for their imports. The serene isolation of Bali was about to vanish for good.[33]

As the *Silver Prince* was steaming steadily across the Indian Ocean, a brine pipe that went through Denis's cabin sprung a leak. By the time it was discovered, the whole cabin was awash in a foot of salt water. A tangled mass of film negative was floating on the surface of the water. The tins containing the precious film were afloat, and a half dozen of them had burst, spilling their contents into the brine that was sloshing gently from side to side with the motion of the ship. Everyone on board came to Denis's aid. The bathtubs were filled with freshwater and all the film that had been affected by the brine was hurriedly washed. Even so, a few rolls were irretrievably damaged because the emulsion had already started to slough off in great patches. But most of the film could still be saved if only an effective way of drying it could be found. Denis planned to stretch ropes from rails across decks of the ship, winding the film from rope to rope to dry. When he tried to do this, however, he soon found that there was a stiff breeze blowing and that it was carrying up enough spray on to the deck to spot the film and make it useless. The captain was most upset and insisted on turning the ship around and steaming downwind for more than a hundred miles until the film had been completely dried and rewound. As he was rewinding the film, Denis noticed that the darkness of the negative, although properly developed, fluctuated regularly every five or six feet. The Balinese who had developed the film did not stir the developer in the deep wooden tanks, causing some sections of the film to be developed far more intensively than others, which produced the fluctuations. By the time they docked in Boston, Denis found the solution to this problem and saved the film. The machine he developed produced a perfect print of all the footage that was saved from the brine bath.[34]

After he left Bali, Roosevelt wrote, "Now, this nation of artists is faced with the western invasion, and I cannot stand idly by and watch their destruction." He was concerned whether Bali would be able to resist the invasion coming from the West and retain its individuality. But whether the Balinese people would be able to keep their individuality, their customs, and their infinite happiness, he believed would depend upon the Balinese themselves.[35]

3. Paradise Gained

E. Alexander Powell, author, explorer, and lecturer, spent much of his life in remote corners of the earth, about which he had been informing the public through his books. One of America's leading globe-trotters, he had also been a war correspondent before and during World War I for several American and English newspapers, and a member of the U.S. Consular Service. He headed the Goldwyn-Bray-Powell expedition to the Far East to make motion pictures of scenes in parts of Indochina and the Dutch East Indies, including Bali, while cruising on the Philippine coastguard cutter *Negros*. His book *Where the Strange Trails Go Down*, published in 1921, which described the expedition, was the first American book to provide information about Bali.

"I went to Bali," Powell wrote, "because I wished to see for myself if the accounts I had heard of the surpassing beauty of its women were really true. The Dutch officials had depicted the obscure little isle as a flaming, fragrant garden, overrun with flowers, a sort of unspoiled island Eden, where bronze-brown Eves with faces and figures of surpassing loveliness disported themselves on the long white beaches, or loitered the lazy days away beneath the palms. But I went there skeptical at heart. Yet, I must admit that, when the anchor of the *Negros* splashed into the blue waters off Boeleleng, I half expected to find a Balinese edition of the Ziegfeld Follies chorus waiting to greet me with demonstrations of welcome and garlands of flowers. What I did find on the wharf was a surly Dutch harbor-master, who, judging from his breath and disposition, had been on a prolonged carouse."

"I was told in Samarinda," Powell remarked carelessly to his companion, by way of introducing the topic in which he was most interested, "that some of the native girls here in Bali are remarkably good looking." "I thought you'd be asking about them," the young Hollander commented dryly. That's usually the first question asked by everyone who comes to Bali. If you want to see them you'll have to cross over to the south side."[36]

Powell's dissatisfaction evaporated rapidly and turned to relief as the visitors ventured inland and discovered that south Bali fulfilled all the traveler's expectations and more. Still, Powell recommended to his countrymen, perhaps with tongue in cheek:

> Instead of going to Palm Beach next winter, or to Havana, or to the Riviera, why don't you go out to Bali and see its lovely women, its curious customs, and its superb scenery for yourself? You can get there in about eight weeks, provided you make good connections at Singapore and Surabaya. With no railways, no street-cars, no hotels, no newspapers, no theatres, no movies, it is a very restful place. You can lounge the lazy days away in the cool depths of flower-smothered verandahs,

with a brown house-boy pulling at the punkah-rope and another bringing you cool drinks in tall, thin glasses ... or you can stroll in the moonlight on the long white beaches with lithe brown beauties who wear passion-flowers in their raven hair. Or, should you weary of so *dolce-far-niente* an existence, you can sail across to Java with the opium-runners in their fragile *prahaus*, or climb a two-mile high volcano, or in the jungles at the western extremity of the island stalk the clouded tiger. And you can wear pajamas all day long without apologizing. Everything considered, Bali offers more inducements than any place I know to the tired business man or the absconding bank cashier.[37]

Lucian Swift Kirtland was a reporter who turned to freelance writing from the Orient, and traveled in the Far East with his wife, Helen Warner Johns, a fellow correspondent. In 1926, Kirtland published *Finding the Worth While in the Orient*:

Once a week throughout the year an antique little packet steamer departs from the harbor of Soerabaja, bound for Eden. Incredible as it may appear, the salon accommodation of this boat is never crowded. One might expect that a vessel with such a destination would be resoundingly advertised and eagerly patronized.

I know from the recorded figures that very few travelers do seek the Island of Bali, the name by which this Eden is known.

Bali remains unnoticed by the multitude, and, therefore, it remains unspoiled. It is possible that you have small interest in naive Edens. But if the idea of discovering a strange and charming by-path does thrill you, then I hope for your own rare pleasure that you will be one of the few who do know Bali.

There must always be a practical side to traveling, even if the destination is Eden. The voyage is really quite a simple affair. You go to the office of the Tourist Bureau in Soerabaja and engage steamer passage. There need be no elaborate preparations, and there can be no extraordinary expenses. But you must pay, out of your treasury of days, a fortnight of time. During your stay on the island you live at the government rest houses. As the servants know no English, it is advisable to take an English speaking servant with you from Soerabaja. The Tourist Bureau will help you with advice.

Words, as Joseph Conrad has the genius to use them, can create in the imagination of the reader the pageantry and mystery of the tropics. But you must be content to allow me to call the beauty of Bali indescribable.

The island has inherited no supreme architectural wonders from the past. Rather should it be said that Bali's temples and palaces are unique curiosities rather than wonders. They are different from anything which you will see elsewhere; and their exotic strangeness makes

3. Paradise Gained

Main entrance to a temple in north Bali. From Aage Krarup-Nielsen, *Leven en Avonturen van een Oostinjevaarder op Bali* (Amsterdam: E. Querido, 1928).

you freshly interested in their architecture even if you are weary of temples. As for the countryside, it is just a little more vivid in its luxury and in its color than nature has granted to other places.

As much of the beauty and charm of this Eden (and distinctly its naivete) exists because the island lies almost unknown and remains so uncorrupted by the white man's blessings, you must not expect to find cosmopolitan or sophisticated hospitality. English speaking servants will not appear.

Otherwise there is nothing to remind you that you are a tourist. There are no professional guides. There are no touts. There are no beggars. There are no fees to be paid at the temples.

You will have in your pocket the map of the island which the Tourist Bureau of Java has prepared. On the back of this folder is printed a list of the most interesting places. The only definiteness which is essentially desirable is to discover all about any special festivals which may be taking place during your visit.

When the last day comes and you stand on the palm girt beach at Bulelang, waiting for the steamer which is to take you away from this paradise back to Sourabaja, you will have lived through not nine days but nine cycles of wonder and enchantment.[38]

4
Dolce-Far-Niente

> And the people kept coming; they came to Bali to create, to be created, to create Bali. They came and wrote of beautiful bare-breasted maidens, timeless villages in a lush paradise, a place of amazing harmony disturbed only by occasional manifestations of wicked witches who were defeated by noble barongs, and of guna-guna the love-magic practiced there. All the world knew that Bali was the enchanted isle of the world's sweetest dreams. And there was another thing. They came because of the beautiful boys. They loved the boys, many of them.
>
> Inez Baranay[1]

Reports began filtering out to Europe and America that Bali, not Fiji or Samoa or Hawaii, was the genuine, unspoiled tropical paradise known as yet, even by reputation, only by the connoisseurs. All of the more affluent world travelers sought to identify themselves as such, as did a number of scholars. The Dutch colonial establishment in Bali was flattered by the attention that the island was beginning to receive and by the generally favorable notices regarding Dutch altruism. The Dutch authorities sought to shelter the travelers from exposure to what might be the irresistible temptation to stay in Bali, perhaps to corrupt—or to be corrupted by—the presumably innocent but hedonistic Balinese. But foreign anthropologists, ethnologists, artists, musicians, dancers, and actors of more or less reputable professional credentials (not to mention numerous adventurers and drifters and occasional diplomats) inevitably and eagerly sought out Bali.

By 1927, the KPM had weekly express service to Bali using two modern liners. KPM advertised all-inclusive tours, covering first-class steamship fare from Surabaya to Buleleng and back, as well as all travel expenses including landing fees, transport by private motor car, meals, lodgings, fees, and tips. The cost was $86 for three days for one adult and $167 for three adults, and up to $155 for seven days for one adult and $264 for three adults.

The Official Tourist Bureau reported that it was instrumental in inducing

The Bali Hotel, Denpasar. Courtesy of the Photo and Print Collection of the Koninklijk Instituut voor Tall-, Land- en Volkenkunde (KITLV), Leiden, Holland.

hundreds of tourists to visit Bali and, so far as they were aware, not one has ever regretted the decision. "No visitor to the Dutch East Indies should fail to include Bali in his itinerary," concluded a message from the KPM. "The additional cost is negligible—the experience cannot be duplicated anywhere else in the world, regardless of cost."

In 1928, the KPM opened the Bali Hotel, replacing the Denpasar rest house and built on the very site of the *puputan* of 1906. The Bali Hotel catered to the rich and famous. Next, the KMP renovated the rest house

4. Dolce-Far-Niente

at Kintamani, and reserved it exclusively for tourists who wished to enjoy the spectacular panorama over Lake Batur.

Tourists came to Bali almost all by sea—the KPM ships putting in at Buleleng or in the event of heavy seas, at more sheltered spots nearby. Padang Bay, in the southeastern part of the island, was outfitted to receive cruise ships. Travel agencies used the alluring name of Bali to attract hordes of tourists for their round-the-world cruises that made a one-day stop at the island. On that day, the tourists were herded to the Bali Hotel in Denpasar to eat their lunch, buy curios, and watch hurried performances by bored "temple dancers"—ordinary village actors who hated to play in the midday heat. The show over, the tourists were rushed back to their ships in numbered cars satisfied to have seen Bali. An average of five or six such cruises unloaded some fifteen hundred round-the-world tourists every winter, which left the Balinese puzzled as to why all those madmen came from so far for only a day. The Balinese would have never willingly left their island, and once an old woman remarked that surely the foreigners must have done something at home that forced them to leave their own lands. The great cruise ships came with more visitors than could be taken care of by the island's limited supply of motorcars, and half the tourists had to remain on board ship until the other half returned. Besides the cruises, every week two KPM boats brought a handful of more enterprising visitors that stayed for three days or even a week or two. Only a few stayed for a longer period.

Travel by motorcars from Java became possible in 1934. A pair of energetic beachcombers started a daily ferry service between Gilimanuk, at the western point of Bali, and Banjuwangi, on the east coast of Java, and a road was put through from Gilimanuk to Denpasar. The trip was strictly for the adventurous. The car ferry took days to arrange and if the current, wind, or waves proved unfavorable, the one-mile crossing might take not half an hour but half a day, and by night the Gilimanuk road was infested with tigers. Air travel became possible in the 1930s, but it was very risky. The first survey flight made by the Royal Netherlands Indies Airways crashed into Mount Batukau, and the first airport, built in Bukit, was too dangerous for landing except in the calmest weather. The KNILM (Koninklije Nederlandsh-Indische Luchtvaart or Royal Netherlands Indies Airways) was known in Malay as *Kalau naik ini lebih mati*, meaning "if you go up in this you will be dead."[2] But starting in 1933 an airline linked Surabaya to Bali and by 1938, with the opening of the new airport in Tuban near Denpasar, there were three flights a week and Bali became a stop on the weekly KNILM flights to Australia and Makassar.

Bali's hotel capacity consisted of seventy double rooms (forty-eight rooms at the Bali Hotel, sixteen at the Satrya Hotel—a Chinese hotel in

Unusual cremation tower. The arrival of the first airplanes made a strong impression of the Balinese, and the tower used to cremate a prince in Tabanan was created in the shape of an airplane. Courtesy of J. F. K. Kits Nieuwenkamp, The Stichting Nieuwenkamp, St Vleuten,

Denpasar, built at the beginning of the 1930s—and six at the KPM bungalow hotel in Kintamani). Thirty-two additional double rooms were made available to travelers in the eight rest houses on the island, although government officials traveling on duty took precedence at all times so that it was impossible to guarantee visitors rooms in any rest house.

4. Dolce-Far-Niente

The number of visitors to Bali increased regularly from 213 in 1924 to 1,428 in 1929. Four hundred eighty tourists visited Bali in 1926. By 1930, as many as one hundred visitors a month were experiencing the delights of the island. After this, arrival stagnated for several years because of the economic depression, and then began to rise again in 1934, reaching an annual average of about two hundred fifty visitors per month toward the end of the decade. This figure did not include the passengers on the *Stella Polaris, Lurline, Franconia, Empress of Britain, Reliance,* and a few other cruise ships that advertised and delivered a day or two in Bali as the high point of their winter schedule. Except on days when the cruise ships put in and some one hundred carloads of sightseers careened about the island, tourism never caused much stir. The cars were hired mainly from private Balinese or Chinese owners, the itinerary was virtually the same and included luncheon—always a twenty-course *rijstafel*, the sumptuous meal of many Indonesian dishes—at the Bali Hotel in Denpasar, and the cost per person was about three and a half dollars. For the other tourists, those who stayed a full two days (long enough to be counted in the statistics) a visit to Bali meant a much more leisurely round of scenic and cultural attractions. Their travel agents provided motor cars (Essex or Hudson five- to seven-passenger

A relief showing Europeans with comic features in an automobile. Courtesy of The Horniman Museum and Gardens, London.

touring cars or sedans, which rented for $10–$15 daily), accommodations (ranging from an austere government rest house at $2.50 to the luxury Bali Hotel at $7.50 double, *tout compris*), and advice and assistance on all incidental problems (for instance, comfort facilities, which frequently meant "the rice paddies for the ladies," and "the coconut trees for the gentlemen"). Admission fees were also charged for entering temples and other sites. Balinese guides who spoke Dutch and English were available for tourists who spoke no Malay, the lingua franca of Bali.

Denpasar was a rambling town of white government buildings, a dozen European houses, and a street or so of shops, surrounded by an outer layer of huts crowded beneath a tangle of trees and palms. The business street of Denpasar leading to the market consisted of squalid shops and a small Chinese hotel. The shops included a line of Chinese grocers, goldsmiths, druggists, photographers, bicycle agents, and a curio stall with mass-produced "Balinese art." There was also a single Japanese photographer, who did little business, but whose shop was strategically placed at the main crossroad. There were also bearded Bombay merchants "dressed like burlesque comedians in tall fezzes, embroidered slippers, pink sarongs, and European vests worn over shirts with tails out." On a side street, Arabs sold textiles and cheap suitcases. In the Javanese ice cream parlor one could buy hilariously colored ices when the electric equipment was in order. There was no church, but the Arab quarter contained a mosque. A small primitive movie house, patronized chiefly by the foreign population, ran Wild West films twice a week.

After dark, in Denpasar, the equipment of the smart young man-about-town consisted of a striped pajamas, a Mohammedan skull cap, sandals, a bicycle, and a flashlight, although he still wore flowers behind his ear to stroll on the main street among the food vendors, the flourishing prostitutes, and the procurers that haunted the streets around the hotels. Colin McPhee described Denpasar:

> During the day there was the incessant clang of bells from the pony carts that filled the streets, and the asthmatic honk of buses and cars forever driving in and out of town. The crowing of a thousand cocks, the barking of a thousand dogs formed a rich sonorous background against which the melancholy call of a passing food vendor stood out like an oboe in a symphony.
>
> But at night, when the shops had closed and half the town was already asleep, the sounds died so completely that you could hear every leaf that stirred, every palm-frond that dryly rustled. From all directions there now floated soft, mysterious music, humming, vibrating above the gentle, hollow sound of drums. The sound came from

different distances and gave infinite perspective to the night. As it grew late the music stopped. Now the silence was complete, only at long intervals pierced by a solitary voice, high, nasal, nostalgic, singing an endless tune; or else broken by the sudden hysteria of the dogs that began in a thin single wail, rose quickly to a clamor of tormented voices and died once more into silence.[3]

The British Journalist Cedric Belfrage described Denpasar as a semi-debauched place. It had a fine market once a week, but otherwise it did not represent the best of Balinese life at all. In the streets were men selling souvenir postcards and, after dark, pimps who could lead the tourist to "the couch of a nice brown girl, very reasonable." Breast-hungry tourists could go home and tell the boys what good sports the Bali girls were, but the girls were simply the same sort of prostitutes that could be found elsewhere. The frankness with which the ordinary girls of Bali revealed their charms did not, to the amazement of some tourists who pursued their investigations further, betoken a willingness to be poked by anyone with a dollar or two to spend.[4]

The relative unimportance of Denpasar was also reflected in the fact that there was only one European doctor, attached to the Bali Hotel (which had to guarantee modern medical service to its wealthy clients). The post was held by a Dutch veterinarian, who had taken some additional courses to qualify as a medical practitioner. Arriving at the small hospital each morning, he would still say, "well, nurse, shall we go into the stalls?" Needless to say, he didn't evoke trust and most patients treated by him would have preferred him to have kept to his former profession.

The post–World War I era of high living and nonstop absurdity had arrived in Bali. Across the oceans, an exotic world beckoned, and those westerners who were wealthy enough to travel responded to its call. The island drew a steady stream of affluent, intrepid, and genteel world vagabonds.

The total "European" population in Bali was 403 in 1930 (out of a total population of 1,101,037); these figures included many who were not colonial officials, such as artists, scholars, and businessmen.[5]

Bali also acquired a reputation as a homosexual paradise. Its image as a haven for homosexuals may be loosely connected to the island's association with beautiful women. It was not surprising, in view of the praise lavished on Balinese women in the tourist literature, that some westerners would find the men equally attractive, and to some extent passive. Hickman Powell saw his duty to report that in Bali, as in all oriental countries, there was a certain amount of male homosexuality. Although he saw no indication of this, he was told that it was widespread and that no moral stigma was attached to it. "Emphasizing peculiarities of sex life," he stated, "would be to tell falsehood by disproportion."

As a homosexual, Walter Spies joined other young men looking for a paradise away from the strict mores of Europe and he believed he found it in Bali. Throughout his Bali years, Spies indulged a personal fondness for young Balinese boys. Not only foreign visitors, but also some Dutch civil servants exploited small boys. Roelof Goris, who served in the Archaeological Service in Bali, was one of the enigmas of the Bali set. Short, dressed in baggy Bombay bloomers, Goris was a shy, odd-looking scholar whose homosexuality separated him from his peers, and whose alcoholism was probably due to his alienation from the mentality of the Dutch civil service. To both Spies and Goris, Bali was a heaven of tolerance in an anti-homosexual world. They both stood for everything traditional if only it was a fitting symbol of Western daydreams.

Miguel Covarrubias had been asked by a native Balinese why it was that white men so often preferred boys to girls. He denied this "strange idea" but later found the explanation when he observed the alarming number of mercenary homosexuals around the hotels at night. He believed that in general the idea of homosexuality was inconsequential to the Balinese. *The Encyclopedia of the Netherlands Indies*, however, stated in a matter-of-fact way that in the Indonesian archipelago, sexual relations between men were widespread and that the Balinese indulged in this "perversion" in a major fashion.[6]

The Austrian ethnologist Hugo Bernatzik recalled that on the first evening of his stay in Denpasar he found that the habits of the Indian mainland had established themselves in Bali, too. A whole lot of half-grown boys offered themselves to him in the street and were surprised that for a long time he did not understand what they were really after. "The natives of Bali seem to a great extent to be by nature 'bisexuals.' But the white men are to all appearances 'monosexual.' 'Today I saw something astonishing,' an old Balinese said to Bernatzik, 'a white child! How do the white men manage to have children when they sleep only with boys?' he asked in all innocence."[7]

Other stereotypical views of Bali's sex life were often repeated. Nudity belonged to the colonial image of Bali, which was commercially exploited. The colonial idea about the Balinese was that they practiced free love before marriage, did not mind nudity, and felt no shame being nude. In a similar vein, Alexander Powell wrote: "Rather than you should be scandalized when you visit Bali, let me make it quite clear that in matters of morality the Balinese women are as easy as an old shoe. Perhaps it would be more accurate to say that they are unmoral rather than immoral. This is one of the conditions of life in Insulinde which must be accepted by the traveler, just as he accepts as a matter of course the heat and the insects and the dirt."[8]

Gregor Krause's photo book prepared the visitors for the pleasant shock of beautiful nude girls and charming little boys. It did not take long before the dirty postcard industry reached the island. The Balinese seemed willing models. The books, but especially the more daring postcards, took their place in the colonial tradition of pornographic cabinet-photo. But some Balinese did not want to sit nude and were angry when they were forced to do so. They agreed because they were afraid to be arrested if they refused. Hickman Powell had an old Balinese servant (whom he called an "old hag") who was angry with him because he had nude girls in his atelier for his artistic friends. He dismissed her and within a few hours was bombarded by applicants for the job. He chose a girl who wanted to do the housework and the sitting as well. And he knew why she had agreed: She had to eat, he admitted, unashamed.[9]

The British anthropologist Geoffrey Gorer stated that as far as his inadequate observation went, the Balinese attitude towards sex was unparalleled elsewhere, they had neither modesty nor immodesty, they were in no way romantic about sex, they treated it as any other part of the ordinary business of life, and it had no more intrinsic emotional importance than eating. This seemed to him the only rational approach. Even Margaret Mead referred to the legendary (but unproven) "numerous love-affairs" young Balinese girls had before marriage.[10]

Richard Halliburton was one of the best-selling American travel writers and well-known lecturers of the 1920s and 1930s, who made traveling, adventuring, and writing his life, and who wrote lushly romantic stories of his adventures while tramping around the globe. Halliburton first heard of the lure of Bali on the docks of Saigon, where he ran across an old tropical drifter who knew "every isle and city on which the sun of the equator blazed." The drifter had been to Bali, and when he spoke of it, he might have been Adam telling Cain about the Garden of Eden. To him it was the most idyllic spot in the Pacific, chiefly because it was almost the only one not blighted by European culture and American tin cans. He assured Halliburton that it was a siren isle, enslaving by its beauty and romance everyone who looked upon it.

When Halliburton arrived in Bali, he decided that to see Bali he must walk and he set forth to explore the island, planning to linger where his "fancy dictated and advance only when the spirit moved." At each village his appearance caused more excitement than had been known in months.

The vast population of pariah dogs clamorously heralded his appearance, and all the villagers ran out to stare as he passed. He found Denpasar less interesting than the wilder aspects of the island, and he turned east, tramping leisurely through terraces of rice and palm-hidden villages hedged with flaming hibiscus. For food he had coconuts, bananas, and mangoes. For a bed, he had the ground, shaded by a grove of trees beside a stream of fresh cool water, or a spot on the shore beneath the fronded palms that stretched out toward the blue ocean.

Halliburton lived in Bali as a beachcomber, wandered the island for a month, and found a place to seek refuge and rejuvenation in "this far-off land of the lotus, this Eden, this idyllic little isle, this Bali."[11]

Moved to verse was Grace Gallatin Thompson Seton, an explorer, writer, and suffragist, who rhapsodized, "Your treasures are straight bodies, lithe/With ivory grace in dance or play."[12] Seton accompanied her husband, Ernest Thompson Seton, a famous naturalist and artist, on many of his travels. As she traveled with him, she discovered her own passion for exploring. Between 1920 and the late 1930s Grace Gallatin Seton traveled in more than twelve countries, exploring places that tourists rarely saw. "I have had a few days in South Bali crowded with sightseeing of the tourist variety," she wrote. "I fed sacred monkeys in Sangeh's Whispering Grove.... I stood in awe amid the giant roots, like a cathedral, of the banyan at Bong Kias. I burned a sheaf of rice straw before the Elephant God in whose cave lingers horrors of old torturing and decapitations. I went through rice paddies to curious rock temples. I ate apple-like mangoes and other strange fruits, and little bits of pork skewered on bamboo sticks; stung the mouth of the scarlet seeds of the Lombok pepper; drunk a native concoction of arak tasting like Lysol. I saw the Bat Temple where the twittering denizens hang like over-ripe plums to the roof of the cave."[13]

Adriaan Jacob Barnouw was Queen Wilhelmina Professor of the History, Language, and Literature of the Netherlands at Columbia University. In 1926, Robert Flaherty, the documentary film producer, sought Barnouw's help in securing the necessary approval and cooperation to produce a film in Bali, and these were eventually secured. Three years later, after Flaherty was introduced to Fredrick Wilhelm Murnau, a well-known German filmmaker, the project appeared set as a Flaherty-Murnau collaboration, and Murnau's yacht—the *Bali*—was ready to sail. But a sudden change of plans diverted the collaborators to Tahiti. Flaherty was apparently determined that *Tabu* would be followed by *Bali*—"the *Ultima Thule of our Desires*, and Barnouw recommended André Roosevelt to Flaherty as an American resident in Bali who was a very able photographer and who had been taking films of life in Bali. *Tabu* was released in early 1931, but

Murnau was killed in a car accident about the same time, and the dream of Bali, only one of the many dreams Flaherty had, remained but a dream.[14]

Hendrik De Leeuw traveled extensively as a representative of the Firestone Tire and Rubber Company. "The final effect of Bali is harmony," he concluded. "A life undisturbed by the cosmic reflections to the purpose that hound us in the rest of the world. Such problems are settled for them by a consoling religion developed especially for them. The effect upon the people, and upon him who comes to see, is one of moving along with the feet just off the ground in an atmosphere of sparkling, brilliant color. No clanging factories belch up clouds of evil-hued smoke to blemish the sky. It is no wonder that Bali has enchanted countless people."

He was one of the many travelers who found Buleleng distressingly European. "Eventually, of course, Bali will be overrun by tourists of the see-and-run type, the type that has made certain spots in Europe and elsewhere an abomination to the serious traveler. This is a shame, for the riches of Bali, physical, mental, spiritual and visual should be tasted by those with proper appreciation of their meaning. It will be a sad day when every other Balinese has learned to speak English!"[15]

Hendrik de Leeuw's daughter, Adele De Leeuw, who served as her father's secretary, accompanied him on his travels to the Dutch East Indies. Traveling to Bali led her to write the first children's book in English about the island, *Island Adventure*, which was illustrated by her brother Cateau De Leeuw.

Hassoldt Davis met Robert Flaherty in Papeete, Tahiti, where he was filming *Tabu*. "You want adventure? You want beauty?" Flaherty asked twenty-one-year-old Davis." There is an island named Bali in the Dutch East Indies. So far it is practically unspoiled. But get there quick before another old beachcomber like me gets his film made. He is André Roosevelt." Davis traveled to Bali with a gloomy neurotic writer named Jeff who, although a competent author of Western stories, had fled there to write a psychological novel. "Our first excited inspection of Boeleleng was markedly disappointing, for here there was little of the beauty we had expected; just the wreck of a bad temple, and crooked, ancient walls, little else. Even the natives, wearing dirty *badjoes* (shirts) and shuffling in battered shoes, seemed to have adopted the worst of tourist–Europeanism."[16]

Davis had difficulty finding a house, as everyone was appalled at the idea that any white man would unnecessarily stay in Bali for longer than his business or his prurient curiosity should compel him. Davis and Jeff chased Roosevelt around the island, from temple to temple and from one rajah's harem to another, until at last they caught up with him. Roosevelt dislodged Davis from the Chinese boardinghouse, which was the best Davis could find in Denpasar. On André's advice he took a house in Kedaton. They were equipped with two serving girls, Mairini, eighteen, and Rinpiog, fourteen. The concrete mansion had been the residence of the high priest, before he died and was removed to a tomb in the backyard, where he was to wait until a suitable mass cremation occurred. Surrounding the house was a garden of orchids, surrounding the garden was a tropical orchard, and surrounding the orchard was an actual moat in which the water flowed green and venomous. "Listen," Davis said to Mairini, "the water circling through the moat makes a pleasant sound, don't you think?" "Why no!" she said. "It is full of dysentery." She explained to Jeff that, since Rinpiog was still under age, she, Mairini, would divide her nighttime service between them. That would cost them a guilder, or forty cents a week, extra.[17]

In Denpasar, Davis met a blond American girl who was sitting in the market on the ground with a pile of oranges before her. "Have a seat," she said, "Help me sell these. Your name is Davis, of course, and mine is Julia Adams. Boston, too. What the devil are you doing here?" "Odd business," she said, "quite odd for Boston. I collect fairy tales. Write 'em. Sell 'em sometimes, and sometimes have to sell the oranges from my garden or the fish from my sea to make ends meet." "I can juggle oranges," Davis said. So he juggled oranges, and the crowd collected about them, and they sold all their oranges. When they later reached Paris, they found that both of them contracted syphilis in Bali.[18]

Davis believed that the result of both climate and wealth made the Balinese lazy, and that the lack of alien needs had made them quite reasonably conservative. He believed that the constantly increasing number of tourists in Bali would never spoil the natives in the manner of the Tahitians because the Balinese were self-sufficient and knew it.

Hermann Norden was a wealthy, much-traveled authority on the witchcraft and ghost lore of Siam, Malaya, and Africa. A retired South Carolina cotton broker, he had devoted his retirement years to exploring the frontiers of civilization. Norden reported that in 1924 a hundred travelers tarried for brief visits in Bali, but in the following year there were many more, "for the increase of tourists is like that of gray hairs—seventeen come in the place of one." But the long isolation left Bali with its original charm untarnished.

According to Norden, the rest house in Kintamani was delightful. The fifty-five hundred feet of altitude put into the air a zest most agreeable to find in a tropic land. He was surrounded by incomparable beauty. Five miles away the crater of the volcano Batur rose above snowy billows of clouds and sent skyward its geyser of mist. Slight persuasion would have been needed to make him believe that a god dwelt on that beautiful fire-protected height. The rest house was a one-story building painted white and looking not unlike a farmhouse in America. Their living arrangements were all the more interesting for their wide swing from primitive to modern methods. Every bit of water that they used was brought by carriers from miles away, but a telephone in the garage kept them in touch with the world.[19]

"Wherein lies the charm of the island? What was the compelling allure of Bali?" Norden pondered those questions. Beautiful of course it was, but not more beautiful than many other islands strewn about the tropic seas. Nor could its culture and customs, interesting as he had found them, account for the spell it had put upon him. "The reason for the enchantment it had for the traveler must lie in the quality of the people: the Balinese—proud, reserved and of exceeding beauty."[20]

William Douglas Burden, an explorer and naturalist who traveled the world collecting amphibians, fish and insect specimens for the American Museum of Natural History, stopped in Bali. He was accompanied by his wife and Emmett R. Dunn, a leading American herpetologist, while on his way to his widely publicized expedition to the island of Komodo. He and his party went looking for the *Varanus Komodoensis* that came to be known as the Komodo dragon. No white man had captured one, and Burden was determined to do so.

> You can feel Bali. The atmosphere of it permeates to the bones. But to feel it is not enough; one must look, also. So, under the influence of the cool draughts of lager, we began to open our eyes. Bali has many attractions. Not the least of these is the nudity, which I should pronounce the most striking feature of an altogether pleasing landscape.
>
> The nudity is really astonishing in both its quantity and quality. There are women, women, everywhere, such round, plump partridges, yet so lithe and graceful, and exhibiting such perfection of form as to inspire the artist.
>
> At twilight we hid by a mossy pool, and watched an entire village come wandering, one by one, down the leafy paths to bathe. There is no false modesty in Bali, and men and women bathe together in a state of nature, with perfect unconcern. The maidens, those exquisite, but rather shy bronze water nymphs, wash and prink and comb their long jet hair, and indulge themselves in the Eastern sport of big game hunting through the wilderness of a friendly scalp; and then, rather languidly, they gird up their loins with the inevitable sarong, fill the water jars, set them gracefully on their heads, and move quietly off through the dark vistas of the jungle.[21]

The American artist Lucille Sinclair Douglass moved to Shanghai after World War I, and, except for several short visits to the United States to exhibit her art and to lecture on the Far East, spent most of her time in China. Helen Churchill Candee, an American author who was an authority on tapestries and Asia, wrote several books, including *Angkor the Magnificent*, for which she was decorated by the French government and the king of Cambodia. Douglass accompanied Candee on their journey to Bali in order to make illustrations for Candee's book *New Journeys in Old Asia*.

Douglass described Bali as a fortunate country, in which there was no struggle for existence, and in which there was food for all to be had with a minimum of labor. There was, consequently, ample leisure that was filled out of a rich imagination of an energetic people with art and music, dancing, and the pageantry of great religious festivals. It was a country where clothes played so small a part, where women were nude above the waist, and where there was a curious lack of sex consciousness.

Douglass wrote: "Many times in Bali I have longed to put into words that which I was striving to say in color, for Bali is not one-dimensional. To savor it fully, one must sense not only color but sound and rhythm." And Candee wrote: "Bali cannot be told. Bali cannot be painted, it cannot simply be seen; it must be embraced with soul and sense. All the antennae of the emotions may come into use but not the intellect. Oh, no, that would spoil it, just as Western progress and improvements would spoil it."

Candee and Douglass reached Bali on a steamer from Surabaya. The time consumed in the crossing was eighteen hours. The cost of the round trip was seventy guilders, or about twenty-eight dollars. On the island, an automobile for two was about fourteen dollars a day, and the rate at the rest houses was about three and a half dollars a day. But one could only bring hand luggage.

"A pack of automobiles like saddled hunters at a meet, absorb each tourist," wrote Candee. "Yes, that is what seekers after beauty become, degraded tourists, and painfully aware of being ridiculous exotics. In Bali you know that the superior ones are the natives, and you but a rude and noisy eccentricity. The hardship will be the leaving of the island at all. There are those who have become enmeshed in the tangles of its joyous beauties and do not leave. But fortunately for Bali they are few."[22]

Franklin Price Knott was widely known was a painter of miniatures, but when color photography came, he laid down his brushes and took up the color plates. In 1927, he returned from a forty-thousand-mile trip to the Orient as an explorer for The National Geographic Society, bringing back several hundred natural color photographs. He made a month-long visit to Bali, making his headquarters in Denpasar. "The quest for photographic adventure along these island paths, past green fields, temples, and

Balinese woman bathing. Illustration by Alexander King, based on a photograph by Gregor Krause. From Hickman Powell, *Bali: The Last Paradise* (London: Jonathan Cape, 1930).

walled villages, is an endless delight," Knott wrote, "unless a carabao suddenly floundered up from the mud to chase the white man." His guide, mixing Dutch with broken English and Malay, only to break out in voluble Balinese when excited, said: "You make picture? *Gewis*! I show you temple, flowers—and much purty girl." But time and again, Knott glimpsed a pretty face and wanted to photograph it, only to have the girl run away when she was asked to pose.

"Bali is a peculiar place," André Roosevelt explained to Knott. "Here books are bound from tree leaves. Religion is the chief occupation. Trial marriage usually takes. It's land of the slimmest women and the fattest pigs. Birds talk and butterflies fly like birds. Praying to pagan gods and fooling pagan devils are the main pastimes. Tourist attractions are many, but tourists few. Our island lies hard by the big path of round-the-world trippers, yet few see it—or even hear of it. It's a social and sociological curiosity, this island of Bali. Its natives are what biologists might call 'sports' in East Indian ethnology. It lies a night's cruise east of Java.... Its women are the fairest in all Malaysia—and a dressmaker would starve."

Knott, who knew many famous models in American and European art centers, recalled few specimens of the human race as easy to look at as the beautiful women of Bali. "Erect, slender-limbed, small of waist and ankle, with tapering fingers, and long, wavy tresses falling over a smooth skin nearly white or light bronze, with perfect, even teeth and a singular grace and dignity of carriage, they had few physical equals among womankind.

> When one stops to think that Bali, with its singular charms, is only a night's run from the tourist path through Soerabaya, one wonders that irresistible civilization has not already upset its primitive life.
>
> Till cheap factory-made sarongs came from Europe, these simple garments were works of art, for at weaving, as at carving and in the fabrication of objects of gold and silver, the Balinese are skillful.
>
> Of course, modernism is bound soon to sweep this primitive isle. Already, the commonplace galvanized-iron roof of the white man's tropic conquest is lifting up its ugliness, and bicycles make tracks on sandy beaches. A few automobiles have come; hotels may soon be built, for tourists are beginning to ask, "Where is this trick island of Bali?"[24]

Oswald Hering was an architect who practiced in New York City. He made a world tour, during which he took what he believed to be the first motion pictures of native life in Bali. "What prompted me to go the Bali?" he asked. "Rumor. The biggest crop raised in the Orient is rumors. Somewhere in India. I heard about the island Eden, in the Malay Archipelago, with its beautiful half-naked women, and as my itinerary included a visit to Java I determined to sacrifice Siam and Cambodia and, instead, spend a fortnight in Bali. In Soerabaja, at the eastern extremity of Java, I found that a small steamer, "the pig boat," made weekly trips to "Little Java," to fetch a cargo of pigs, the island's chief export to Java and Singapore, for the consumption of the pork-loving Chinese. The little boat has three or four staterooms, near the bow, and when the wind blows from that quarter aft, where the pigs are lodged, one can make the overnight trip with fair comfort."[25]

Hering's story was mainly concerned with the beauty and art of southern Bali, and with its simple, devout, undefiled, and unspoiled people. There was plenty of good food on the island for everyone. There were no bread lines in Bali. The Dutch were satisfied to levy a small tax and leave the island to the cultivation and enjoyment of its people. The male population of Bali did very little work. So far as Hering observed, their main occupation was training their brilliantly plumaged cocks for the weekly fight. Cockfighting was the national sport, and, "curiously enough in a heathen country," the feathery combats took place only on Sundays. The Dutch had officially prohibited cockfighting, but just as in "civilized" countries, the sudden prohibition of a long-time inviolable custom was nullified, and the cock fight throve in Bali as freely as the speakeasy on Broadway.[26]

Hering observed that the island received an average of fifty visitors annually. He inquired if there were any resident Americans. There was one, he was informed, André Roosevelt. There were about a half dozen antiquated Fords on the island, some battered bicycles, and a few dilapidated Dodge buses rattled back and forth on the main roads. These were the only means of getting around, short of hiking or riding on the back of a horse. Produce and merchandise were carried on the head, chiefly by women. A Balinese woman toted on her head a load of fruits and vegetables, sometimes three feet high, with far more grace than the average New Yorker ported her inevitable handbag.

Desiring to take a motion picture of a *lelong* dancing performance, which was done only at night, Hering paid twenty-five guilders in order to have it done during the daytime. The entire village populace turned out to witness this unique performance of the *lelong*, especially for the American *Tuan Raja* and his magic camera that took photographs of people while they moved. "Little did I imagine the dire consequences of that occasion," he wrote later. "My poor Bali! I, thy devoted, bungling, stupid lover, have unwittingly seduced thee! I, thy adorer, to gratify a selfish desire, have taught thy beautiful people how to turn art into guilders, with which no doubt thy lithe and stalwart men will not buy pants, to replace the wholly adequate loin cloth, or the comfortable and graceful sarong; and *bajus* and

Cockfight. From J. C. Lester, *Landschap, Bevolking, Godsdienst, Gebruiken en Gewoonten, Architectuur en Kunst van het Eiland Bali* (Harlem: Droste, 1932).

cotton waists will cover the matchless beauty of the breasts and bosoms of thy lovely women! Woe is me!"[27]

Hubert Jay Stowitts, dancer and self-taught painter, who joined Anna Pavlova's dance company and ended his dancing career at the Folies Bergere in Paris, also lived and painted in Bali. In October 1930 he wrote to his mother from Bali:

> We are here on the magic island where the other culture makes one positively scorn vulgar white Aryans. The so-called white race is mechanized but really not civilized. These people have much more real culture and inherent good manners and are completely devoid of everything that is course and vulgar. All the arts are alive and thriving, but none of the arts are done for money, but simply out of instinctive necessity. They have their symphonies every night, and even when there are no feasts the dancers rehearse just for the thrill of it. None of them are paid. The leader of one of the orchestras and one of the composers are both chauffeurs, and the best dancer is a fisherman during the day. Many of the children can recite whole plays from the Mahabarata and Ramayana by heart.
>
> However, the island is already ruined by the uncultured white man! The Balinese men wear white or striped shirts instead of a beautiful colored scarf as formerly and ugly cowboy hats and hideous gold caps instead of their graceful turbans.[28]

The sculptor Malvina Hoffman was asked by Stanley Field and Marshall Field III to create sculptures for an exhibition named "The Races of Man." The task required the artist to travel to remote corners of the world searching for authentic models. She was accompanied by her husband, Sam Grimson, a photographer who took photographs of the models for the statues and kept notebooks of body measurements. He was also her secretary and her plaster caster. Melvina's unflagging energy and interest in every aspect of "native" appearance and custom was combined with uncritical acceptance of the most timeworn clichés.

"Bali," Melvina wrote, "by its isolation and lack of accommodation for the casual tourist, and because of the wise policy of the Dutch which has left Bali for the Balinese, has retained its individuality and primitive character. The people seem more like unspoiled children of Eden than any other race I have yet had the opportunity of studying. Surrounded as they are by gardens as beautiful as an earthly paradise can be, creatures of sunlight and music exude a mellow satisfaction of life that seems too good to be true. Bali is an island where gods still sanctify existence by their presence, and the people like their religion instead of preaching it."[29]

The German artist, art historian, and author Elisabet Delbrück spent her time in Bali at the rest house in Kintamani, where, for days at a time, she was the only European. Back in Germany she held many lectures on her experiences in Bali. The American painter Dana Pond, who traveled widely, had a charming house in the Balinese quarter of Denpasar. The American painter and etcher Elisabeth Telling stayed two months in Bali, much of the time at Tirtha Empul. Reviewing her exhibition in New York a year later, an art critic wrote that Bali, which was attracting an increasing number of American tourists, seemed to be luring American artists as well. "Telling ranged up and down the social scale," he wrote, "from a ricefield worker to princesses and from dancers to Buddhist priests. One who has never been to Bali leaves her exhibition with the conviction that she portrays its citizens with insight and without flattery." The French illustrator and cartoonist Oscar Fabrès, born in Chile but living and working in the Netherlands, visited Bali and produced some of the best cartoons of the island. Angelica Schmitz ("Gela") Archipenko, a sculptor and wife of the sculptor Alexander Archipenko, also visited Bali, as did the Austrian painter Emil Rizek, who spent several months in Bali.

Henry Eichheim, violinist, conductor, and composer, made several trips to the Far East resulting in a collection of much musical material and musical instruments. Eichheim visited Bali with Leopold Stokowski, conductor of the Philadelphia Symphony Orchestra, who was also on a trip to the Orient. Stokowski relished the wonderful metallic sounds the gamelans produced, and obtained in Bali gongs that he took back to Philadelphia. Eichheim memorialized their experience by writing a series of brief tone poems, using a number of gamelan instruments in the percussion section of the orchestra. One of tone poems, *Bali*, which Colin McPhee dismissed as "dished-up impressionism," was first performed by the Philadelphia Orchestra under the direction of Stokowski, who frequently performed the work, and even recorded it in 1934 on an RCA Victor label. The Russian violinist Alexander Mogilevsky arrived in Bali from Moscow. He became madly enthusiastic about Balinese music and promised to tell the composer Igor Stravinski that all European and modern music was like a pointless children's game compared with what was being done in Bali.

John Charles Van Dyke served for many years as a professor of art history at Rutgers University and head of the library at the New Brunswick Theological Seminary. Widely acclaimed as art critic, he moved freely in the "best" of New York City's social circles. Despite his teaching and library work, his duties were light. Armed with a growing reputation as an art critic, he went on extensive travels abroad, stopping at the island of Bali for a week. "Bali is at once declared to be the most wonderful of all the islands," he stated. "Perhaps it is—at least the wonder does not die out on closer acquaintance. One goes ashore at Boeleleng, submits to the suggestion of the tourist agency there, and allows himself to be hustled around the island on an automobile, like a ride in a whirligig, and yet still comes away with an impression of beauty, perhaps seen only out of the tail of his eye as he turned this sharp curve, or shot down that precipitous valley."

The greatest interest in Bali for Van Dyke was the Balinese themselves, their natural beauty, their fine detachment from Western civilization, and their naive unconsciousness of their own qualities. Every one of the Balinese was apparently well-fed, clothed, housed, contented, and even happy. Van Dyke praised the superb physique of the Balinese and the fact that the Balinese were quite perfect in type and development. The only badly set-up people that he saw in Bali were Dutch officials and American tourists.[30]

Ruth Page, a dancer and choreographer who pioneered and developed the opera-in-ballet, a bold new form that became her forte, toured the Orient in the fall of 1928. Her performances included an appearance in Tokyo at the enthronement ceremonies of Emperor Hirohito. Then she came to Bali. "To me," she wrote, "all of Bali seemed like an orchid-haunted garden of dreams; sounds, flowers, people, are soft and sweet. There is a delicious moment between consciousness and sleep in which a simple impression gathers about itself a strange and luminous logic—a moment in which apparent facts are seen and understood through a lens of magic atmosphere. When I recapture that twilight and look through it again, I am tempted to say of Bali that its music, people, and flowers are imbued with a single enchanting spirit which haunts them all. And though I can recall quite accurately the days of my enchantment in Bali, to me their reality is but the outward expression of my dreams." On her return to the United States, Page performed *Two Balinese Rhapsodies*, which she choreographed to original Balinese themes (arranged by the American composer Louis Horst).[31]

Hickman Powell, one of the top reporters at *The New York Morning World*, took a leave for a trip around the world. Powell did not seek adventure but respite from the strenuous pace of modern life. "I hardly know why I went to Bali," he later wrote. "Perhaps it was to satisfy myself that other men had lied."

Powell described Buleleng as "corrugated iron roofs. Chinamen in white pyjamas. Bombay traders, lost tribe of burlesque show comedians, with their shirt tails hanging out. Sweat and mosquitoes. Tin cans, through all the East the worst malfeasance of the Standard Oil Company. Dutchmen in peaked official caps, with high-buttoned choking collars." He then asked: "The belles of Bali, where were they? I had seen men leer, and nudge, saying: 'They don't wear any shirts.' Men's voices had grown deeper and their eyes dim, as they spoke of chaste dryads in a tropic Arcady."[32]

As we descended, the air softened to a balmy warmth that kept the freshness of the mountains. Then appeared a solitary female figure, swinging toward us up the road. The sun shone russet on an earthen pot above her head, matched to the strips of a bold *sarong* trailing easily from waist to feet. A scarf fell carelessly from a shoulder, and the bronze bowls of maiden breasts projected angular, living shadows. She walked majestically, with slowly swinging arms, with never a glance for

Young Balinese woman. From Aage Krarup-Nielson, *Leven en Avonturen van een Oostinjevaarder op Bali* (Amsterdam: E. Querido, 1928).

staring eyes that now rolled past her. And all at once she was but a part of a vast spreading wonderland, embodies dreams of pastoral poets.[33]

"I had glimpsed the beauty of the earth's end," wrote Powell. "She was a slattern, soiled wench; and pursuit gave way to sad depression. I scarcely sought beauty any more; but now I found Bali. I had found a tiny spot that is different from any other place in the world."

Powell came to Bali for the usual three days' tour, but met André Roosevelt, and decided to remain. He made his home with a native family in Bengkel, a village in southern Bali. From this vantage point he could watch the pageant of the Balinese as yet unspoiled and unself-conscious. Powell was struck by the culture of the Balinese; their religion fascinated him. He had been charmed by their wonderful music and had spent hours admiring their dances.

After an hour or two spent with Powell, André Roosevelt realized that Powell was a keen young American newspaper man who had assimilated in a few hours infinitely more than the average person would have in the same number of months. Powell had the peculiar knack that is characteristic of the good newspaper reporter of digging deep below the surface and delving into the psychology of things unseen; he had the soul of an artist, and he could also write. When Roosevelt suggested that Powell remain in Bali to write the first book in English about the island and its people, Powell could not resist the temptation. His stay on Bali formed the basis for his book, *The Last Paradise*, which attracted many more tourists to that island. Alexander King, who illustrated the book, although he never visited the island of Bali, became a Bali enthusiast from listening to the stories of Bali told by André.

Helen Eva Yates was the women's editor of the *China Press* in Shanghai and writer for the Dutch East Indies government in Java. She wrote *Bali: Enchanted Isle; a Travel Book*, dedicating it to Lowell Thomas, at whose suggestion the book was written. "This is not meant to be a guide-book," she wrote, "but I hope it may tempt you to go forth and 'adventure' for yourself in Bali as I did."

> It is difficult to write about Bali. One has to see the island to understand its peace and tranquility and exotic tropical atmosphere. Even the lucky travelers who visit it seldom have time to remain long enough to study the mystery of Balinese life. If they can stay a month or two, they may learn a great deal about the customs, of course. But even if they were to live in Bali a long time, they would not fathom the secret inner life of the natives.

Two weeks in Bali gives the traveler a picture of this idyllic isle of mythical people. That is time enough to make impressions that will last a lifetime, and fill one's memory with glowing pictures to recall on less happy days. As in all traveling, the more you read and bring to a country in the way of study and interest, the more you carry away in experience and understanding.

Each month of the dry season, during the full moon, there is a continual round of entertainment, dances, shadow plays, and temple ceremonies. So the new visitor should certainly hunt up an almanac and be sure of a full moon during the time he is visiting Bali, if he would see the island at its beautiful best.

The best months in which to see cremations are the dry months of late summer, during August, September, October, and November, when there is little rain.[34]

5

"Saint" Walter

> *Saint Walter. He was amazing and aristocratic bold and benevolent creative dedicated engagé enlightened fascinating famous gifted historical influential intellectual inspiring just judicious kind lucky musical noble original pioneering popular persecuted queer rich successful talented vital wise extraordinary and young when he died, too young, yet who is to say when life is completed? He turned his back on the white overlords, refusing to be one of them, although he accepted their honours, for it did not occur to him to despise colonialism itself, only that it was too often brutal, too rarely enlightened. But his admiration was reserved for the brown-skinned people he found here, and his admiration was unreserved: their beauty, their delicacy, their natural aristocratic grace, their artistry, the harmony of their lives, the richness of their culture.*
>
> Inez Baranay[1]

Despite the enduring popularity of sensationalist images, a markedly different perspective on Bali also began to emerge in the late 1920s. The main catalyst in this formation was Walter Spies, who had taken up residence in Ubud, where he was joined by his friends and associates.

Walter Spies, painter, musician, photographer, choreographer, linguist, *bon vivant*, host to scholars, celebrities and millionaires, and lover of young Balinese boys, who was later dubbed, with some justification, "the Gauguin of Bali," was certainly the most flamboyant westerner to live in Bali. Born in Moscow to German parents, he spent his youth there, in privileged diplomatic circles. But when World War I broke out, his family was interned in a small town in the Ural Mountains. After the war, he returned to Germany. Largely a self-taught painter and musician, he lived and worked in the company of the great German expressionist painters and avant-garde composers, studying art and music in Dresden and Berlin, and leading the life of a young Berlin homosexual. He became the lover of Friedrich Wilhelm Murnau, one of the three directors on whose work rests the fame of the German cinema of the 1920s. In 1923, at twenty-eight years of age, fleeing the clasps of the older and very possessive Murnau, Spies signed up as a sailor on a freighter sailing to the Netherlands Indies and jumped ship in Java. He first settled in Bandung, was employed as a pianist in a Chinese cinema, and then moved to Yogyakarta, where he became master of the sultan's music and conductor of his orchestra.

It was at the invitation of the prince of Ubud that Spies made his first visit to Bali in 1925, and it was in the prince's palace that he set up his first house—with his piano, bicycle, and butterfly net—when he decided to establish himself in Bali two years later. Soon thereafter, he built a house in Campuan, at the edge of the village, on land belonging to the palace. "Walter Spies's choice of Bali, and of a continuing light involvement with Balinese male youth, seemed part of his repudiation of the kind of dominance and submission, authority and dependence, which he associated with European culture. The very dissociated impersonality of Bali gave him the kind of freedom that he sought," was Margaret Mead's assessment of him. In Bali, Spies found that finally he was at home. Spies called his life in Bali "my eternal birthday."[2]

Louise and Robert Koke visited Spies in 1936, and Louise described the house:

> A dark, two-storey house clung to the side of a steep ravine. Dense foliage screened it from the road and made a secret stillness. Below the house an oval swimming pool lay half hidden among the trees, fed by a bamboo pipe from a hillside spring. The house was decorated with Balinese paintings and antique carvings. One of the Mr. Spies' own paintings, a forest scene in great detail with great shafts of light casting long shadows, hung in the living room. There was a grand piano as well—a remarkable find in such a place.
>
> At the swimming pool, the servants brought a low table laden with bottles, glasses and ice and set it in water at the shallow end of the pool. Mr. Spies, lying partly immersed, poured the drinks. I sat up to my waist in the cool, mountain water, holding a glass of Holland gin and imagining what exotic parties could take place in that hidden ravine. At night the wooded slope would be mysteriously lit by burning wicks set in hanging coconut shells. Metal threads in the servants' garments would shimmer in the warm glow. The air would be little heavy with burning incense, and the odour of coconut oil in freshly washed and anointed hair. That was an impression to take away.[3]

At the back of the house Walter built a studio. When the muse of painting was upon him, he would put on shorts and a half gourd on his head and went into hiding to paint. Nobody ever saw him place the brush on canvas. He would paint for hours on end in complete seclusion, coming out only when he got hungry. It took months to finish a picture. Miguel and Rosa Covarrubias always wanted a painting of Walter's but never managed to get one as he never had more than one at a time, and that one was always sold in advance.

Spies became the flamboyant figurehead of the Western colony of artists and scientists. His house in Campuan became a busy salon abuzz with curious foreigners. Spies's influence in Bali was derived as much from the nature of his personality as from his artistic achievements and original insights. He was sensitive and somewhat reclusive, often shutting himself away for days when working on a new painting, but the sincerity of his devotion to cultural matters won him many friends, both among the Balinese and the expatriate community. He not only found Bali aesthetically rewarding but, as a homosexual, was also attracted by the islanders' comparatively tolerant attitudes. For the Balinese, homosexuality was merely a pastime to be enjoyed by young unmarried men and not a matter for moral condemnation.

Spies was interested in Balinese music and transcribed it, he painted Balinese landscapes, he photographed, he was well mannered and showed the governor-general of the Netherlands Indies the wonders of Balinese art during the latter's visit in 1937. He was one of the few foreigners in the Dutch Indies who could get on with the typical Dutch civil servants who were provincial, thorough, and strict. Some of them, inevitably, envied Spies: his relations with the Balinese people were better then theirs, and to foreigners he was a charming, cosmopolitan, and intelligent host. He attracted all the people who really did matter who visited the island, and he managed his affairs rather well. He was not after money, but he had a talent for commerce. At the same time, he was a romantic who detested the influence of strangers on "his" Balinese. He was communicative, yet aloof. He was the center of "European" life in Bali—all whites in Balinese eyes being from Europe. He was impressive. He was the kind of man that was missed the moment he left the room. His contemporary, Edgar du Perron, described him as "a Balinese institution." The westerners believed that the Balinese needed Western guides to teach them how to remain authentic Balinese, and Spies was one of these westerners. He assisted in creating dances that were to be performed for tourists on the ground of the Bali Hotel. He wanted the dances to be real Balinese and yet harmless to the Western eye which was not used to the outlets of ritual "violence" so characteristic of trance dancers.

Martin Birnbaum, an art dealer, described Spies as an excellent musician, a good naturalist, and a painter of remarkable pictures that breathed

Walter Spies with his Cockatoo and pet monkey at Campuan. Courtesy of The Horniman Museum and Gardens, London.

the very spirit of Bali. Spies's house, built in part without nails was a storehouse of Balinese art. In the garden he had a veritable menagerie of pets, including monkeys, doves, cockatoos, dogs, and even a python. He had made careful piano transcriptions of the music of various gamelans. Whenever he found a hitherto undescribed spider, slug, or dragonfly, he made scientifically correct watercolor drawings of it. Sculptors, weavers, draftsmen, and carvers of bone found in him a ready purchaser of their best products.[4]

"In daily life it was almost impossible to communicate with Spies in other than playful, semi-jocular ways," wrote Claire Holt. "And if on some rare occasions he could be led into a serious conversation, it would soon end by his slipping out of it as from an uncomfortably high chair. He loved to play with and at everything."[5]

Walter went on to build an enviable lifestyle for himself in the cool foothills of Ubud, where he was waited on by handsome boys and kept amused by his cockatoo and pet monkey. Bali's image crystallized around him and his social set, and for many, Walter Spies came to represent all the charms and graces of Bali. The rich, the famous, the titled, and the simply curious beat a trail to the famous house in the hills of Ubud. He would open his house to usually very wealthy, and frequently noble, paying guests. When short of funds, Walter would rent his house to guests, moving into cheaper accommodation. When he had money—usually from patronage—he would build a new one. By these means he acquired five or six guest houses which could be let out.

Spies's charm was legendary. Anyone of any importance who came to Bali in the 1930s came to visit him. His lifestyle was irresistibly chic. He was the host and guide to scholars and millionaires, to artists and to Hollywood stars. He had many Balinese dancers and musicians friends, and could command astonishing performances to entertain his guests. Johan Fabricius, a Dutch adventure novelist, wrote that Spies's "whole soul was bound up with the island to which he had come in search of happiness; he was, perhaps, the only white man who ever succeeded in finding it there, though one should remember that, being partly Russian by birth, he already had a touch of the Asiatic about him."[6] Miguel Covarrubias called Spies "Bali's most famous resident," and in his book on Bali, he acknowledged his debt to Spies. In his charming devil-may-care way, Spies was familiar with every phase of Balinese life, and has been the constant source of disinterested information to every archaeologist, musician, or artist who had come to Bali.[7]

Theodora Benson described Spies as "a sort of uncrowned king of Bali." "He is clever and nice," she wrote, "and knows more about it than anyone." An authentic friend of the Balinese, he contributed more to the prestige of the white man in Bali than the Dutch colonial "despots." He gave Miguel and Roas Covarrubias his time and his knowledge for the pure love of it. He knew every village and all the people in it, the days of their temple feasts, the names of their dancers, musicians, actors, and artists. Margaret Mead described Walter as "a perfectly delightful person, an artist and musician who has welcomed and entertained all the interesting people who come here. He has done a great deal to stimulate modern Balinese painting and has painted Bali himself and in general has worked out a most perfect relationship between himself, the island, its people and its traditions. Spies is a delightful host and I shall not soon forget the days I spent with him."[8] Leopold Stokowski called Spies "a rare personality," and described him as a "handsome man with brilliant expressive eyes and flexible physique." He was also gifted as a linguist and spoke well the two languages of Bali, so that he penetrated deeply into the life and arts of the island. On the other hand, Spies's love for the Balinese was not contradicted by his quiet appreciation of colonialism and his stance against modernization.

As the years passed, Ubud became a byword for hospitality and culture. On one occasion, two American women were said to have arrived at the house with the express purpose of shaking the hand of Walter Spies. Having achieved their objective, they drove off. Some visitors had learned of Walter's way of life through his reputation in the salons of Europe and North America, others were passed on by mutual friends. Moreover, he was employed by the colonial authorities to promote Bali's image abroad and played a role in the development of the Balinese contribution to the Colonial Exposition in Paris in 1931.

Walter disliked the pettiness and officiousness of certain Dutch civil servants, but he was never entirely opposed to imperialism, and, like many of his circle, regarded enlightened colonialism as the way forward. Walter and his circle were closely associated with the more culturally aware members of the colonial service, such as Roelof Goris. Goris was, however, somewhat isolated from the colonial mainstream, not only through his alienation from the mentality of the Dutch civil service, but also because of his homosexuality and alcoholism.

Spies's house was often so crowded that he could hardly find time to pursue his painting, music, and other interests. It depressed him so much that he had a cabin built in the mountains near Ideh to serve as a quiet retreat where he could escape when he wanted to work in peace. Spies was temperamental when he went into seclusion to paint; he would work incessantly for months on one of his canvasses. They were snatched by prosperous art-loving travelers who were lucky enough to find Spies with a finished painting. There were never two paintings in his house at once. Walter's paintings fetched higher prices than those of any of his colleagues in Bali. In the 1930s, the average oil painting cost between three hundred and six hundred guilders. Walter Spies's prices were "somewhat' different: between twenty-five hundred and three thousand guilders per painting! He supported himself by painting and by unabashed sponging off the rich and famous. Mornau continued with his generosity toward Walter and sent him money every month. In return, Walter sent him paintings. Spies also received a bequest from Mornau, large enough for him to live on for two years. At one point, Spies wrote that it was time he started to earn a little less money.

Since his aim was to withdraw for long period of time, he had to find someone to manage his house at Campuan during his absences. Spies got seriously in trouble when his house was rented out as a hostel. Two Germans, Walter von Dreesen, author and illustrator, and Fritz Lindner, Vicki Baum's stepbrother, who were Walter's guests at the time, agreed to look after the house as a hostel for paying guests. Dreesen was tactless and arrogant with the servants, insisting on being addressed as "Baron," and the Balinese mocked him behind his back, calling him "the big belly with the little head." The behavior of this management, to which Spies handed over the house and that of the clientele, shocked even the Dutch authorities. Criticism was leveled at the "new boarding house," and it did not escape the attention of the colonial authorities that the tone of the house had declined.

When Spies was accused of letting his once romantic home at Campuan become an important cog in the machinery of the Balinese tourist industry, he replied that romantic Bali depended on tourist guilders, and that he came to his senses and no longer put everyone up for free. "Unfortunately I am not able to live solely from painting," he wrote, "and the tiny trickle that Campuan brings in with its paying guests is just enough to keep alive." The less idealistic, but more commercial, reality of life in Campuan in the late 1930s, appears all too clearly in a letter he wrote to Jane Belo (Colin McPhee's wife) in February 1938 in which he described Campuan as "always full of guests, till now not very nice, I must admit, and last month we made over a thousand guilders!! Isn't that fun!"[9]

Most of the foreigners who lived in Bali during the 1930s acknowledged how much they owed to the competence and goodwill of Walter Spies. It was to him that André Roosevelt and Baron Victor von Plessen owed the enduring allure of their films *Goona-Goona* and *Die Insel der Dämonen*. To a large extent, the myth of genius surrounding Walter had been self-cultivated through the careful assessment of those people he could best use for the realization of his projects and goals. While Spies was not manipulative, he knew what he wanted and how to get it. Spies's charisma showed in his ability to sell his paintings for many times the price that any other artist in Bali would have dared to request. If he was asked how he decided on the price of a painting, Spies would simply say that he "just plucked it from the air." Two of his Balinese paintings were sold for over one million dollars apiece at recent auctions in Singapore.[10]

Walter was too occupied in his hideaway to be concerned with mundane matters. Perhaps because he was so engrossed in his work, he failed to grasp the full significance of the events in Europe and Pacific Asia. Persecuted as homosexual, his tragic death only added to his romantic myth. When the Germans invaded Holland, Spies was interned by the Dutch in Java and later in Sumatra. Shipped with other German civilian prisoners in January 1942 to Ceylon, his ship, the *Van Imhoff*, was hit by a Japanese bomb and sank.

The Dutch artist Rudolf Bonnet studied art in Amsterdam and then left for Italy, where he met Nieuwenkamp, who told him about Bali and convinced him to travel there. He arrived in Bali in January 1929 and was soon enthused by the dance and pageantry and decided to stay. After two months in Tampaksiring, he moved to Peliatan, and later took over Spies's water palace in Ubud (when Spies moved to a new house in Campuan), setting his studio there. Bonnet was often maligned as a colorless man, incredibly reserved, and rather stiff, but at the same time, he was a man of grace, sensitivity, and wonderful organizational skills. He felt limitless love and respect for Bali and the Balinese. His knowledge of Bali and Balinese art and culture was immense. He was at heart a *bon vivant*, who found Bali the perfect setting in which to live his dreams. He stated that one could live happily in Bali if one was content with oneself. He became involved in community work such as healthcare, education and art development, and particularly with the Bali Museum and the *Pita Maha*, a society of young Balinese artists.

Bonnet worked hard. He painted from 7 A.M. to 12 A.M. and again from 1:30 P.M. to 4 P.M. and no one could disturb him between those hours. But after 4 P.M. anyone might come and many artists visited him. The first two pictures he exchanged for a car—a Durand. Walter Spies, on the other hand, just worked by order. He commanded such a high price that one painting gave him enough money for him to live a year in Bali.[11]

Bonnet's relations with Spies were founded on comradery rather than on real friendship. Bonnet got to know Spies *too* well. "What a pity," he wrote, "that so much genius and such insipidness should be combined in the same person."

Bonnet not only produced his own work but also encouraged young Balinese artists, promoting their work all over the world. Together with Spies and Tjokorda Gde Agung Sukawati, a royal patron of the arts in Ubud, he founded the *Pita Maha*, whose aim was to maintain a high artistic level of its members. The society's stated purpose was to support artists and craftsmen working in various media and styles, and to encourage experimentation with Western materials, theories of anatomy, and perspective. Thanks to his devotion, members of the *Pita Maha* produced work of high quality during its short time of existence. Spies and Bonnet's influence on Balinese art turned out to be a crucial one. Spies had been the "PR man" of Balinese painting—he had allowed himself to be affected by the island and its people without trying to unduly affect them in turn. Bonnet had been the "guide," the teacher, trying to show his pupils the right direction in theory and practice, but never attempted to "recreate them after his own image." Spies and Bonnet also collaborated on projects concerning the preservation of true Balinese art. Spies was the curator of the Bali Museum and Bonnet was the sales director. They turned the Balinese into "professional" artists by striving to control the artistic quality of the works they marketed and helping them to direct their works toward the budding tourist market. At the same time, Spies and Bonnet stimulated the making of small-sized paintings that fit into tourists' suitcases. While Spies was flamboyant, Bonnet was a nuts and bolts man who made sure that the plans worked.

Bonnet and Spies, as unattached homosexual men, could easily immerse themselves in Balinese life and develop close contact with individuals while encouraging and supporting the talented artists surrounding them. Bonnet's dedication to the Balinese and their art had no peer. They represented two polarities of the Bali expatriate homosexual lifestyle of the era.

Baron Victor von Plessen, German artist, zoologist, filmmaker, and member of the Kaiser's Corp of Guards during World War I, subsequently studied art in Berlin and Munich and became a versatile and talented artist. He later studied ornithology and ethnology in Germany, learned Malay, and undertook five expeditions to the Dutch East Indies. "Why be a big butter and cheese man in Schleswig-Holstein when there are wild beauties to be painted in the tropic seas, strange customs to be learned, flamboyant birds to be collected?" he asked. Son of one of Prussia's greatest families, he mingled with the humblest laborers as a friend, and the Dutch officials were puzzled and called him a socialist. The natives called him *Tuan Raja*. From time to time, von Plessen visited Spies; they would hold long conversations, drink whiskey, or watch dances. Von Plessen also turned out to be one of Spies's patrons. From time to time he would buy some of Spies's paintings and traded his car for two canvasses. "I think the fineness of the pictures exceeds that of the car," Spies wrote his mother, "yet I could do with a car. It is a beautiful car, very strong, and climbs the mountains like nothing else. I am learning to drive now." Von Plessen produced the motion picture *Island of Demons* in 1930–31 with Spies's help. He created the outline for the motion picture, but Spies was the principal adviser.[12]

6
Last Paradise

Bali rapidly developed into one of the most romantic destinations and the most romantic stop on the tourist itinerary for cruise ships and yachts. As the 1930s progressed, the image of Bali that emerged was one of a splendid place for romantic foreigners looking for an Eastern paradise. Bali became synonymous with beauty and sensuality (bare-breasted women) and artistic talent (every Balinese was by nature an artist), mixed with glimpses of exotic anger (trance).

Dutch theologians ridiculed the colonial concern with Balinese culture, calling Bali an artificial would-be-authentic tourist place and a cultural reservation. The Dutch Christian author Mary Pos wrote sarcastically about the veneration the white residents in Bali pretended to have for Balinese tradition while "they drive in an open convertible with a bunch of lover-boys on front seat, back seat, and hood."[1] But the dissident voices were drowned by the great chorus of administrators, artists, travelers, and journalists who continually reinforced the images that constituted traditional Bali. These images gained credibility every time they were reiterated. When travelers went to Bali, they saw what they wanted to see.

Photographic prints published in popular magazines, postcards, tourist advertising, and travel accounts were especially important in establishing a romanticized and formulaic presentation of Bali. These images motivated others to visit or study the island, resulting in an ongoing stream of new photographs that, in turn, inspired still more to take the journey, and to literally reproduce the island's paradisiacal character.

Margaret Mead, however, believed that the steamship companies that advertised Bali in the 1930s tried and failed to make it the lineal descendant of Tahiti in the romantic 1920s, with the slim figure of a high-breasted, scantily clothed girl as the symbol. "The average tourist—the businessman from Milwaukee, the college boy from California, the schoolmistress from New England—came away from Bali talking not of undressed maidens but of happiness and art. For even the cursory three-day tourist visiting the

Dutch East Indies in the 1930s recognized in Bali the very opposite of the pleasant, sensuous idling away of which the romancers had imputed to the South Sea Islands."[2] But a glimpse of the "Garden of Eden" promised in the widely-distributed tourist images of the day was sufficient to convince the disoriented, disenchanted, wealthy, and famous to make the long trip by ocean liner or by yacht to experience paradise for themselves.

Paul Drennan Cravath, an American lawyer best known as the chief architect of the modern large corporate law firm, traveled widely after his retirement and visited Bali twice. He was accompanied by Alfred Rutgers Whitney, a retired construction engineer, yachtsman, and traveler. Cravath wrote:

> Bali is the best advertised of the Dutch East Indian Islands. I ran across several Americans who planned to visit Bali without any idea of visiting Java or any of the other Dutch Islands. The average American does not know why he is so anxious to visit Bali. It is the result of clever propaganda, and is perhaps not disassociated from the fact that the Balinese of both sexes wear no clothes above the waist.
>
> A short visit to Bali had been part of my program from the start. When I reached Surabaya I found in circulation the exciting rumor that there was to be a grand cremation in Bali the following week. The hotels were filled with Americans who had come from far and near for the event, and the K.M.P. Steamship Co. had arranged to run three steamers instead of one, to carry the throng of tourists to the cremation.[3]

"Alas, the serpent of Western civilization has entered this Eden of Bali," Cravath continued, "and the inevitable process of modernization has already set in. The flocks of tourists are already having their influence. A few of the children have taken to begging. The ladies of North Bali are already aping their Caucasian sisters by wearing jackets, with dire effect on the picturesqueness of the crowds and the cost of living. Those interested in the popularity of the island for tourists are warning the natives of south Bali that if they take to wearing too many clothes the Island will lose its chief attraction to tourists."[4]

When Cravath returned to Bali three years later, he could not see much change in Bali except that a large proportion of the women now wore jackets. He found that Bali was still the mecca of all tourist steamers that visit that part of the world, and in time the simplicity and modesty of the Balinese was bound to succumb to the baneful influence of the American tourist.[5]

Paul Morand, French novelist and diplomat, was granted a leave of absence from the Ministry of Foreign Affairs and spent several years traveling around the world.

6. Last Paradise

In 1925, when I went round the world, I had never heard of Bali, and neither had most people. Cruises did not stop there, travel agencies did not mention it, the shipping companies did not evoke it in the soft colors of their advertisements, and after a night of dancing till dawn the ladies did not say, with a sigh: "Shall I go to bed or fly to Bali?"

During the last three or four years the movies have drawn the attention of the world to Bali. Astounding burials, terminating in truly Wagnerian flames, strange ceremonies in which the participants stabbed each other, and many other delightful or mysterious rites, abandoned elsewhere, were thus revealed to our *blasé* gaze.

The rumor quickly spread, in a world sick and tired since the war, that in Bali every day is a holiday, as in Venice in the time of Casanova. First it was included in one or two American cruises; then, at the Colonial Exposition in Paris in 1931, we were charmed and surprised by the Bali dancers. Nowadays a visit to Bali is compulsory; it is the Capri of 1932; it has taken the place of languorous Tahiti in the minds of college boys and in the hearts of women of forty.

A colonial hotel and bungalows have already been built in Den Pasar; Chinese merchants are installing themselves like worms in fruit; batiks are manufactured in Manchester; the inlaid porcelain in the walls of the temples is Czecho-Slovakian; opposite the coast of Java the women have ceased to go naked and cover their breasts. Let us hasten to talk of Bali, for tomorrow it will be only a memory, so true is it that men always kill what they wish to love.[6]

The guide to Bali prepared by G. H. von Faber in 1932 declared that Bali had been drawn out of its isolation and was coming more and more under Western influence, and that Bali boasted electric light, cinemas, hotels, largely ugly advertisement hoardings, telegraph and telephone service and tourists who pour in from far and near. The guide advised readers to take time over their visit. It stated that it was advisable to travel light, a portmanteau could hold all that was needed for a stay of a couple of weeks in the island. Ordinary washing could be done everywhere but soap must be taken because none of the hotels or rest houses provided this important requisite. A blanket would be useful because blankets were either not available in the rest houses, or not available in sufficient quantity, or sufficiently clean.[7]

Julius Fleischmann, executive for the Fleischmann Yeast and the Fleischmann Distilling companies in Cincinnati, whose chief hobby was yachting, took his family and friends on a thirty-six-thousand-mile trip around the world aboard his yacht *Camargo I*. The trip lasted twenty months. Of the many features of Bali which were outstanding, Fleischmann thought that probably the most striking was the people's great food staple: rice.

"The rice paddies form the face of the landscape and are to the countryside what beautiful features are to a person. From now on, rice will conjure up a memory of one of the most beautiful motor trips I have ever taken."

"Our last day in Bali," wrote Fleischmann, "was the most spectacular of our visit—a fitting climax to all we had seen before—cremation ceremony. Throughout the whole ceremony the excitement of the crowd was intense. This holiday mood remains as one of my lasting impressions of Bali." "Life in Bali," he concluded, "seems to be one perpetual holiday!"[8]

Donald C. Starr, a Boston lawyer and assistant attorney general of Massachusetts, and a "cruising man," arrived in Bali on his eighty-five foot schooner *Pilgrim*. Harold Peters, the captain of the schooner, wrote: "In our nine-day stay in Bali we attended a religious festival at Běsakih, part way up the 10,308-foot peak of Bali (Agoeng), saw monkeys, cockfights, countless rice terraces, gorgeous costumes. Best of all was the exquisite dancing of some little girls, apparently about twelve years old, in blue and silver dressed and tall headgear." Horace W. ("Hod") Fuller, chief engineer of the schooner, wrote in his journal: "The people are very childlike in many ways. The men fly huge kites about eighteen to twenty feet high with bamboo cords. They also tie little wooden whistles to the birds' necks and then let them go and the whistles blow as the birds fly about. The women and girls sure are easy to look at & some of them are very beautiful. They have fine figures and wear nothing above the waist. They have long black hair, delicate features and very white teeth when they don't chew betel nut."

The question which Starr had been asked more often than any other about Bali was whether Bali was overrun with tourists. He reported that the proportion of whites seen in the streets of Denpasar, where there were several hundred Dutch officials, was so small as to be scarcely noticeable, and it was certainly far from what could be called "overrun."[9]

Templeton Crocker, member of a family renowned for its contributions to the first transcontinental railroad, was more interested in exploration than in the South Pacific Railroad, and many museums profited from his sense of adventure and his generosity. On his 118-foot yacht, *Zaca*, with five friends and a crew of ten, Crocker traveled a year around the world. Crocker remained seven weeks in Bali while the boat was undergoing a general overhaul in Singapore. Geoffrey Dodge, a bachelor who was a commission broker in antiques, an interior decorator in Paris, and a member of the *Zaca*'s party, claimed that he had visited Bali before, but Stowitts warned Crocker that Dodge was regarded in Paris as an opportunist and an adventurer. Stowitts found Crocker and the other members of the *Zaca* appallingly insensitive to native culture, and when Crocker invited him to sail back to Europe on the *Zaca*, he declined, preferring the company of strangers on a passenger ship.

Crocker found the Hotel Bali to be the abode of any tourists who happened to be grazing on the island and he decided that it was no place from which to really see Bali or the Balinese. "There is always the glamour of fresh charm," he wrote, "always a satisfaction that it is indescribable. Who can adequately express the beauty of a native gathering in the markets; or under a banyan tree at meal-time, where brown bodies with coloured cloths move through shadow and sharp sunlight, each in a pose as if directed by a master? What brush can paint the green of growing rice, a *djanger* scene at night; the life in cremations; or the colour of a temple feast?"

"We pass a flock of light-brown ducks busily following the flag of their keeper. All day they have eaten, swam, quacked, and waggled their tails in the rice-fields, and now are pattering homeward as fast as they can. Their ungainly armless bodies wiggle as they keep up an incessant chatter which none of them listens to." It is no wonder that the artist Oscar Fabrès compared the tourists to these ducks.

It was wrenching to leave Bali, Crocker concluded. The Balinese were an incredible people, artistic, unspoiled, happy, and had an innate desire for color and beauty. Money was not one of their gods. Yet they were doomed to an ever-increasing contact with the world. It was to be deplored that so many tourists rushed through. Bali was a place to be visited alone, slowly and reverently. It was not a stage to be seen through lorgnettes, nor was it a place to be compared with any other in the world.[10]

Barbara Hutton, granddaughter of Frank Woolworth, the five- and ten-cent store pioneer, was worth more than $50 million when she came of age. Her early life was lonely and tragic, but she refused to accept the label of "poor little rich girl," which she carried throughout her life. Soon after being presented at the Court of St. James in 1931, Barbara and her friend, Jean Kennerley, daughter of Lord Alfred Simpson-Baikie, went to the movies and saw a film about Bali. When it was over, Barbara announced, "I'm going to Bali. You and Morley must come." Barbara, of course, offered to pay their way. "Barbara," recalled Jean, "was famous for deciding on a change of scene on the spur of the moment. She didn't need a reason to pack her bags and go." Morley Kennerley, Jean's husband, was an American publishing executive.

Barbara and her companions sailed on the steamer *Lurline* for the Far East. The real purpose of the trip had been to visit Bali, and Barbara found everything there she had hoped to find: beaches, dusky village lanes, terraced paddy fields, Hindu temples and shrines. It was remote and exotic, with a culture frozen in time. They remained a month in Bali.

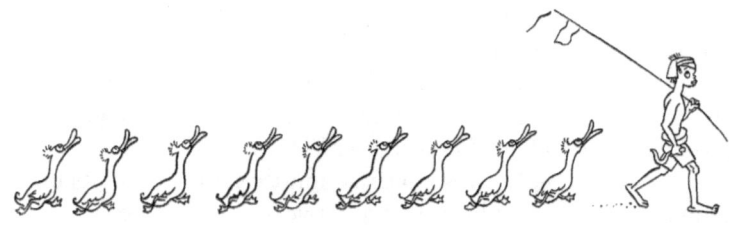

"A Bali—Tourisme." Cartoon by O. Fabrès. From *Aux Indies Neerlandaises* (Amsterdam: P. N. van Kampen & Zoon N. V., 1934).

"No one had really gone to Bali," Jean Kennerley remarked. "There were no tourists. There was no electricity. Most of the people there had never seen a wristwatch before, they burned incense to the deities and told time by the sun. Everywhere were these beautiful, smiling, bare breasted native girls in sarongs. Morley's favorite part of the trip was when Barbara and I went native—long sarongs and no tops. Barbara joined them in their ceremonial dances and quickly picked up the subtle, precise movements of the eyes and hands performed to the unearthly music of the gamelan, an ensemble of bamboo xylophones. It was a kind of religious ballet, all fire and light." They befriended Walter Spies, and visited his home many times. Jean described it as one of the loveliest on the island. Like the island itself, it was primitive in its elegance, and one washed by pouring well-water into a rigged canvas bag and read by kerosene lantern. When they left, Barbara financed Spies's swimming pool.[11]

Doris Duke, the American heiress known at the time as "the richest girl in the world," visited Bali in her extended world-encircling nonconsummated honeymoon trip with her husband, aspiring politician James Henry "Jimmy" Cromwell. She arrived in June 1935, on board the yacht *Sea Belle II*, chartered from the government of the Federated States of

Malaya in Singapore. While she remained most of the time on the vessel, film survived showing her frolicking in the spring-fed pool of Walter Spies's house in Campuan, a monkey on each shoulder.[12]

The life story of Laura May Corrigan, who came to Bali in 1934, was one of the most fabulous in the annals of international society. Born in Wisconsin, her father was said to have been an "odd jobs" man and herself to have once been a waitress in Chicago. These stories, despite the lack of any stigma pertaining to them, caused her exclusion from Cleveland society after her marriage to James William Corrigan, president of the Cleveland Steel Company. Snubbed in Cleveland, the Corrigans went to New York, but met the same treatment there. Mrs. Corrigan spent hundreds of thousands of dollars in an attempt to get into New York's social swim, but shortly after World War I she moved to London. Her mansion there was a mecca to princes, ambassadors, and dukes. She became one of England's best-known social leaders during the period between the world wars, and was virtually one of London's society arbiters.

Mrs. Corrigan's party, which included the Vicomte de La Rochefoucauld and the Marquis Talleyrand de Perigord, flew out of Paris to Batavia, where she leased a ship for one thousand guilders a day. They had the whole ship, which included a swimming pool and a tennis court, just for themselves and traveled through the East Indies. Spies was asked by KPM to show them around Bali, and was paid twenty-five guilders a day. He arranged dances and everything else required by Mrs. Corrigan and her party.

Spies found the "foolish Corrigan party" to be very nice people with whom he immediately became friendly. Corrigan was a cheerful and amusing person who climbed with her party in deep ravines, waded through streams, and, at times, was covered with dirt and mud from head to foot. During the cremation ceremony, when it rained the whole day and they were soaking wet all over, she joked the whole time. Corrigan bought many precious and costly antiquities including wood carvings, gold bowls, krisses, and gamelan instruments for museums in Europe and America. She also gave money to various Balinese gamelan and dance groups to buy new costumes and jewelry. Her gifts to Spies included hundreds of liters of gasoline, three crates of food and drink, medicines, cigarettes, a beautiful old silver bowl, and, since she could not buy the painting that Spies just completed because it was too large, she gave him another five hundred guilders, which helped him pay all his debts and taxes.

By virtue of his position as Bali's most famous hotelier, Walter Spies became Bali's tourist officer. Quite a few other famous names found their way to his door and stayed a few days with him, including various members of the British aristocracy. Finding Bali's romantic surroundings a pleasant relief from the rigors of the London season, they had made the charms of Bali known to their companions, including the Duke and Duchess of Sutherland, Lord and Lady Plunkett (she the daughter of Lord Londonderry), Lord and Lady Beatty, Lord Louis Mountbatten and his wife Edwina, Lady Ravensdale, daughter of the viceroy of India, Sir Bolton Meredith Eyres-Monsell, the first lord of the admiralty, Viscount Evan Frederic Morgan Tredegar, poet and painter, and Harold Nicolson, British diplomat and author.[13]

Harold Acton, British historian and aesthete, known as "the last of the old crowd" and a representative of his generation, wrote:

> The island's chief attraction for tourists was its wealth of feminine bosoms: every conceivable shape of bosom was displayed, since women walked nude from the waist up, but owing to the insolent curiosity shown by visiting aliens the women in the larger villages now covered themselves at the approach of a motor. Those processions of women with pagodas of baskets on their heads had been painted and photographed often, yet their dignity had not been spoiled by reproduction.
>
> An indigenous passion for dancing, an indigenous rhythm, had made it impossible for these people to move awkwardly. Islam had not dulled their spirit, and everybody seemed a potential dancer. Their temples, the buildings of which were small and thatched with elaborate gates, were not remarkable as architecture, but they were harmonious settings for the dances and plays performed there. Nearly always they were built near a stream or lake or gigantic banyan tree. The banyans on the island were the real cathedrals, the centers of village life. Very wisely the Dutch had left the island alone for the benefit of the tourist industry, and since there were few tourists this year, the place showed no signs of pollution.
>
> For the next three weeks I heard nothing by gamelan music and devoted all my attention to Balinese dancing. The showers of the gamelan rarely ceased. Not since Diaghileff's ballet have I seen such syncopated perfection: arms, hands and fingers played a greater role than legs—the finger movements were specially significant.[14]

In July 1938, for example, Spies wrote to Lady Mary Delamere, sister of Countess Mountbatten of Burma and granddaughter of Sir Ernest Cassel: "It is so nice to hear you are coming back to Bali soon. What fun we will have! You must come and stay with us for a time, not only in Kuta. Do you like hunting? Shall we shoot a tiger? In west Bali, the most exciting and marvelous country of the world? We will go there in a small native trigger sailing boat, camping in tents along the north coast. And there are the lovely coral reefs and coral gardens, where one gets absolutely crazy with excitement."[15]

Spies's network of correspondents ensured his familiarity with American artistic and high society—an important factor in his becoming a key element in the propagation of the romantic image of Bali in the West and in the promotion of Bali as a tourist destination. Spies, the international culture broker, could interpret Bali to the West in its own modern, transatlantic terms. His friend Dr. Willem Stutterheim described Spies's role with more irony, suggesting that his "fame as a tourist officer is well known in Europe and I heard there that you are starting a Balinese Greenwich Village, with snakes, monkeys and almost nakedness as big attractions as they have not got in New York." It was more or less true.

Spies and his romantic dream house at Campuan had become an important part in the machinery of the burgeoning tourist industry. The transformation of Campuan from home to a de facto hotel was an inevitable result of the constant flow of visitors that Spies attracted as a focus of the transatlantic imagining of Bali as a romantic bohemian paradise. The less idealistic—not more commercial—reality of life at Campuan in the late 1930s appears all too clearly in a letter written to Jane Belo, in which Spies described Campuan as "always full of guests, and last month we made over a thousand guilders!! Isn't it fun!" Spies's opinion regarding many of the tourists was not generally favorable. "It is funny," he wrote to his mother, "that so few of the interesting people one meets here in Bali, such as great artists or scientists or posh aristocrats, should be likeable as well." Many of the celebrities who visited Spies carried off a completed painting by him, thus affording him the wherewithal to continue living the good life for several months. To all of them, Walter was gracious and helpful in orienting them to what interested them most in the island, whether it was the natural beauties of the landscape, the wildlife of the jungle areas, the wonder of the coral reefs, or the ways of the people themselves.

Cole Porter, his wife, his collaborator, the playwright Moss Hart, the actor Monty Wooley, and several other companions including two maids and a valet, sailed on the Cunard line *Franconia*, using this world tour to collaborate on a musical which was to become *Jubilee*, and one of the songs in this musical was inspired by the music of Bali. The New York *Herald Tribune* reporter quoted Porter as saying: "I find on reading Cunard literature that I am to get inspiration in out-of-the-way places; I supposed this is really what I am after. I will look. Mr. Hart will look, and perhaps we will capture something in Bali, although I have never seen Bali before."

As a testament to Cole's fame, everywhere he and his party went abroad the *Franconia* they were bombarded with renditions—frequently very bad ones—of his tunes. It was the fate of Cole Porter and his entourage, as Hart remembered it, "to be plagued by hotel orchestras hidden behind potted palms manfully blaring out "You're the Top" in Bombay, in Zanzibar, in Rio, and even—by what miracle of communication no one of us could fathom—in Tahiti and Bali." Moss Hart described Bali:

> Bali is a traveler's paradise. Just as one's first glimpse of Venice is exciting and satisfying because it actually lives up to the postcard pictures of it, so Bali delights the wanderer and fulfills the wanderlust—for the reason that it is practically all things to all travelers. Here, at last, is what you had hoped the trip was going to be like on that far-off afternoon as you pored over the travel prospectus with a chill December wind whistling outside the windows. You looked at pictures of Bali then and you didn't quite believe them—too much as been written about Bali—too many people have come and gone to leave it unspoiled—yet, in some curious fashion, it has succeeded in remaining lovely—I hate to use a shopworn phrase, but say it I must—Bali is sheer enchantment. Every turn in the road, each face, every little house is cameo-like—a perfect thing in its way.
> No doubt of it. Bali is the top.[16]

Noel Coward spent three weeks in Bali, staying with Walter Spies in his beautiful house on the edge of the jungle, with a monkey and cranes in the garden and two Steinways and a phyton indoors. Spies enjoyed Coward's company, finding him cultured, nice, and cheerful, and the stay was very amusing. Spies painted a vivid picture of Coward's ten day stay in Campuan. "I liked Coward," Spies wrote, "*nya* very much. He is very amusing! We just roar with laughter from morning to evening! Noel sits mostly at Colin's Steinway and sings all the newest songs of Porter, himself, Gershwin, Berlin, etc., and so it goes—and goes." Coward, however, was angry when he found that Spies did not have any paintings for sale, and was absolutely furious when he found out later that Barbara Hutton and Charlie Chaplin already had several![17]

To Isabel Anderson, American author, and Larz Anderson, U.S. minister to Belgium and ambassador to Japan, visiting Bali was one of the chief objectives of their long journey to "the other side of the world." They wanted to see Bali before the inevitable catastrophe that the impending horde of tourists would surely bring, inasmuch as the world tour organizations were threatening to include the island in their schedules. European adventurers to Bali wrote of the sex appeal of the people, their music and dancing, intimating that the life of the island was one continuous and somewhat hectic holiday. While this legend had added to the desire of travelers to visit the island, it had spread an unjust reputation of the Balinese.

When the Andersons reached Bali, they found "a most attractive hotel (at least to look at), in which we spent the night. And what a night! Our room was small, stuffy, hot, notwithstanding the fact that the door and window were open and the electric fan going. On the bed were a mattress and sheet, but no covering. The heat beneath the netting was stifling, and all the mosquitoes in Bali, I am sure, were holding a convention under it. Lighting my torch, I killed a great many without the slightest appreciable effect on the horde. I was so bitten there seemed no possible escape from a bout with malaria. And as I gave battle, I exclaimed bitterly, 'Bali is no Paradise, after all!' Even if there had been no mosquitoes I could not have slept, for the dogs fought outside all the first part of the night, stopping only when the cocks began to crow. And at that time activities in the kitchen, near which was our room, began with a vengeance. The bath was a small tiled reservoir from which to dip water to pour one. The natural impulse is to climb into this high tub, but because strangers do not know any better, broken glass is put in the bottom, and so one has to be careful. The proper procedure is to soap in a side basin, and then, with the dipper that is provided, pour the water over one. I found this method satisfactory and quite refreshing, and no water wasted. Because of the many tourists it was difficult to get much to eat, and what there was, was not good. The coffee was served black and cold in Dutch fashion, and could be heated only by the addition of hot milk."

When they returned to the ship, they were amused to listen to the various reactions of the sightseers to Bali. So cultured! said one. So pagan! contradicted another. Such artistic dancing! declared a third. So tiresome! said a fourth. In fact, there were almost as many opinions as tourists!"[18]

James Saxon Childers of Birmingham, Alabama, was professor of English literature and creative writings at Birmingham–Southern College. He was also an author. A romantic bachelor, his English literature class always filled early, especially with young ladies who reputedly found it hard to resist his lanky good looks, dramatic lectures, and travel stories from around the world. Writing about Bali, Childers could not have been more wrong when he wrote:

> The dream of all dreamers has been of a fertile land tilled by a contented people, a society of primitive simplicity in which the individual and the group are spiritually and economically benefited. Such a dream is a reality in Bali. In Bali, man carries on the business of living with just enough work to remain economically independent, physically and mentally sturdy. The rest of the time he is dancing under

the trees, or playing in the village orchestra, or bathing in clear pool, or making love to some pretty girl who lives exactly the same life as he. I have found in Bali that even a traveler can fill his lungs and stretch himself.

Bali is only a speck of an island, a hundred miles long and fifty miles across, but a million men and women live there, and I envy them the simplicity of their lives and the serenity of their souls; there is no neurasthenia in Bali. Wealth is so equally divided that there is no poverty and no man is the servant of another. There is little illness, no political jealousy, and no committee to care for public and private morals, no Sunday. Each man has his own bit of soil and works it with his own hands, raising enough rice to feed his family and to barter for the few essentials he can not make for himself. He wears only a piece of cloth, and sometimes he forgets to put it on. He is ignorant of the laws of convention and free from stultifying mental and spiritual domination: he is his own priest, taking his turn in serving before the altar.

And Childers concluded: "Tomorrow, Mac, I'm going away from Bali. I'm going back to Singapore, to clothes and motor trucks and adding machines. Here in Bali I walked erect, laughed with the stars and trees, caught a glimpse of an earthly Indraloka; I kept a tryst with beauty. And tomorrow I'm going away. I shall be stripped of my coat of gold. I shall lose the flowers from my hair. Once more I shall wear a Manhattan shirt and a Stetson hat. And I am sad, even though I know that in the long years ahead my memories of Bali will partially lullaby my discontents."[19]

Alan John Villiers, Australian sea writer, sailed the fully rigged ship *Joseph Conrad* some sixty thousand miles around the world with a crew largely consisting of young cadets. Having arrived in Bali, Villiers wondered what manner of reception the vessel would have. He had some vague idea— or hope, rather—that Bali was still to some extent a preserve from odd wanderers and tourists and the like. He soon found his fear and his hopes both groundless. The tourist manager from the KPM was first on board, distributing maps labeled "Tourist Routes in Bali," and wanting to book passengers for round trips of the island by automobile. "Good Lord!" Villiers thought, "They *want* tourists—and I had thought this the last unspoiled island."

"We'ave two sousand a mont," exclaimed the man from the KPM with great pride; he asked how many of Villiers's boys would like to go on the round trip of the island. He mentioned a sum that, even in gold guilders, was most reasonable. The dancing would be ten guilders extra. "We had heard of Balinese dancing, no? It was very good." Yes, they had heard of the Balinese dancing and indeed it was exquisite. The man from the KPM went on about the delights of a visit to the Forest of Sacred Nutmegs and the Elephant Cave and the second largest banyan tree in the entire world.

Villiers's heart sank at this recital and he found himself looking sadly upon the tourist maps and things. "It is, I suppose, the cruising liners that have done it. There is scarcely a round-the-world cruise these days that does not include a stop at Bali." When he got back on board, he heard that two female runners had been out from a local harlotry seeking customers, and the connoisseurs reported that the place was not so bad. "But Buleleng is a port, it is not Bali or Balinese. Sooner or later all ports become much the same, offering the same 'attractions.'" "Poor Bali!" Villiers thought. "I had heard so much and here it was, just a Dutch Hawaii." Still, Villiers stayed in Bali ten days, and made the round-the-island tour.

> I went on the bureau's conducted tour to Den Pasar in the south of the island, the royal tombs, the nutmeg tree, and all that—six of us in an open car. The route lay along good Dutch roads past labeled villages and tired dogs; we went at speed, for it was a long way, and watched the inoffensive Balinese, walking gracefully along the dirt and grass by the roadside, scurry frightened out of the car's way. If I were a Balinese, I should be angry with that; some of them looked sullen, most indifferent, and many scared. This is their home—their beautiful and lovely home, wherein they have followed their quiet and cultured lives peacefully through many generations. They need neither the motorcars nor the roads, and the gaping sightseers who cavort past bring them no benefit. They stand in need of little we whites can bring; they know how to live, and this is more than we do.[20]

Villiers commented that Bali was still a long way from being spoiled, because there were as yet few beggars and no "rackets." But at Buleleng and Denpasar, the roadside merchants hopefully offered large selection of photographs of their womenfolk half naked and unashamed. Into the little café at Denpasar came a guide of sort, speaking some English, inquiring whether Alan was interested in "nice girl 'ores." He arrived at the hotel and ate heartily; but he could not help still thinking of the incongruity of that asphalt road and the motorcars while he gazed around him at the usual assemblage of globe-trotters. "Why do so many of these round-the-world wanderers wear discontent so heavily upon their features? It seemed to me that the sophisticated perambulating white, dissatisfied with himself but not knowing why, possessed every advantage money can bring him, and only dimly aware there is much money will never buy, can be a more harmful and more dangerous influence among native races than the roar of

Dancer and gamelan orchestra. Illustration by Alexander King. From Hickman Powell, *Bali: The Last Paradise* (London: Jonathan Cape, 1930).

guns. "In Bali as elsewhere, one hears faint whispers of some of these ambassadors of our culture—the homosexuals, the queer, the near-insane, the blatant and the foolish; though the worst of them do not come as tourists, but usually with the intention of staying. I wish the Hollanders would *close* Bali to all sight-seeing and neurotic whites."[21]

In the 1920s, the management of the rest house at Denpasar had the novel idea of entertaining its guests by organizing dance performances created especially for them and staged on request. After the opening of the Bali Hotel these performances became a regular attraction presented every Friday evening to the tourists freshly disembarked from Buleleng, and a pavilion was built for this purpose on the terrace of the hotel. The orchestra and dancers came from the neighboring village of Belaluan. Soon afterward, other performances were organized for the tourists on Saturday morning at Kedaton on the outskirts of Denpasar. The troupes formed for the KPM soon became famous among the visitors. Thus, the orchestra of Belaluan was proclaimed "the finest gamelan of Bali" while Kedaton was described as "the home of the best dancers of the island."

It was only after the Bali Hotel began to entertain their guests with performances of "native dancing" that Balinese dances were deemed worthy of being recommended to tourists in guide books and travel accounts. Balinese dances acquired their prestige only after becoming tourist attractions. In the brochure that the KPM commissioned from Roelof Goris and Walter Spies for the 1931 Colonial Exposition in Paris, prospective visitors were informed that: "Thanks to the activities of the manager of the Bali Hotel in Denpasar it is now possible to attend the excellent concerts, which are given every Friday evening by this famous orchestra on the front terrace of the Bali Hotel. They were often accompanied by interesting dances."

"In the evening," wrote Villiers, "after the big meal, there was a dance—a grand orchestra; a man who expressed grace and rhythm superbly with his hands; little girls sedate and lovely with their supple grace and quiet beauty; and two men in masks who harangued each other at great length but utterly beyond my comprehension. The performance was given on a concrete stage before the hotel, lit by a solitary electric light. In the best places in front of the stage were ranged the seats of the whites. They sat there, staring. Beyond a wire enclosure were the Balinese—hundreds of them, permitted to be there by the grace of the management. Interested and animated they watched, while the heaven-sent sat scowl-faced and overfed, and afterwards discussed the rhythm and meaning of it all. I strolled over to a native bazaar and drank some Balinese beer.

"In the morning there was a dance in a temple courtyard close to Denpasar. Here again the tourists sat and the Balinese stood. The curiously assorted crowd included now a score of Japanese students, photographing furiously with German cameras manufactured in their own country, and making copious notes in little books. They were dressed queerly in some kind of European fashion, and were led by a paunchy gentleman of their own race with a cheap cigar drooping from his gross mouth. Behind them stood the Balinese—not many, for most of them were at work.

"The tourist business warp our minds, until we think every pious act and ritual of a conquered folk a poppy show to assuage our insatiable lust for entertainment.[22]

"I liked Bali," concluded Villiers. "I was glad I went there. It is worth visiting even though it is well upon the road towards becoming a kind of Dutch Hawaii." He left Bali with the stirring strains of the gamelan gong in his ears and saw again the infinite grace of the small girls dancing, hoping to God no fool was ever permitted to take them away for a season in Hollywood or on Broadway.

As Bali developed into one of the most romantic destinations, the earliest tourist images, which capitalized on Bali's most famous attraction, its bare-breasted women, gradually became more complex. A barrage of new books and articles appeared extolling the island's cultural and natural features. The bare-breasted women faded into the background as the dancing girl became Bali's new leitmotif. Bali became fashionable for its dances, music, clothes, and climate. Rich British and Americans flocked there and came back with gaily colored Bali-esque prints.

The images that found favor with the tourist industry were often those that dwelt on the more extreme and unusual aspects of Balinese culture. Thus, photographs of burning cremation towers, frenzied trance dancers, courtiers in dazzling brocades, and grotesquely masked performers were all grist to the mill in the dash to create the ultimate in exotic holiday destinations. Films, popular books, postcards, and magazine articles reinforced the notion that Bali was somehow different, that it possessed an extraordinary culture that had to be seen before it was too late. Not all the "publicity" was vulgar, especially the high quality travel literature, but much of it depended on stereotyped images designed to lure, and perhaps titillate, the potential visitor. Tour guides wrote about temples, rice terraces, and religious ceremonies, about cock fights, and, of course, about the cremation ceremony. Fleischmann wrote that his last day in Bali was the most spectacular of his visit—a fitting climax to all he had seen before—because on that day he observed the magnificent cremation ceremony, "probably one of the most remarkable things" that he had ever seen.

The romantic notion that all Balinese were artists was often repeated. No cliché proved more pervasive. André Roosevelt wrote, "with a feeling of neo-colonial self-righteousness," that the Balinese were the greatest artists of this world, and still more, that every Balinese, man or woman, was an artist. "The people turned to art as a pastime," he wrote. Whether sculpture, painting, music, or dancing, they simply had to produce or to give breath to all these, since they could not help themselves. Martin Birnbaum wrote that almost everybody was an artist in Bali, and Miguel Covarrubias proclaimed that "everybody in Bali seems to be an artist. Coolies and princes, priests and peasants, men and women alike, can dance, play musical instruments, paint or carve in wood and stone." The Dutch archaeologist Dr. Willem Stutterheim said, with more honesty, that "to a certain degree every Balinese is an artist, but, as elsewhere, there are only a few artists who really create significant things of beauty."

While most accounts by foreigners praised the performances organized by the KPM, a few discordant opinions were voiced. Crocker reported that during a gamelan and dance performance at the Bali Hotel by I Mario, the greatest dancer in Bali, an American sitting near him said, "Well, I guess a little of this goes a long way." His companion answered, "The same goes with me too," and they left. Robert Hamilton Bruce Lockhart, a British diplomat, recalled that the dances were long, and before the end he found himself yawning. And without a genuine expert to explain things, he believed that most Europeans found it hard to sit through a whole evening's performance, especially in the artificial surrounding of a European hotel. Ruth Masters Rickover remembered that the performance of the Friday dances at the Bali Hotel struck her at once as artistically perfect yet not wholly satisfying because the audience and the setting were artificial and out of place. Philip Hanson Hiss, architectural designer and photographer, realized that it was inevitable that some of the first music that he heard and some of the first dances that he saw after he came to Bali should have been at the Bali Hotel. These were, in fact, the only dances that many tourists did see. The KPM, which monopolized the tourist trade, did much, perhaps too much, to make the dances and music both dramatic and interesting. A beautiful pavilion was built in the hotel courtyard, and at least one night a week dances were given for the tourists. When Hiss first saw these performances, he was interested in the sheer virtuosity of some of the music and dances. But he had already seen many stage shows more elaborately presented, so he was not impressed. This was not very different from Broadway or Hollywood. Later, after he had seen dozens of performances in the different towns throughout Bali, he understood why these performances at the Bali Hotel, though by many of the same gamelans and dancers, appeared to lack something essential. The stage setting of the KPM was too overpowering and in some ways too artificial an atmosphere for Balinese dance and music. But most important of all, the people who formed the natural background for all Balinese performances were missing. The KPM had also attempted to inject as much sex as possible into the dances, and sex was the one quality that was almost entirely absent from the Balinese dance, therefore its appearance struck a false note. The dancers and the orchestras had been playing to an uncritical audience that had little notion of whether the performance was good or bad. Consequently there had been a steady slackening of effort, and it was small wonder that many tourists returned to their homes feeling bitterly disappointed with "paradise."[24]

Robert Hamilton Bruce Lockhart concluded that the Dutch genius for tourism and the lurid advertisements of the shipping companies had completed the work of popularization. Those who sought a resort where an old-world civilization remained intact had to come quickly. The conversion of "the last paradise" into the newest hell was proceeding apace, and all too soon Bali would become a second Port Said.[25]

7
Goona-Goona

> When Hollywood had heard of Bali, where women were said to go around exhibiting the most beautifully developed mammary glands in the world, the race to can them on reels of celluloid for retailing to the boobus Americanus at twenty-five cents an eyeful was on. It had been an edifying commentary on the sudden interest in Bali that the first of these films to be widely shown was called Goona-Goona, which means "magic" in Balinese, but that within a month or two the term "Goona-Goona" had been incorporated in American slang as a new term for the mammary gland or glands of the human female.
>
> Cedric Belfrage[1]

The 1931 International Colonial Exposition in Paris dramatically proved the world's receptivity to the lure of the legend of Bali as a paradise island through the tremendous success of a Balinese troupe of dancers and musicians. They were the sensation of the exposition. It was the first time that live performances of Balinese music and dance were heard and seen in Europe. The troupe captivated the imagination of the surrealist artists and the general public alike. Colin McPhee, Jane Belo, and Beryl de Zoete all caught their first glimpse of Balinese dance in the Colonial Exposition.

Commercial recordings of Balinese music, however, were already available a few years earlier. Representatives of the German recording companies Odeon and Beka were sent in August 1928 to Bali to record Balinese music, which were made under the guidance of Walter Spies. Five of the sides made at that time were included in the early anthology of non–Western traditions, *Music of the Orient*, by the German scholar Eric M. von Hornbostel. These records were the first exposure to Balinese music for many people—the general public as well as potential ethnomusicologists. Some of the Odeon/Beka recordings eventually appeared in Europe and America, but the majority had been intended originally for local sale in Bali. For this reason, the information on the labels was printed in Malay, and in some cases even in Balinese script. The ambitious plan to develop an indigenous market was a complete failure, however, since few Balinese were interested in this new and expensive technology, especially when there was a world of live performances happening daily in the thousands of temples and households throughout the island. Colin McPhee was the only customer to purchase these 78 rpm records in an entire year from one frustrated dealer. McPhee's collection contained most of the copies that are still preserved to this day, for the Balinese dealer later smashed the remaining stock in a fit of rage.

Movie cameramen were especially unpopular in Bali. The islanders, out of sheer willingness to be agreeable, had posed and acted for movie breast hunters, and had been rewarded with the most niggardly payment. The movie men, cockily barging in directly from Hollywood, were blissfully convinced that any native ought to bow down and kiss their feet for a chance to work all day for a few cents. It did not occur to them that if they had first taken the trouble to make themselves agreeable, the Balinese might have been happy to work for almost nothing, just out of friendship.[2]

Goona-Goona was produced in Bali in 1928 and 1929 by André Roosevelt and Armand Denis, with assistance from Walter Spies, and with a native cast including the Royal Balinese Gamelan Gong orchestra of Belaluan and the Legong Dancing Girls. Much of it was refilmed in 1929 after a processing accident. The film was also known as *Love Powder* and was released in Europe as *The Kriss*.[3]

The title *Goona-Goona* (the Balinese term for "magic") refers to a strange drug which is given to the heroine, Dasnee, by a sister of Prince Nonga. The prince returns from Europe and becomes enamored of Dasnee, whose father is a lowly carpenter. The prince's father is eager to have his son marry Princess Maday. Wyan, a coolie (unskilled laborer), is in love with Dasnee, whom he subsequently marries. When Nonga comes of age, his father presents him with a dagger, called a *kriss*, which figures into the plot of the story. For through it, Wyan discovers that Nonga has visited Dasnee at night. The coolie avenges the wrong by killing the prince after a desperate struggle, and the prince's father eventually kills the coolie with the *kriss*.

Die Insel der Däemonen (The Island of the Demons), also known, confusingly, as *Black Magic*, was produced and directed in 1931 by the German Baron Victor von Plessen, for which the casting and choreography were done by Walter Spies. With the American dancer Katharane Mershon, Spies choreographed for the film the *Kecak*, the so-called "monkey dance," which became a tourist staple (and presumed by many, some Balinese included, to be a traditional Balinese dance), that enthralled and amazed visiting tourists. The film tells a fictional story of young lovers thwarted by

Poster for the Théatre Balinais at the Dutch Pavilion at the International Colonial Exhibition, Paris, 1931. Courtesy of the Koninklijk Instituut voor de Tropen, Tropenmuseum, Amsterdam, Holland.

greed and black magic in a politically correct ethnographic background. Spies had specially rescored the original gamelan composition for two pianos to be used in this film, but was disappointed after he saw the movie because typical 1930s movie music was substituted for his score.

Goona-Goona: an Authentic Melodrama of the Isle of Bali, opened at the Cameo Theatre New York City on September 16, 1932, and ran for nine weeks. The reviewer in *The New York Times* wrote: "In spite of the explanation of the doings of the native characters by a screen voice, the action is often rather vague. This, however, is counterbalanced by the beauty of the scenes and the ingenuous acting of the natives. It is quite a poetic little tragedy and although it is not unfurled with the expertness necessary in telling a shadow story, it has the charm of the customs and traditions of the Balinese and the background of their enchanting bit of land."[4] *Variety* emphasized the fact that the native cast of Goona-Goona was excellent because not one of its members was camera conscious, and much of the native beauty of Bali, including scenery and customs, was interwoven with the story. It also noted that, although 'Goona-Goona' was number four on the list of Balinese topicals, it "was essentially for the subsequent run theatres. Houses with odd policies, formerly known as arties should be able to retain it profitably for a week."[5] Baltimore censors objected to a display advertising for the film in which two Balinese women nude above the waist were shown.

The Isle of Paradise was produced by Charles Tillyer Trego, who hailed from New York and attended the Wharton School but did not graduate, and was connected with advertising and publicity for the Cunard Line. An amateur photographer, he shot the film during a six months vacation in Bali. It was shown initially on July 20, 1932, in a special charity performance at the Vanderbilt Theater in New York City.[6] The report in the *New York Times* described the film as "a record of the daily life of the Balinese, set against pastelle skies, rice fields, shadowy lagoons, mountains and the pounding surf of the Pacific." Bali was shown as a land where "every task seems a pleasant one" and where "the process of being happy is a graceful and every Balinese knows the secret."[7]

The reviewer in *The New York Sun*, wrote that "the average movie audience may find it a bit dull, tho beautiful; but for those who have an interest in beauty for its own sake, for relative degrees in civilization, for a look into the estate of civilization which belongs far, far back in the distant past and which, due to isolation, has remained unchanged in an industrialized world, *Isle of Paradise* is enormously interesting."[8]

Virgins of Bali, made on the island of Bali with an all native cast and produced by Deane H. Dickason, opened on December 7, 1932, at the

Cameo in New York City. *Variety Bulletin* commented: "Exploiting two pairs of shapely maiden breasts through nearly six reels of celluloid, if backed by a modern story, this film would undoubtedly prove very obnoxious, and probably never get by the censors."[9] *Variety* speculated that a theater showing *Virgins of Bali* so closely after another Bali picture would indicate that management "figures the demand for bust pictures is still lively. At half past seven the opening day the house was nearly full and not a score of women in the three hundred seater." It further stated that the story was inconsequential and what the picture had to offer was good photography and girls bare to the waists. "Where the previous pictures have played, this one will stand up. Where the others have not yet reached, this will be a stag standout if properly advertised. Advertising angle is the manners and customs, with the photographs doing the real selling." The film "will probably draw little fire from the censors and no reason why the scissors brigade should butt it."[10]

William K. Vanderbilt, president of the New York Central Railroad and a lieutenant commander in the U.S. Naval Reserve, his party, his crew of fifty-one, and his 264-foot yacht *Alva*, which was called a floating palace, visited Bali in 1932 as part of twenty-nine-thousand-mile world cruise. *Over the Seven Seas*, a motion picture record of his cruise, was presented for a single performance for the benefit of the American Christmas and Relief Fund at the Plaza Theatre in New York City on December 15, 1932. *Variety* reported that the motion picture included "magnificent scenic passages and innumerable picturesque touches ... not to speak of what may be called goona-goona touches of native dancing girls in ... Bali."[11]

"The remote little island only became news to the rest of the Western world," wrote Miguel Covarrubias, "with the advent, a few years ago, of a series of documentary films of Bali with a strong emphasis on sex appeal. These films were a revelation and now everybody knows that Balinese girls have beautiful bodies and that the islands lead a musical-comedy sort of life full of weird, picturesque rites."[12]

The films were significant as important aspects of the creation of Western romance and of Bali as paradise. *Goona-Goona* started an American craze for things Balinese. Vicki Baum claimed that "Bali has become the fashion. There is an invasion of Bali bars and Bali bathing suits and Bali songs." Perhaps the most popular of the songs inspired by the motion picture was "On the Beach at Bali Bali," with words and music by Abner Silver, Jack Meskill, and Al Sherman, which was recorded by several American bands in 1936 alone, including Tommy Dorsey and Jimmie Lunceford, among others.

"Goona-Goona: a Balinese Love Song," was also inspired by the motion picture. The lyrics were written by Mitchell Parish, and the music was written by Serge Walter. "I Wanna Go Back to Bali," with lyrics by Al Dubin, who was best known for "Lullaby of Broadway," and music by Harry Warren, was one of the numbers in the motion picture *Gold-Diggers in Paris* which was released in 1939.

"Goona-Goona" became a popular phrase for tropical sensuality, and Bali's highly eroticized pull became even stronger. In 1930s Hollywood, the impact of the film and the delight of film producers in the beautiful women of Bali was such that the topless look was called "Goona-Goona." "Goona-Goona" also became at the time New Yorkese for "sex-allure," and the "Sins of Bali" was the name of a New York night club. When the motion picture opened in a Broadway theater, the milk bars in the drugstores around Times Square were soon selling Goona-Goona sundaes. Recipe: Two scoops full of chocolate ice cream, side by side, topped with two maraschino cherries.[13]

Legong: Dance of the Virgins was produced between May and August 1933 entirely on location in Bali with an all-native cast by the French Marquis Henri de la Falaise de la Coudraye, who was Gloria Swanson's third husband, the husband of actress Constance Bennett, and the head of Bennett Pictures Corporation. The film opened on October 1 1935, in New York City. A thirty minute print of this film was in circulation in Great Britain until the late 1940s and was primarily used to titillate audiences.[14]

Man's Paradise was filmed in Bali in 1932 by Grace Goodhue Huntington, but was released only in 1938, because the Production Code Administration of the Motion Picture Association of America did not confer a certificate of approval of the film in part because they noticed "at least twenty-one shots in which the bare breasts of women are completely exposed. Many of these are close-up shots at angles which accentuate the bare breasts of these women. In addition, there are one or two sequences in which children appear completely nude." *The Hollywood Reporter* noted that the cockfight in the film, "in which one of the birds finally is slain after being hamstrung, will interest many in this country, as heretofore no such scenes had been allowed on the screen."[15]

8
Living Treasure

> *Created, the legend of the paradise island spread quickly, amalgamating the oriental mystery of Shangri-La and the romanticism of Gauguin's Tahiti with the promise of the Garden of Eden. The ready Western receptivity to its lure was proved dramatically by the tremendous success of the Peliatan dance and gamelan troupe at the 1931 Colonial World Fair in Paris, which captivate the imagination of the surrealist artists and the general public alike.*
>
> Bruce Carpenter[1]

A small community of foreigners resided in Bali; for the most part they were artists and scholars, along with a handful of expatriates. These foreign residents constituted an avant-garde as well as a cultural guarantee for the elite tourism. They served as mediators between the Balinese and the tourists. Not only did they certify and disseminate to the West the image of Bali as paradise, they also identified Balinese society with its culture, which they mostly saw in terms of its artistic and religious activities. They helped popularize the villages in which they lived, primarily Ubud, Sanur, and Kuta, which would become the island's major centers of tourism. They brought a decisive energy to the renewal of Balinese art by encouraging Balinese artists to produce works that would appeal to foreigners and could be sold in the tourist market. The remote little island only became news to the rest of the Western world with the advent of the documentary films of Bali with a strong emphasis on sex appeal. These films were a revelation; everybody knew that Balinese girls had beautiful bodies and that the islanders lead a musical-comedy sort of life, full of weird, picturesque rites.

Since the 1920s the island of Bali has been described to the point of exhaustion as a true Garden of Eden, the cradle of a traditional culture that has remained aloof from the vicissitudes of the modern world, and a place where exceptionally gifted inhabitants devoted most of their time and wealth to staging sumptuous ceremonies for their pleasure, for that of their gods, and for the greatest satisfaction of their visitors as well. To some visitors Bali was smart place to go, one of the many places visited in a round-the-world cruise; to others it brought a mental image of brown girls with beautiful breasts, palm trees, rolling waves, and all the romantic notions that went into making a South Seas island paradise.

Advertising its tours to Bali in 1932, the Rotterdam Lloyd's Royal Mail line brochure described Bali as a marvelously beautiful island with a culture entirely its own. The lovely scenery was beyond description, and the Balinese were a fascinating race, cheerful, friendly, and helpful. The time of the year to visit Bali made little difference as it was delightfully cool in all seasons, particularly in the hill section where the air was always bracing and refreshing, and the nights were cool enough to require blankets. If there was an opportunity to see a cremation ceremony, the brochure said it should not be missed.[2]

> All those who visit Bali, be it only for a few days, are certain to have an opportunity of attending some religious celebration. In addition to the many ceremonies, which are held in accordance with the religious calendar such as temple festivals and village ceremonies, there are a number of customs in the home and family life, which are solemnly observed. Among these, cremation is certainly the most important in addition to being the most expensive. The cremation of persons, belonging to the higher castes costs many thousands of guilders and some ceremonies have known to cost from fifty thousand to one hundred thousand to guilders. The man of low degree often awaits for years until he is able to cremate a deceased relation. The estate of a father, mostly consisting of rice fields, is usually wholly or partly sold in order to defray the cost of the cremation.[3]

Winning the National Art Directors' medal for an advertisement he had done for piano manufacturer Steinway & Sons, Miguel Covarrubias used the cash prize that came with this award to take his wife, Rosa, on an extended honeymoon to Bali. He spent the six-week voyage from New York to the Dutch East Indies on board the freighter *Cingalese Prince*, taking daily lessons in Malay. Mexican-born Miguel was an illustrator and caricaturist and one of the stars of the social scene in New York City. His wife, Rosa, was a dancer. They were both inspired by Gregor Krause's "splendid album of Bali photographs," and developed an irresistible desire to see Bali for themselves. The actress Claudette Colbert and her husband, actor-director Norman Foster, American leading man of the stage and Hollywood films of the 1930s, accompanied the honeymooners to Bali, and probably stayed a week. John Ford, the movie director for the Fox Film Company in Hollywood, also visited Bali at the same time, as did Nelson Rockefeller and his bride on their round-the-world honeymoon trip.

Miguel described his first unforgettable glimpse of Bali at dawn: "...a high dark peak reflected a sea as smooth as polished steel, with the summit of the cone hidden in dark, metallic clouds." He described Buleleng as a place of narrow streets lined with dingy little shops of cheap crockery and cotton goods run by emaciated Chinese in undershirts or by Arabs with forbidding black bears. Javanese in black velvet skull-caps mingled with Dutch officials in pith helmets and high starched collars, but the beautiful Balinese of steamship pamphlets were not to be seen anywhere. Denpasar was a glorified Buleleng.[4]

The room in the Bali Hotel was clean and sanitary, albeit with a hospital bed, through the middle of which, lengthwise, stretched a hard, round bolster, the so-called "Dutch wife," but the Covarrubiases could not stand for long the stolid prudishness of Dutch hotel life, nor could they afford the high rates. They also knew that they were not getting a true picture of the island in their Dutch-influenced hotel in Denpasar.

On the veranda of the Bali Hotel at tea time, Balinese girls sold curios, plainly junk. But they were not to blame. They had discovered that the tourists generally preferred hideous statuettes made by beginners or the gaudy weavings dyed with anilines to the fine old pieces of woodcarving or to the sumptuous ancient textiles. Balinese sculptors were turning out mass-produced objets d'art for tourists. Sculptors began working for a new public: tourists who had little appreciation of the technical perfection demanded by the Balinese. This necessarily introduced the mercenary element into Balinese art, until then non-existent. Alan Villiers complained that the indiscriminate and intelligent scramble for "souvenirs" was a poor way to foster local arts. If there was sufficient demand for inferior products, they became more inferior, and that had been the case in Bali.[5]

In the KPM publication to promote tourism in Bali, published for the Colonial Exposition in Paris in 1931, the Dutch anthropologist Roelof Goris wrote: "Regrettably, during the last few years tourists have been offered silver trinkets for sale, such as silver corks, powder boxes, *bonbonniers* etc. These, however, have no real artistic value. Of course, everyone should be free to purchase what they wish. But still, we believe we should advise against buying such articles, for two related reasons. First, there is the self-interest of the tourist who believes he is getting something truly Balinese and instead he is getting a mass-produced article of no real value. Second, there are the interests of Balinese craftsmen; in the face of the demand for such trinkets, silversmiths neglect their real handiwork, and the diminished production of real Balinese works of art makes it harder for tourists to acquire them."[6]

G. H. von Faber complained that Bali's arts and crafts were degenerating. A large proportion of the products of these were destined for the foreign visitor, and Western tastes were taken into account by the artists. Woven fabrics and the products of the silversmith's art were also suffering. The finish of such articles left much to be desired. The Balinese turned out articles which they themselves would never use, and they reckoned on the inability of the tourist to discern the difference between good work and bad. It was often painful to see how the cunning female hawkers inveigled the foreigner into parting with a fairly large sum of money in exchange for worthless rubbish. The world took these products for specimens of Balinese art, and the good name of Bali suffered.[7]

Some years later, the Austrian ethnologist and explorer Hugo Bernatzik complained similarly that in Denpasar, carved wooden figures were exposed for sale. They were badly executed and a much too brilliant gloss excited his attention. The polishing of carved wood was a special art in this country, the objects being rubbed and worked for days until a delicate silky sheen covered them. But a Caucasian trash specialist had shown the carvers that one could save labor by varnishing the figures. Like that they shined even more and the tourists bought them altogether indiscriminately. A few years ago they were still cheap and good, then cheap and bad, and finally expensive and bad. "How can you sell such horrors?" Bernatzik's companion, a lady living in Bali, reproached the dealer. "Have you sunk so low that you call this art?" "Not at all," was the ready answer. "For the tourists it has to be hideous or they won't buy it." And unfortunately the dealer was right.[8]

After the first bewildering days, when they had recovered from the shock of the initial distressing impressions, Miguel and Rosa Covarrubias quickly dropped the organized sightseeing program to go out and "discover" the real Bali. As they became more and more familiar with their new life, as their ears grew accustomed to Malay and they were able to converse in that language, they made friends among the Balinese. Looking for another place to live, they settled in one of the pavilions in the compound of one of their Balinese friends, who was a prince by birth, a carpenter by profession, and a musician by choice, and the leader of a prestigious gamelan orchestra in the tiny village of Belaluan, just outside Denpasar. The manager of the Bali Hotel loaned them two beds, two chairs, and a table. They also bought a decrepit Chevrolet for eight hundred guilders, and gave themselves up to the full enjoyment of the island, going to feasts, dances, and ceremonies.

The Covarrubias's Bali experience was greatly enhanced by their friendship with Walter Spies, and Rosa stated that Miguel and she could not have done anything or known anything without Walter. The months flew past while they roamed around the island with Spies. They watched strange ceremonies, enjoyed the music, listened to fantastic tales, and camped in the wild parts of western Bali, as well as the Sanur coral reefs.

Miguel had an extraordinary curiosity about everything, especially the Balinese culture. It was a lovely coincidence that Belaluan was one of the island's cultural centers at the time and Miguel was introduced to the best-loved artists of the day—the dancers, musicians, painters, mask-makers, silversmiths, and puppeteers of the region. The news spread rapidly through Belaluan and neighboring villages that friendly, inquisitive foreigners were living there, and soon it became common for dozens of visitors to come and meet the newcomers, to talk, and to play music.

Miguel and Rosa were profoundly affected by the island and developed a deep enthusiasm for the Balinese lifestyle, which struck Miguel as the opposite of the living he had been doing in New York. Life in Bali was simple, natural, highly spiritual, creative, and aesthetic. Miguel liked the Balinese and was immediately comfortable with and admiring of Balinese simple nobility, good nature, serenity, and gentility. On a very personal level, he felt a deep response to the place and the people. Miguel threw himself into the Balinese life. He traveled to nearby villages and temples, to festivals and all-night shadow puppet plays, and to tooth filings, the Balinese rite of passage out of puberty. He was interested in seeing everything—cockfights, a house under construction, farmers in the fields, and women planting rice in the brilliant green terraced rice fields. These sights were recorded in sketches, and the information carefully collected.

"The roads were particularly infested with miserable dogs, the scavengers of the island that barked and wailed all night in great choruses. The Balinese were not disturbed by them and slept peacefully through the hideous noise. The mongrels were supposed to frighten away witches and evil spirits. Such dogs were undoubtedly provided by the gods to keep Bali from perfection."[9]

Rosa accompanied Miguel on many of his excursions, but she also pursued her own interests, food being a major one. Rosa enjoyed visiting the outdoor marketplace by herself, discovering exotic fruits, vegetables, and herbs she had never seen, engaging the vendors in conversation, asking for the names of the foods she did not recognize. After making her purchases, she liked to linger at the market, photographing the women and their wares. The cook taught Rosa how to prepare the Indonesian dishes for which she became well known in later years in Mexico. Miguel was also interested in food. "Balinese food is difficult for the palate of a westerner," Miguel wrote. "Besides being served cold always, food is considered uneatable unless it is violently flavored with a crushed variety of pungent spices, aromatic roots and leaves, nuts, onions, garlic, fermented fish paste, lemon juice, grated coconut, and burning red peppers. It was so hot that it made even me, a Mexican raised on chili peppers, cry and break out in beads of perspiration. But after the first shocks, and when we became accustomed to Balinese flavours, we developed into Balinese gourmets and soon started trying out strange new combinations. Most Europeans, used to beef and boiled potatoes, simply cannot eat Balinese food, but on the other hand, no Balinese of the average class can be induced even to touch European food, which is *nyam-nyam* to them—that is 'flat and tasteless.'"[10]

Balinese dance was of the most interest to Rosa, and this passion was also shared by Miguel. Their interest in dance attracted new visitors, especially the youngest Balinese dancers. They danced for Rosa, and she danced for them, and they were fascinated by the modern and interpretive demonstrations she made for them. She spent a great deal of time with the youngsters of Belaluan, playing with them, learning their games, teaching them games she remembered from her own childhood, and photographing them.

As a man, the idyllic beauty of Bali's women, who, in his opinion, were entirely free of self-consciousness, enchanted Miguel. They were as "stately and graceful as goddesses," he told one journalist. "Tawny-skinned, with dark glowing eyes, proud red mouth, erect bearing." They were ideal models. Miguel was concerned that the absence of beggars was threatened by tourists who lured boys and girls with dimes to take their pictures. He found that in places frequented by tourists, people were beginning to ask for money as a return for a service.

The Covarrubiases thought they would spend three months in Bali; they spent nine. On their way home, they stopped in Paris and visited the Colonial Exposition, where they met Jane Belo and Colin McPhee, who were on their way to Bali. Miguel transformed his sketches into gouache and oil paintings on the crossing home. They became part of a one-man show of thirty-one Balinese pieces in a New York gallery.

Miguel and Rosa could not be happy until they were able to return for a longer period, and they did return to Bali two years later, partly assisted by a generous scholarship from the Guggenheim Foundation. At first they were disappointed. The tourist rush was in full swing, and Denpasar was full of tourists. In Denpasar, a great many women had taken to wearing clumsy blouses, the young were developing contempt for Balinese ways, and the people complained of poverty, which Miguel saw as "another novelty in Bali." To escape tourist-ridden, commercial Denpasar, they accepted Walter Spies's offer to share his beautiful home in Campuan, and they remained there for several months. Once settled, Miguel went to work in earnest, collecting material for his book. Later they moved back to the old house in Belaluan. There, they had an open door to the frequent local festivals, and within their compound they had opportunity to observe the daily life of the Balinese and to collect firsthand information.

After a year stay in Bali, with many hundreds of pages of notes containing such stories and details on home life ranging from house construction to the four ways to prepare a festival dish of sea turtle, scores of sheets of illustrations from floor plans to kitchen utensils, over a thousand of Rosa's photographs, and an eight-millimeter film they had shot, the Covarrubias returned home.

Miguel's book, *The Island of Bali*, was published in 1937 and became the standard description of Bali read by an increasing number of tourists who visited the island. It was described as the "latest, liveliest, and by far the most alluring of the many books that have been written about that enchanting island east of Java." Miguel summarized the images that had by now been established and brought them together in a well-rounded synthesis: the image of the noble elite from foreign Hindu-Javanese descent, the village as age-old traditional community, and the balance and equilibrium of the Balinese character, added to advertising descriptions of the arts and exotic rituals. The book was a best-seller, causing a fit of Balimania in New York and elsewhere for years. It also turned out to be great tourism promoter for Bali.

Walter Spies wrote to Miguel and Rosa after reading the *Island of Bali*. "I am very ashamed to read all that glorifying nonsense about me in the introduction and I must say that it had already added to my publicity! Every new coming tourist knows everything about me, and I had already two orders for pictures again through your book!" Spies wrote further that he saw every tourist carrying Covarrubias's book. "It is just the thing everyone wants to have! And to everyone who asks me something, I say: look in Covarrubias."[11]

Like many other visitors, Miguel also believed that, undoubtedly, Bali would be soon "spoiled" for those fastidious travelers who abhorred all that which they brought with them. "Even when all the Balinese will have learned to wear shirts, to beg, lie, steal, and prostitute themselves to satisfy new needs, tourists will continue to come to Bali to see the sights, snapping pictures frantically, dashing from temple to temple, back to the hotels for meals, and on to watch rites and dances staged for them." The Balinese would be guides, chauffeurs, and bellboys to the tourists to be tipped; dancers were on salary; curio-dealers and tropical beauties could be photographed blouseless for a fee.[12]

The life of Al Hirschfeld, America's great theater caricaturist, followed a singularly circuitous route from St. Louis to New York, and then, at the age of twenty-one, he sailed to Paris. After returning to New York and deciding to seek an earthly paradise, he and his wife headed for Tahiti in the tracks of Paul Gauguin, in search of the usual inspiration, creative stimulus, and local color. He ran directly into disillusion. Tahiti was overwhelmed with tourists. The "natives" were strumming Portuguese ukuleles and singing Irving Berlin tunes. "It was a depressing place," he said. "The food was European, the music was from 46th Street, and most of the cloth came from England or 14th Street." But the light was like nothing he had ever seen.

His friend Miguel Covarrubias was luxuriating in Bali while Hirschfeld was suffering in Tahiti. In his letters to Hirschfeld, Covarrubias presented glowing accounts of life in Bali that drew Hirschfeld to the island. By the time the Hirschfelds arrived in Bali, the Covarrubias had been gone for a month but Miguel left for the Hirschfelds everything in his house—his bicycle as well as kitchen equipment and the domestic staff. Hirschfeld rented the house from a Balinese nobleman and lived there for fifteen dollars a week. Two dollars a week paid for a cook, the food she provided, and six houseboys who cleaned, laundered, shined shoes, and performed other domestic chores. Clearly an artist could live like a king. Hirschfeld fell in love with Bali—with the people, the landscape, and the island's natural theatricality. "From morning to night, they had kite-flying, beetle-fighting, dancing of all kinds, puppet shows, silhouetted things with oil lamps and shadows thrown onto a screen. The whole place was a giant theater." During the next eleven months, Hirschfeld explored Denpasar and its environs on foot and on bike. It was in Bali, not on Broadway, that he discovered what was to become the essence of his art. "Up until Bali," Hirschfeld recalled, "I wanted to be a sculptor. After Bali I decided that sculpture was a drawing you tripped over in the dark." The Balinese sun bleached out the color and flattened forms. He fell in love with pure line. He began to "see in lines," and shifted to illustration in black and white. The elimination of color did not happen consciously. Looking back, he said, "I don't know when the peculiar alchemy took place." Partly, he credited Bali's climate. "There's something about the sun that takes out all the color and leaves shadows. There's very little color left on the beach. It's all black and white, and you begin to think in terms of line." The people became line drawings walking around. It was in Bali that his attraction to drawing blossomed into an enduring love affair with line.[13]

Despite his affinity for Bali, Hirschfeld decided to return home after a year, but by that time he was short of money. An extra–Balinese event made his departure possible. Charlie Chaplin, who was visiting Bali, was so appreciative of Hirschfeld and admiring of his talent that he bought four of his watercolors. That purchase allowed Hirschfeld to pay for his transportation back to the United Sates. "He saved my life," Hirschfeld said. "If he hadn't come by, I would probably still be on Bali."

The first time Charlie Chaplin heard of Bali was during a conversation with his brother Sydney. They were discussing the general unrest of the world. "If it comes to the worst," Sydney said, "I'll go to Bali. That is an island untouched by civilization, where you can sit under the sweltering palms and pick the fruit off the trees and live as nature intended. There one doesn't worry about depression. The problem of living is easy. And the women are beautiful."

The subject came up again when the Chaplins were en route to Japan. Sydney brought Charlie a book on travel, which included an interesting article on Bali. Charlie read the chapter and was sold. The Chaplins then had a talk with two young American artists who had been studying in Italy and were going to Bali. "It's no use going back to the States now," the Americans said. "We'd only join the ranks of the unemployed. So we thought we would save what little money we had left and go to Bali. You can live there for five dollars a week," they added, "and that's what appeals to us."[14]

Charlie's first glimpse of Bali was in the morning—"silvery downy clouds encircled green mountains leaving their peaks looking like floating fairy islands. Majestic landscapes and smiling inlets passed until we reached our destination." The governor of Bali invited the Chaplins to his residence where they met several other Dutch officials. To his horror, Charlie discovered that they had seen one or two of his pictures. "Good heavens," he thought, "have I come all this way for another Rotary Club welcome?" But after tea at the governor's house, they got into their automobile and sped along the road to south Bali.

The further they traveled the more beautiful the country became; green rice shoots were growing in silver-mirrored fields, and wide green steps terraced down the mountainside. Suddenly Sydney nudged Charlie. "Look there, quick!" Along the roadside was a line of stately young women, dressed only in batiks wrapped around their waists, and their breasts bare. Looking picturesque, they carried baskets laden with fruit on their heads. The male of the species was just as admirable. From then on, they were continually nudging. Some women were quite pretty. Their guide, who sat in the front with the chauffeur, was most annoying, for he would turn with lecherous interest to see their reactions—as though he had put on the show for them. Arriving at the Bali Hotel in Denpasar, they found the sitting rooms were open like a veranda and partitioned off with sleeping quarters at the back. "How nice to be away from civilization, relieved of stiff shirt fronts and starched collars." Charlie made up his mind to go around native-like with just a loose shirt, a pair of trousers and sandals. He was most indignant when he found a notice posted in the room which read that all guests must be fully dressed when entering the dining room, and dined deliberately without changing his clothes or shaving.[15]

Al Hirschfeld, who met Charlie several years before, invited the Chaplin brothers to his house for dinner. Before the day was over, they all became fast friends. After dinner, the entertainment began. There was a gamelan orchestra, and all the workers in Hirschfeld's compound danced. To the Balinese, who saw him in the flesh, Charlie was simply a funny man who came to Bali with his brother and who, after watching a Balinese dance, took the stage and imitated what he had just seen, performing for them a hilarious parody of that dance. They screamed with laughter. On discovering his anonymity, Charlie decided to carry out an experiment. The pith helmet he carried with him served just as well for this research in laughter. He played it like a drunk. He put on the helmet on his head and it flipped up in the air, seemingly with a will of its own. Undaunted, and with a wide-eyed look of nonchalance, he tried it again. And again the hat flew off his head. The Balinese howled with laughter, thinking his hat possessed demoniac powers. When the simplicity of the trick was exposed to them, they tried desperately, amid great hilarity, to snap their turbans in the air in the same way. The clowning instantly communicated it to the audience. Charlie had wanted to see if the Balinese would laugh at his pantomime. They did, proving that his comedy could transcend all barriers, and Chaplin was ecstatic. On his first day in Bali, Charlie Chaplin had earned for himself the descriptive title of "funny man," while Hirschfeld was known in Bali as "the bearded man."

Hirschfeld recalled a conversation he had with Chaplin. To Charlie, movement was "liberated thought." He said this slowly, as though he had discovered a great truth. A Balinese girl is like this, and with the elegance of a ballet dancer he hopped about in staccato movement, his finger nervously describing a delicate Chinese fan, his head imitating the detached, boneless, easy rhythm of a cobra. There she was, the little Balinese dancing girl, clear as a drawing.

After the performance, they strolled over to Hirschfeld's house and sat out on the veranda underneath a myriad of stars. That was Charlie's first night in Bali. "How different," he thought, "from anything I'd ever seen. How far removed I felt from the rest of the world. Europe and America seemed unreal—as though they never existed. Although I was in Bali only a few hours, it seemed I had always lived there. How easy man falls into his natural state. From these facile people one gleans the true meaning of life—to work and play—play being as important as work to man's existence. That's why they're happy. The whole time I was on the island I rarely saw a sad face." Later in the evening, they strolled down to the village for a cup of coffee at a store kept by an old Chinaman who sold everything from ladies' garters to canned asparagus. Returning to the hotel, Charlie noticed a pretty Balinese girl walking ahead of them. She would occasionally look over her shoulder, sending furtive glances in their direction. She wore a little cotton jacket. He was told that in the south of Bali only women of the streets covered their breasts.[16]

In the morning, breakfast was served on the veranda where they reclined in their pajamas and took their pineapple and mangosteen and enjoyed the morning sun. The Chaplins decided to abandon ship and prolonged their stay in Bali. The daily routine would start after breakfast by taking automobile excursions to various parts of the island. They would return before lunch, and in the afternoon they would take their siesta. In the evening, thanks to Spies, there was always some form of entertainment, which would complete their day. One festival lasted all night. It was given by a rajah who was celebrating because he had paid his debts to the government and was now free from the threat of imprisonment. "An appropriate reason to celebrate," Charlie thought. It took place at night on the outskirts of the forest and hundreds came from all parts of the island. There were fireworks, a barong play, and a kris dance. Most elaborate preparations were made, the cost of which, according to Chaplin, would again endanger the rajah with threats of imprisonment. Charlie took motion pictures of many of the Balinese ceremonies.

Walter Spies called on the Chaplins and had lunch with them at the hotel one day. He played Balinese music for them, which he transcribed for piano. "The effect was like a Bach concerto played in double time." Chaplin found Balinese music cold, ruthless, and slightly disturbing; "even the deep doleful passages had the sinister yearning of a hungry minotaur." After lunch, Spies took them into the interior of the jungle, where a ceremony of flagellation was to take place. They were obliged to walk four miles along a jungle part to get there. When they arrived, they came upon a large crowd surrounding an altar about twelve feet long. Young maidens in beautiful sarongs, their breasts bare, were queuing up with baskets laden with fruit and other offerings. A priest, looking like a dervish with long hair down to his waist and dressed in a white gown, blessed and laid the offerings upon the altar. After the priests had intoned prayers, giggling youths broke through and ransacked the altar, grabbing what they could as the priests lashed violently at them with whips. Some were forced to drop their spoils because of the severity of the lashings, which were supposed to rid them of evil spirits that tempted them to rob.

The Chaplins went in and out of temples and compounds as they pleased, and saw cockfights all hours of the day and night. They left one at five o'clock in the morning. "Their gods are pleasure loving," wrote Chaplin, "and the Balinese worship them not with awe but with affection. Bali then was a paradise. Natives worked four months in the rice fields and devoted the other eight to their art and culture. Entertainment was free all over the island, one village performing for another." Charlie Chaplin remained eighteen days in Bali and "every moment was interesting." Anything after Bali was a letdown.[17]

9

Imaginary Museum

> *Balinese surprise Western observers by their lack of "soul" even while the focus of their death rites is the soul of their dead. Proof of their lack of feeling was laughter and gaiety during cremation ceremonies, their completely impersonal execution of dances and dramatic plays, a seeming indifference in times of crisis that in some other parts of the world call forth a display of emotions.*
>
> Claire Holt[1]

Bali in the early 1930s began attracting a steady stream of intellectual personalities and artists, along with a colorful crowd of truth seekers, dilettantes and casual tourists. Almost overnight, Bali became a focal point for serious westerners in search of new experiences and a state of grace. Bali had become a metaphor for paradise—a luscious, tropical retreat.

Claire Holt, student of dance and sculpture, was born in Riga, Latvia, and came to the United States at the age of twenty. She studied sculpture, and was *The New York World*'s dance critic. In 1930, Claire embarked on a trip around the world. When she reached the Dutch East Indies, what was intended as a brief visit turned into an extended stay and a lifelong involvement with Indonesia. She spent the greater part of the decade there and published articles on Indonesian art, culture, and life. She assisted Dr. Willem Stutterheim, the Dutch archaeologist and art historian, who became her mentor, in his archaeological researches and pursued her own studies of Indonesian performing art. Her introduction to the performing arts took place at the court of Surakarta, where the traditional arts flourished in the thirties. She also became Dr. Stutterheim's companion and escort, although the Dutch establishment was shocked to learn that Dr. Stutterheim was living with his young American assistant.

Claire Holt's exposure to Indonesia left her with an overwhelming and enduring impression of a complete integration of art in the spiritual and daily lives of its people. It was this pervasive interplay that held Holt there for ten years. She had lived beside, worked with, and pitted herself against many of the Western scholars who worked in Indonesia during the thirties. She also forged a significant alliance during this time with the Swedish impresario and patron of the arts and ballet, Rolf de Maré, who was also wealthy dance aficionado and the founder and director of Ballets Suedois in Paris. Developing an interest in folk art, music, and dance, he traveled to collect primitive art. Holt accompanied de Maré on a sweeping tour that included Bali, documenting, filming, and photographing traditional dances for Les Archives Internationales de la Danse in Paris, which he founded.

Colin McPhee was a Canadian-born composer and ethnomusicologist who studied in Paris and then lived in New York City, taking part in the modern music movement. It was in New York that he had an opportunity to hear the first recordings of Balinese music, which were brought to him by Claire Holt and Gela Archipenko, who had just returned from a visit to Java and Bali. Colin was enraptured by this music and was enchanted with the sounds.

Colin and his wife, Jane Belo, decided to travel to Bali, and were able to live in Bali only because Jane had money. Since foreigners could not purchase land in Bali, Colin and Jane leased the property. Jane was the legal owner of the house. She paid for the house in Sayan and provided all the capital for the project. Indeed, Jane completely supported Colin financially during their marriage. In his later years, he called his trip to Bali "an escape from the vulgarity of America, the sordid materialism, the competition, and all the modern virtues." But there is little doubt that McPhee's idyllic years on the island of Bali were prolonged as a deliberate escape from his many personal problems and career insecurity. Colin, although homosexual by inclination, married Jane, an intelligent woman rich enough to take him to Bali and support him while he researched its music. Perhaps the end justified the means.

While McPhee intermittently exhibited a charm that beguiled well-wishers other than his long-suffering wife, his tirades about the state of the wicked world (especially in reference to his own talents), his self-absorption, and his infantile petulance proved increasingly tiresome. Colin was a homosexual whom Margaret Mead described as having a "very dissociated impersonality which gave him the kind of freedom he sought," who didn't "exercise a single conjugal duty of bed, board, or companionship." In his first person singular account of life in Bali in the 1930s, *A House in Bali*, Colin did not even hint at the existence, much less of the close proximity of Jane, who shared with him both the house and the enthusiasm for Balinese culture, as well as her financial support. Colin also concealed the real nature of his relationships with the young male dancers, musicians, and house boys who were the principal cast of characters in his book (although this is quite obvious if not explicit).

9. Imaginary Museum 121

Jane Belo was the child of wealthy Texans. After her father's death in her early childhood, she traveled in Europe with her mother and sister and then settled in New York City. As a student at Barnard College, Jane became absorbed in anthropology. Margaret Mead called Jane "one of the most gifted observers and interviewers whom it has been my good fortune to know," and credited Jane Belo's earlier writings on Balinese art and ritual, published during the 1930s, for her own decision to go there. Jane seemed to have been attracted to the island as an opportunity for fieldwork as Colin was to music.

Jane was fully aware from the beginning that Colin was homosexual, and knew her own inclinations toward women. But Colin and Jane were married and in 1931 they sailed for Bali via Paris, where they ran into Rosa and Miguel Covarrubias, who gave them a firsthand account of life on Bali as well as a letter of introduction to Walter Spies. Most likely Colin heard the Balinese gamelan that was performing in the Dutch pavilion at the International Colonial Exposition. Both Colin and Jane remembered the early morning approaches to the island as breathtaking. "We never found anything as lovely as our beautiful Bali, and, as we returned, we always stood on the deck at sunrise, just as the ship which bore us was coming in to port, and saw the mountains looming in the early mist behind the stretches of beach and waving palms."[2]

As soon as Colin and Jane reached Bali, they headed for Denpasar. Although they stayed at the Bali Hotel, the usual haunt for westerners, they kept their distance from tourists. When Colin sat in the front seat of the car, where he could talk with the chauffeur as they drove, the hotel manager strongly disapproved. For in this little gesture anything apparently was to be read, possible friendliness and intimacy, and even worse, equality, which was so abhorrent from the colonial point of view. "You must keep your distance," said the manager; "The correct place for a white man is in the back seat. In the old days," he continued, "Hollanders married natives; today it is different. Take them to bed if you like, but see they come at the back door." He spoke in heavy earnestness, but without hatred. He bullied his boys, sometimes in roaring fury, sometimes in tired routine. "Lazy!" he complained. "You can teach them nothing. Ten years I've been here," he moaned. "If it weren't for the girls." He had a final word for Colin, "If you really must sit in front, drive the car yourself and let the chauffeur sit behind." Colin continued to sit the way he pleased.[3]

The hotel offered daily itineraries for guests who wanted to cram visits to the sights of Bali into a few days. But Colin avoided such common junkets; he preferred to drive at random through the island, getting lost in the network of back roads that ran up into the hills where, as he looked down towards the sea, the flooded rice fields lay shining in the sunlight like a broken mirror. He was mesmerized by the sound of music forever in the air. As the days passed, the seductive appeal of the music increased, and Colin gradually realized he could not leave. He and Jane broke out of the hotel's stuffy European environment and rented a small house in the village of Kedaton, just north of Denpasar. The house was immediately outfitted with servants, and the couple settled into a peaceful tropical existence.

This first house was small and square, with a roof of corrugated tin and walls covered inside and out with damp white plaster. It had four rooms and a cement floor, and in traditional Balinese style, the kitchen and bath were in a separate building. Light came from coconut oil lamps, and servants brought water up from the springs. "The doors creaked; the rooms were musty; the place had been shut a year. But from the deep veranda in front you looked out through the palms over gleaming rice fields and caught a glimpse of the sea beyond."[4]

When Colin and Jane returned to Bali two years later, Colin commented: "Many people from God-knows-where are building houses. Every one wants to be Robinson Crusoe, and takes other footprints in the sands as personal insults," but "the music was still marvelous." Colin wrote to Aaron Copeland, a well-known American composer, that he was really glad he came back for there had been loads of material to absorb. They immediately also began looking for property, and Colin searched for a spot in the hills, where it was cooler, quieter, and more conducive to work. The site he found was all that and more. It lay in the outskirts of Sayan, a small village perched on a mountain ridge not far from Ubud. The property overlooked a deep ravine, at the bottom of which rushed a broad stream. Terraced rice fields lined the other side, and the mountains of Tabanan were visible in the distance. The view was stunning. In choosing a village such as Sayan, Colin and Jane reconciled themselves to a life that would conform to Balinese customs. Sayan was small and a bit off the beaten track; it was quiet and conservative, "a peasant village, not very old, but running according to old Balinese law." There were no shops, only "a small market every two days." Few there spoke Malay, so the McPhees had to start learning the Balinese language.

The McPhees's house in Sayan was built in Balinese style out of bamboo with a thatched roof. They constructed at least four buildings: a "large house" with a veranda, dining alcove, studio, and balcony; a "bedroom house" with two verandas and two bedrooms; a "bath house"; and a "kitchen house." There was also a separate garage. Teak, durian, nutmeg, coconut, and "several other untranslatable woods" went into the structure.

9. *Imaginary Museum* 123

A panorama of the Sayan house built by Jane Belo and Colin McPhee. Photograph by Colin McPhee. Courtesy of the UCLA Ethnomusicology Archive—University of California, Los Angeles.

Colin was a talented cook and had two kitchens built on the property. One was fully outfitted for preparing an array of international cuisine. The other was "purely Balinese." Jane was accustomed to this grand life. Coming from an affluent family, she accepted servants as a usual part of daily existence, yet she was not considered arrogant or ostentatious by friends. Like other Westerners in Bali during the 1930s, they had a large retinue of servants—twelve servants,—"all beautiful and naked to the waist." There were six servants in the McPhees's kitchen alone: several to carry water up from the river, one to wash clothes, others to cook.

Colin and Jane rented Spies's house while their own was being built, and Spies stayed in another building on the property. In a letter to his mother, Spies described his carefree days with the McPhees: "The McPhees and I live together very quietly and happily. He has brought a Steinway grand piano, and so we play much two-piano music. We have a lot of fun at home." Spies went on to call McPhee an "exceptionally good cook."

Despite the McPhees's household establishment, life in Bali was rugged in a number of ways. There was no plumbing or electricity and few shops or cars; travel to the West involved a twenty-day trip by ship, and access to the materials needed for research was difficult—books and paper were at a premium, and even newspapers arrived two months late. Mail was delivered not to their door but to the Bali Hotel in Denpasar. Colin combined a pleasant existence with a determination to document the musical culture around him. Although he had no formal training in fieldwork or any aspect of scholarship, he fell into anthropological research with natural ease. The secure comforts of a gentleman scholar gave a firm foundation to his efforts. He described life in Bali as "lazy and unproductive. I leisurely collect Balinese music and make notes for a book, and the rest of the time plant trees and flowers, or ride the horse." Yet the quantity of his transcriptions and the quality of his writing on Balinese music show that the pace, if "leisurely," was nonetheless dogged.

During their years in Bali, the McPhees not only observed the culture but also became active community members who adhered closely to local customs. They were liked by the people of Sayan. They took part in temple ceremonies and were accepted as part of the community. Hugo Bernatzik gave a westerner's perspective on Colin and Jane's, as well as Walter Spies's, sympathy for the Balinese: "Among all the whites whom I met on my travels they were the only ones who, amid the beautiful tropical scenery, did not live in barracks and had not, though their means would have permitted, built themselves houses in the loud colonial style. They had real artistic natures, whose whole endeavor was to encourage and maintain the good characteristics and disposition which the Bali people so richly possess."

"In the circumstances," wrote Bernatzik, " it was no wonder that I soon made friends with them and gladly accepted the invitation to stay at one of the two houses. My new friends knew the land well and most kindly put their knowledge at my service. Thus in a few weeks I got to know the country in first-rate fashion, and my planned eight days' stay expanded into many delightful weeks." The Steinway grand piano in the front room of his house in Sayan was an object of delight for many Balinese, helping to make his home a favored meeting spot for well-known Balinese musicians.[5]

Jane concentrated on the study of ceremonial life, trance and other aspects of religious behavior, and children's art. Colin turned more and more to the study of the gamelan. He traveled across the island searching out as many varieties of gamelan playing as he could find, and learning about Balinese music by working closely with musicians on the island.

After several years of intensive study of the gamelan, Colin described himself as being entirely absorbed in his work. "Everything seemed of greatest interest, from the detail of the 'flower parts' in a far-off village by the sea, to the bare and simple melodies of the mountain gamelans." As the days passed, he found himself thinking less and less about composing. He began a work for orchestra, but he knew that he would never finish it. He wrote a few short pieces and forgot about them a week later. The urge to write music had left him, and composing had become an "oppressive responsibility." As the drive to write music left, he felt "free and happy, liberated from something in which he no longer believed," although Virgil Thompson, the noted American composer, considered McPhee to have been a fine composer "before he got screwed up and went all Balinese." Yet even though he stopped composing for a time, he never fully saw himself as a scholar but as a composer working within a brotherhood of fellow musicians, inquiring how persons like himself functioned in another culture. McPhee learned about Balinese music by working closely with musicians on the island, several of whom played prominent roles in his life there. Yet, when he tried to launch what he believed to be his masterpiece, *Tabuh-Tabuhan*, a work for a large orchestra based on his piano transcriptions of Balinese gamelan, the piece was not performed in New York. That was left to Carlos Chavez in Mexico City, where *Tabuh-Tabuhan* was a momentary sensation.

Sampih was a Balinese child of about eight when McPhee first met him, while the house was being built. The two struck up a tentative friendship, and soon Sampih was stopping frequently at the McPhee house. Eventually he came there to live. McPhee probably never adopted Sampih officially. One day, quite by accident, McPhee discovered that Sampih had talent as a dancer. Sampih was a lively, precocious child, with a personality as wild as the *kebyar* dance he improvised. McPhee loved the boy intensely and was devoted to giving Sampih every opportunity to grow as a dancer. McPhee also organized several gamelan groups, including a children's gamelan group. He later turned the story of the founding of the children's ensemble into a charming children's book, *A Club of Small Men: A Children's Tale from Bali*.

Even though Jane had known from the beginning that Colin had male lovers, she eventually found this intolerable. In his Bali notes Colin occasionally alluded to affairs with Balinese men, but he was mostly discreet and extremely private. But several of his friends suggested that one of the appeals of Bali for McPhee was its openness to homosexuality. The breakup of the McPhees's marriage while they were still in Bali was due to Jane's increasing humiliation from Colin's ever more flaunted homosexuality. Walter Spies, McPhee's closest European friend on the island, mentioned what must have been a contributing factor, that McPhee "drank heavily and had an ugly temper when drunk." (He died of cirrhosis of the liver.)

Colin later described at least one reason for the end of his relationship with Jane: "My alliance with Jane was broken off by me in a final fit of stubbornness, and on the whole I don't regret it, for she had turned into what for me was a prig, probably because she was tired of my untidy and carefree attitude towards life. Anyway, I was in love at the time with a Balinese, which she knew, and to have him continually around was too much for her vanity. So it all ended as I had foreseen at the beginning, and Jane was unbelievably loyal long after there was any reason for it."[6]

Colin stayed alone in Bali for nearly a year after Jane left. He left in December 1938. A number of factors conspired to make him leave. The first was a lack of money. Although Jane seems to have supported him for a time after their divorce, she would not do so indefinitely. When the Dutch authorities mounted the "witch-hunt" against homosexuals, and many westerners in Bali were under suspicion, McPhee must have also been the object of such suspicion, and the timing of his departure from Bali, only five days before Walter Spies was arrested, suggests that he was in such danger. Besides, he had not allowed Jane to tell anyone that they had been divorced the previous summer. McPhee later wrote: "Everyone carries within him his own private paradise, some beloved territory whose assault is an assault on the heart. For me it was Bali, for I had lived there a long time and had been very happy."

Jane returned to Bali not long after Colin left, to finish her research on Balinese trance, and found it quite different. On one level it was hard "to pick up the life again without Colin to make things interestingly difficult." On another, all westerners on the island were being harassed by the Dutch authorities as part of a general crackdown against the growing movement for Indonesian independence. En route, in Sydney, Australia, she met Margaret Mead and her husband Gregory Bateson, who had just finished their fieldwork in New Guinea. The situation in Bali was unsettled enough that they decided Jane should not travel alone. So they accompanied her and spent six weeks following up on work they had done a year earlier. The three moved into the house in Sayan, and the villagers celebrated her return.

Colin McPhee was able to describe Balinese music in great detail and to bring Balinese music to the West in a way that could be understood and used, but his story has an air of pathos about it. His abiding passion for Bali, so well conveyed in his autobiographical account, was a love affair doomed to separation. He spent most of his life missing opportunities and deadlines—particularly for his magnum book, *Music in Bali*—and in penury, as if blighted by a longing for the island he was able to conjure up in music and words.

9. Imaginary Museum

In July 1936, the Museum of Fine Arts in Brooklyn installed an exhibition of McPhee's collection of Balinese art, the most comprehensive collection that ever reached the United States. "'There are, however, a number of omissions from the McPhee *kain gambar* (paintings on cotton cloth),' demure Miss Christine Krehbiel, in charge of the exhibition at the Brooklyn Museum, explained. 'The Balinese have no Will Hays to censor their art.' And with a tolerant smile: 'They have unusual ideas of what are sacred subjects and ... well!'"[7]

Katharane and Jack Mershon were professional dancers. Katharane began her dancing career in her late teens by touring the United States as a ballroom dancer. She later studied and taught ballet, was director of the Pasadena Playhouse, and acted as administrator of the Denishawn Company schools. Jack Mershon was also a brilliant photographer and an expert gardener who had an independent income.

A friend of theirs had a motion picture that he wanted them to see, and they went to his house to see it. It was picture of a man in Bali dancing and the dancer's name was I Mario, the greatest Balinese dancer of all time. When Katharane saw him dance, she said, "My goodness, we've got to go to Bali to see Balinese dancing." So they picked up and went to Bali to stay a month. They remained nine years.[8]

They first rented a house on the seashore at Sanur. "And so there we were with a house, a cook, a garden, a *babu* (maid)—and no language! It seemed incredible that one could undertake such a responsibility. But then we were to be in Bali merely two months, and during that time we'd be the only non–Balinese for miles around. Adjustment was not simple. The language barrier was baffling."

They settled in the village of Sanur, where they built a house. It was a beautiful house built Balinese style: it had a thatched roof and the main room opened out onto a lawn, where modern bamboo furniture sat on the porch. Beyond the room there was a terrace, and then growth all along the seawall to hold the sea back. The Mershons enjoyed Bali, largely because they kept themselves busy. Jack had raised a splendid garden in the sandy, often drought-stricken soil, and Katharane ran an improvised but effective free clinic for people afraid to go to the government hospital in Denpasar. They spent their spare money on medicines and took turns every day treating scores of people, who often came from afar with the most frightful sores. The disinterested work of the Mershons made them the idols of the neighborhood and they were known as *tuan doctor* and *nyonya doctor*. There was of course a fine modern hospital in Denpasar, but the Balinese preferred the more informal, sympathetic clinic of the Mershons. The Mershons took great interest in Balinese music and dancing, and had intimate knowledge of the life and tradition of their Balinese neighbors.[9]

Theodora Benson reported that the Mershons's house, like most European houses in Bali, consisted of a group of small houses, a little collection of pavilions. Here, as in most of them, there were some lovely antiques, chiefly from Bali, including the lovely carved and painted doors. "When you sat on the porch of the house," wrote author Cedric Belfrage, "their Balinese neighbors would come uninvited and squat by you, glad of a friendly chat if you speak their language but quite happy just to sit and be unobtrusively companionable. The Mershons couldn't tell you just how many there were in their household, the kitchen quarters were more or less open house for anyone who cared to drop in and attach himself. They had hired one or two servants and others kept adding themselves on, happy to help about the place in odd ways for no wages because they liked the Mershons and it was fun."[10]

"I was out one day with Walter Spies," Katharane recalled. "We heard some music sounds in the distance. It was explained to us that these sounds were designed to drive away smallpox. I told Walter that I thought it would be a wonderful idea to choreograph some of the movements I had developed for the Pasadena Playhouse production of *Lazarus Lost* to these sounds. I proceeded to do that and worked with the dancers, and that's how I came to choreograph the *Kecak* (Monkey Dance)." Dressed in full Balinese regalia, Katharane also joined in a graceful dance in perfect harmony with the Balinese dancers, swaying to the rhythmic pulsations of the gamelan.

Mershon was the guest of the rajah of Karangasem. Upon arrival at the palace, she was delighted by her accommodation in the south palace, which consisted of a private sleeping room, a bath, and a kitchen. To show to what extent the rajah had extended himself to please his guests, her kitchen had plates and utensils of non-Balinese origins, butter (not used by the Balinese), tinned milk, canned corned beef (Libby's!), tea, sugar, European vegetables—potatoes, carrots, cabbage—as well as a great variety of Balinese ones. Bread and cookies were provided from the prince's palace.[11]

She was helped by a small boy who lived nearby, who took the task of improving her language, and who stayed more and more at her house. She adopted the four-and-a-half-year old boy, named Murda. For many years she became known as "mother of Murda," and was accepted by the Balinese. Through Murda, she learned high and low Balinese. He was constantly correcting her because she would use high Balinese to the wrong people and low Balinese to the wrong people and so forth.[12]

There were two houses in Bali that were really establishments that ran like homes should run, having lots of servants. One was Jane Belo's and the other Katharane Mershon's. Belo had a beautiful house in the middle of the island; Mershon had one on the seashore. Between the two of them, they entertained everybody who was of any note at all who came to Bali. (In October 1986, Katharane's ashes were sent to Bali for the final ritual in the Balinese life cycle ceremonies that she so vividly portrayed in her book about Balinese rituals, *Seven Plus Seven: Mysterious Life-Rituals in Bali*, so fulfilling her final wish).

"In Bali, nothing ever took place according to plan," wrote Beryl de Zoete, but "something always happens in Bali to revive your spirits if something has happened to depress them, and as we sit disconsolate on the loggia of the priest's house we are told a version of a play which opens up a new world to our investigation." Long after nightfall, the dance that the travelers expected to see in the afternoon "is really starting, and it proves so good that we forgive it for not being the one which we spent all the day in trying not to miss."

Beryl was described as beautiful in youth, young-looking in middle age, gypsylike, with dyed black hair and rings on every finger, in old age. She had cool carillons in her laughter and an indomitable spirit that glowed in her piercing erudite eyes. She had been the companion of Arthur Waley, "the whale of Chinese translators" and assistant keeper in the British Museum, who had taught himself Chinese and translated Chinese poetry. She was regarded by his family and friends as his wife in all but name until her death. Theirs was a flexible arrangement, allowing scope for separate living quarters on occasion as well as for her constant adventuring abroad with one or more appreciative male friends. Ten years older than Arthur, Beryl had means of her own.

Even in her fifties and sixties her looks remained striking and her figure supple. Harold Acton said as late as the 1930s that her belly dance could still rival the Moroccan girls' in the *quartier réservé* at Casablanca, and her performance of the *danse du ventre* put the professionals to shame despite the disparity of age. She had been a pupil of Émile Jacques-Dalcroze, originator of the eurhythmics system of musical instruction. She traveled widely in the Middle East and Far East while Arthur stayed home, fluently spoke French, German, and Italian, and was widely recognized as an excellent translator. She was a dance critic for the *New Statesman, The Daily Telegraph,* and Richard Buckle's *Ballet;* but her strongest claim to fame, much talked of at the time, laid in her three pioneering books on the dance and drama of Bali, Ceylon, and southern India.

A forceful and flamboyant personality, able, impetuous, and demanding, Beryl was accustomed to getting what she wanted. Beryl lacked inhibition, she liked success and found it stimulating. Beryl was described as "original, unconventional and unworldly, often very amusing, and her gaiety and enthusiasm made her personality very attractive." Her disarming and humorous caprices—demanding "freshly-baked insect hoppers filled with honey," or yak's milk at a cocktail party—seemed thoroughly tiresome to people who remained unmoved by her "blend of sibylline agelessness with virginal amazement." She could, in her bad moments, be silly and clumsy and insensitive and selfish. She was generous and kind as well as loyal to her friends. She could irritate, but she could not hurt because there was no malice in her. Beryl aroused Margaret Mead's wrath and Mead found that Beryl had an "acid tongue" and a gift for destructive criticism that intensified the conflicts which were apt to arise among the members of any expedition. Mead identified Beryl with the witch, a prevailing Balinese figure. Beryl was possessive, and tried to appropriate the people she liked and keep them under her wing.[13]

Beryl's passion was the dance in all its forms, but more especially the ritual dances of the East. She traveled extensively to study them on the spot and thus satisfied her other passion, traveling. Beryl was taken by the Balinese dancers at the 1931 Paris Colonial Exposition. She resolved to visit the country in which such a great and mysterious dance art was home. In Bali, she conducted almost daily excursions to watch ceremonies, either performed in accordance with the calendrical cycle or performed to order.

Walter Spies was Beryl's instructor in things Balinese as well as her collaborator. During a fifteen-month sojourn in Bali, Beryl was Spies's guest. They worked well together and their partnership survived the occasional rifts between them, resulting in their book *Dance and Drama in Bali*, which Beryl wrote and Spies's photographs illustrated.

Beryl de Zoete credited Gregor Krause with Bali's reputation as "an earthly paradise in which a favoured race of men live in Utopian harmony with their own kind, with nature and their god." But de Zoete continued:

> As if to make some return for the extraordinary richness of sensation which every visitor to Bali experiences, some travelers have gone so far as to fill the sky and cover the earth with birds and beasts and plants which are not found there; they have sentimentalized its people, and added a touch of mustard to a savorless perfection by allusions to frantic rites behind closed doors, in which naturally the writer did not participate. Others who have not been there suggest that Bali is too spoiled to be worth a visit. For how, they ask, can so small an island have maintained its integrity when thousands of tourists are

9. Imaginary Museum

Beryl de Zoete noting dance movements at Campuan. Courtesy of The Horniman Museum and Gardens, London.

washed up yearly on its shores, raced along excellent roads to its catalogued beauty spots, and supplied with *objets d'art* specially fabricated for them? One can only reply that the Balinese have a non-resistant way of resisting what does not suit them which is far more powerful than protecting stubbornness, and which has been illustrated by their method of dealing with missions. There are a few converts in a few very poor villages which have been neglected by their priests; there is more than a sprinkling, alas, of dirty European shirts and tin roofs. But the interest of the men of Bali in their own life is too great to be diverted by the sea-drift of tourism, which is, by the way, responsible neither for shirts nor missions nor tin roofs.

Bali was neither a last nor a lost paradise, but the home of a peculiarly gifted people of mixed race, endowed with a great sense of humor and a great sense of style, where their own traditions are concerned; and with a suppleness of mind which had enabled them to take what they want of the alien civilizations which have been reaching them for centuries and to leave the rest very successfully. The swift tourist did not even scratch the surface of Bali; indeed, one might drive about for months and would do no more than that.[14]

10
Oh, Noble Breasts of Bali

Visitors had fun writing paeans and poems of praise to Bali in the visitors' book of the Bali Hotel, and many have written their opinions of Bali in doggerel verse. The most famous, attributed to Noel Coward, complained: "As I mentioned this morning to Charlie,/There is far too much music in Bali..." as well as too much dancing, perhaps a few too many bared breasts, and "too much artistic endeavour.[1]

Some of the visitors had been unable to refrain from bursting into song. The effort of another poet, an Englishman of Singapore, stirred to inspiration, was entitled "To Batoer and Agoeng and the lesser Peaks of Bali," the most poignant item in the visitors' book:

> Oh, noble breasts of Bali,
> Erect and proud you stand,
> A bronzed and rhythmic setting,
> To green and fertile land!
> Ye beauteous breasts of Bali
> To which thy children cling
> And draw their living substance
> From mother nature's spring!
> Oh, laughing breasts of Bali,
> That youth aspires to climb,
> To stretch themselves upon thee,
> In ecstasies divine!
> Oh, welcome breasts of Bali,
> By age forever blest,
> Where weakly heads are pillowed,
> In everlasting rest!

Frank Clune, one of the most prolific and colorful Australian travel writers, commented that, as any intelligent reader could see at a glance, the pure-minded poet was naturally thinking only of the volcano-cone mountains of Bali.

George Walter Caldwell, a retired surgeon and author from Hollywood, California, after reading the foregoing poem, dashed off "under extreme provocation," the following:

> A rhyme-making Babbitt came out of the West,
> Of beauteous Bali he saw but a breast,
> He saw not the charm of the magical night,
> Saw nothing at all when a breast was in sight.
> He heard not the music of gamelan gongs,
> Or the temple-maids chanting their mystical songs,
> He saw not the temples of flame-trees aglow
> Nor banners of palm-trees—his eyes were too low.
> When Venus and Juno walked gracefully by
> It was only their breasts that attracted his eye.
> The doctors will say, "He has breasts on the brain,"
> When he has returned to his home town again.
> If he goes to heaven—he will not I fear—
> God spares the angels his lecherous leer!

An unknown scribe then commented on the way in which the Californian spelled his penultimate word:

> The Poet says of Bali
> Of how her bountiful breasts
> Will nourish all who dully
> Obey her God's behests.
> The Philistine is moved to jeer
> At what he calls the Poet's leer,
> It seems to stir him to invoke
> God's wrath upon his lecherous joke.
> I will not judge between the two,
> Though Philistine he called so well:
> Yet this I feel is mainly true—
> At least the Poet knows how to spell![2]

Three other tourists from California wrote: "Even to a visitor from Los Angeles Bali seems beautiful"; "We have nothing like this in California" and "Even the man from California was silent."

The visitor's book provides a cross section of tourist reactions to Bali. Clune further commented that not being a poet or a Philistine, he did not add his paean or his growl to the visitor's book. "Inspiration causes perspiration," he stated, " and it's too hot in Bali to versify." Theodora Benson was another traveler who glanced through the visitor's book, and "smiled and smiled at its naive shrieks of praise." She almost wanted to find Bali overrated. "The gem of the Orient....." "In sweet and tender remembrance of a few days delightfully spent in unique Bali." "*Bali, l'île des rêves, lacs mystérieux ... un souvenir ineffaçable dans ma vie.*" Quotations too: "A thing of beauty is a joy forever," and even "A beauty is a joy for ever." It struck a rather welcome note to come upon the simple comment: "I hate Bali!!! Signed N. Ipple, Pres: Amalgamated Brassiere Co., Boston, Mass." But "scientific study" revealed something phony about it. Several of the poems were mostly ecstatic. Two of the lines in one poem went:

> Where man is good to the rooster and cow
> And women and dogs live anyhow.

The visitor's book offered Benson one other escape from the mainly ill-expressed ecstasies. Someone had written. "I saw the real Bali; not for tourists." Benson certainly did not lay any claim to any such thing. She knew that she was a tourist all right.[3]

Major General Lord Edward Gleichen, English soldier and diplomat, and grandson of Queen Victoria's half sister, wrote: "May the Lord long preserve this beautiful people from the horrors of 'civilization' and 'missionaries.'" An Australian visitor echoed this sentiment: "God spare these delightful people from the vices of the white man."[4]

The Marquis Henri de la Falaise de la Coudraye wrote in the visitor's book: "*Six semaines de Bali! Un rêve trop court! Je reviendrai!*" A typical Frenchman wrote, "*L'Hôtel du soin, l'Ile du sein*" (Hotel of care, the Island of breast), and from many visitors' point of view he has said everything.[5]

The dogs—poor starving beasts—were the only feature of Bali that came in for sustained criticism if not to say hatred and scorn, in the visitor's book, for their continued barking.

11

Little Grass Shacks on the Beach of Bali

Muriel Walker, Vaneen Walker, Muriel Pearsen, Manx, Mrs. Manx, K'tut Tantri, and Surabaya Sue; her ancestry was bizarre enough to match her string of names. She was born Muriel Stuart Walker in Glasgow, Scotland, but considered herself "full-blooded Manx, or rather a mixture of blood from the Viking pirates who swept down from the North in the Thirteenth century and the kings of the Isle of Man." Thus, she was widely known to the westerners in Bali by reference to the island she claimed as her spiritual origin. Many of her erstwhile Bali contemporaries referred to her as Manx or Manxy or Mrs. Manx, but Robert Koke, the owner of the Kuta Beach Hotel, believed that she took the name Manx because it sounded exotic.

She went with her mother to the United States, adopted the name Vaneen Walker, settled in Hollywood, and earned a living as a screen journalist. She married an American, Karl Henning Pearsen, and remained married to him until he died. Her first images of Bali were those in the movie she saw in the cinema in 1932. It was a rainy afternoon and, walking down Hollywood Boulevard, Muriel stopped before a small movie theater and on the spur of the moment decided to go in. The film was entitled *Bali, the Last Paradise*, and she became entranced. The picture was aglow with an agrarian pattern of peace, contentment, beauty and love. "Yes, I had found my life," she later wrote. "I recognized the place where I wished to be. My decision was sudden but it was irrevocable. It was as if fate had brushed my shoulder. I felt a compulsion, from which I had no desire to escape." She sailed from New York City in November 1932, and as she wanted to paint in Bali, she acquired a two-year supply of canvasses, brushes, and oils.[1]

She registered at the Bali Hotel but found the lounge and the dining room so crowded with white men and women that it was not difficult to

imagine herself again in New York or Hollywood. The people were mostly Dutch, of the colonial administrative type; there was a sprinkling of American tourists. A Dutch official told her that artists did not stay long and that foreigners got fed up with the island after a while. While many artists came to Bali, they quickly got tired of the place and went home. "We have a Belgian," he continued, "he's living with a Balinese woman—set himself up in a lost paradise of his own." "We expect Americans to be a little odd, but when they're Dutch they're beyond the pale. But in no case do we like it when the whites become intimate with the natives. It is bad for our prestige."[2]

After she arrived in Bali, she dyed her naturally auburn hair black, to avoid appearing like Rangda, the archetypal red-haired Balinese witch. She lived in the guest house belonging to the rajah of Bangli, near his palace. It was a simple "modern" concrete house, "more like a garage." She was given the name K'tut Tantri (fourth-born child). Here, she said, she studied traditional Balinese culture, became a member of a royal court, studied the Balinese language, and painted. She became a close and firm friend of Anak Agung Ngurah, the rajah's son who was Dutch educated. It was hardly surprising that the relationship between Manx and Ngurah was very close, that this relationship was construed as romantic and even sexual, and that she was considered Ngurah's Western "concubine" (given the common colonial presumption that the Oriental man's greatest aim was to have sex with a white woman). Nor was it surprising that the suggestion of such relationship, whether true or false, would result in Manx's identification by the Dutch authorities as a subversive, or at least an undesirable element who was "at one with the natives." She was said to have "gone native" by wearing native sarongs, an accusation that, on the island identified in the West as "the Isle of Bare Breasts," suggested nudity and promiscuity. In fact, although she claimed to have worn traditional costume in public on several occasions (always "covered up"), her usual dress was far from revealing. She certainly wore batik and other sarongs, but they had been made into long neck-to-knee dresses, known as "Mother Hubbards," and it was in this garb that she was photographed. Manx saw herself as a lonely, romantic dreamer, who found herself betrayed and abandoned, her life in tatters, and without any real family. The Dutch also hounded her, and because they wanted foreigners to remain under the watch of Dutch eyes, they were against foreigners living in the villages.

Opposite: Rangda, queen of the witches, the powerful symbol of evil in the Balinese world. From the back cover of *Bali*, a travel brochure published in 1930 by the Officieele Vereeniging voor Toeristenverkeer in Nederlandsche-Indie in Batavia, Netherlands East Indies.

By the 1930s, interracial sex was seen not just as a cause of racial degeneration but also, in political terms, as a betrayal of the whites. Half-caste children or adults were very rarely seen in Bali. Few westerners married Balinese women, and there was only a French girl who had married into Ubud's royal family when she wed the Balinese prince Cokorda Gde Raka Sukawati, who organized and led the Balinese dance and gamelan troupe to the Paris Colonial Exposition. The girl, Gilberte Riviere, had grown up in the French countryside but moved to Paris. She got a job at the 1931 Colonial Exposition in Paris, where she met her future husband. She followed him back to Bali and insisted upon living with him. The Dutch took a dim view of her because the prince already had four or five wives, and she did not know that, according to his tradition, he was entitled to have more than one wife. But Princess Gilberte Sukawati didn't count them because they were all Balinese. Emilio Ambron, and Italian artist, described her as "a little pale with tousled blonde hair, rather attractive but with a bewildered expression." She was treated from a distance, because neither the westerners nor the Balinese approved of mixed liaisons. The attitudes of Western Bohemians regarding sexual relations with the Balinese were often ambivalent, if not even hypocritical. In fact, sexual relationships between the Western Bohemians and the Balinese were not uncommon in 1930s Bali.[3]

In 1936, Manx's relations with the rulers of Bangli had apparently deteriorated. This was probably the result of the rumors of a sexual relationship between Manx and the prince. The Dutch Resident attempted, later, unsuccessfully, to deport Manx as an "undesirable alien," running a "hotel of low morals," but was defeated because she had valid immigration papers. Manx could always be counted upon to harass the Dutch officials she hated and despised. She, therefore, made a point of invariably wearing *pakaian* in public. Nevertheless, she was largely tolerated by those "narrow-minded" authorities, although she was barred from the grounds of the Bali Hotel.

Robert Koke, who learned photography and other skills while working for Metro Goldwyn Mayer in Hollywood, and his future wife, Louise Garrett, a talented artist, arrived on the island in 1937. Koke, a tennis pro and film editor, met Louise Garrett, painter and then wife of film maker Oliver Garrett in Hollywood. After Garrett returned from a trip to Hungary with a mistress, Louise obtained a divorce and left Los Angeles with Bob without bothering to marry. They disguised their relationship because they relied on Louise's alimony payments from Oliver Garrett as a major source of income. They did not marry until after their return to the United States.

11. Little Grass Shacks on the Beach of Bali

Koke was assistant director to King Vidor on the 1932 film *Bird of Paradise*, filmed in Hawaii. Here, Koke enthusiastically embraced American beach culture, learning to surf on massive eight-foot boards at Waikiki beach and developed a passion for riding the waves. He later also worked as a special effects expert on Irving Thalberg's film, *Mutiny on the Bounty*.

The visit to Bali was to be the "big adventure" on their round-the-world travels. Louise would paint and Bob would take photographs for two restful months before they went on to India and Europe. They reached Denpasar, staying at the Bali Hotel, which Bob described as "something out of Miami Beach." The manager greeted them with military heel clicking and offered them an accommodation which included a modern bathroom with running hot water. Inside the hotel, not an inch of Balinese decoration was to be seen. Instead of the strains of one of the Balinese gamelan orchestras, they heard static from the radio.

The following morning they investigated the streets of Denpasar, with its weather-beaten board shack housing, Chinese grocery shops and restaurants, curio and art shops, Bombay-style textile bazaars with silk and batik, and huge native market. The hubbub was terrific as excited shoppers passed each other laughing and arguing with the merchants. Louise and Bob were enthralled by the energy and humor of the place and by the good-natured banter of the women. Already they were beginning to like the Balinese, but Denpasar was not very different from many other outposts of the White Man's empires.

One day, when they were exploring the island on their hired bicycles, they pedaled through a coconut grove and came out on the most beautiful beach in the world, "clear surf lapping miles of white sand fringed with palms, and no trace of human habitation as far as the eye could see." After months of traveling through Japan and China, they were in a mood to stop. They had fallen in love with Bali and the beauty of the beach, and decided that Kuta Beach was the place for them. It was Kuta Beach's resemblance to Waikiki and its possibilities as world-famous surfing destination that directly inspired Bob's decision to attempt to build a hotel there similar to ones he had experience with in Hawaii. Bob knew only too well that Americans, heavily conditioned by fantasies of Pacific liberation, would happily "spend ten thousand dollars to live in a coconut grove." He wanted to recreate Waikiki and reap the profits of Kuta. The Kokes decided to build a hotel on Kuta Beach. Within three weeks they had leased part of that beach, and in four months they had built on it the Kuta Beach Hotel.

The Kokes met Manx in Denpasar shortly after arriving in Bali and agreed that she would guide them on some of their tours. Later, Manx helped the Kokes with the arrangements to lease the land on Kuta Beach and to get their hotel built. She was also, for a while, a tour guide for the hotel. In return for these services, a house was built for Manx across the road from the Kokes' bungalow. She continued to assist the Kokes as tour guide until a dispute erupted between them, causing the relationship to be severed and leading Manx to open her own bungalow as a hotel in direct competition with the Kokes. Both parties then wrote each other out of their accounts of their lives in Bali, and both sides ran their hotels in frosty competition, the situation being more absurd than acrimonious. With no separate signs, Manx's hotel was easily confused with the Kokes' hotel with which it shared a road. The KPM and Dutch officials were at first hostile to the would-be American hoteliers, but realized gradually that the Kuta Beach Hotel catered to a different kind of tourist and brought in trade that otherwise would not have come at all.

By the summer of 1938, the hotel had running water and a telephone, cars for hire, and a small golf course. The initial investment was two thousand dollars (each guesthouse, completely furnished, cost three hundred dollars). The hotel was not "a contrivance of concrete and plumbing." The Kokes built it native style—little guesthouses of bamboo and tatched roofs, bamboo furniture and batik curtains and couch covers. At the Kuta Beach Hotel, people could sleep in a bamboo hut soothed by the rattle of palm leaves and the soft swish of the Indian Ocean. Soon they were turning guests away.[4]

Their first guest was one Bill Dunbar, a young American touring the world. He insisted on staying with the Kokes, even though the only place in which they could put him was a couch on the crowded porch. He never returned from his visits to Denpasar without a block of ice in his dogcart. For months after he left, occasional travelers who had heard about the Kokes from Bill, would turn up asking for lodgings. They came in dogcarts, not in taxis, and always brought a block of ice. Ruth Masters Rickover described the Kuta Beach Hotel:

> We found ourselves presently in a small cottage, strangely reminiscent of shelters along the Appalachian Trail. Everything needed was there but no unnecessary frills. We used kerosene lamps because the hotel had no electricity. The washing facilities and WC were in a small building. To get there one wandered through a coconut grove with a beautiful beach on one side where the surf rumbled constantly. It was all most satisfying and exactly what one would like to find on a tropical island.

11. Little Grass Shacks on the Beach of Bali 141

Kuta Beach Hotel. Illustration by Louise Koke. From *Our Hotel in Bali* (Wellington, N.Z.: January Books, 1987).

The Kokes planned the hotel with the typical American longing for tropical romance in mind. The guests slept in individual small cottages nestled in a coconut grove. Each had a charming front porch overlooking the beach and a high-ceilinged bedroom. With windows and doors open—all of them screened, of course, for it was an American enterprise—it was wonderfully cool at night.[5]

Robert Koke founded surfing in Kuta. He said that one reason for his fascination with Kuta Beach was its waves, so much better than those at Waikiki. He and Louise incorporated the surfing motif into their letterhead, built boards in the long and heavy fashion of the time, and encouraged both visitors and their own Balinese workers to have a go. Because the Balinese at that time instinctively feared the sea, it was a measure of the Kokes' influence that they succeeded. Bob and Louise also encouraged their workers to display their cultural skills—even when serving dinner. Directly after the boys had served their guests, they ran toward a trio of *jegogs*—queer bamboo xylophones set in frames that were carved in the shape of serpents—and played a minor air, which sounded like a soft wind blowing through the palms, as the guests ate. Then they broke off to serve the next course and return to play another soft accompaniment to the meal. Frequently cooks, gardeners, and visiting drivers would join in as musicians. Following tradition, the customs obliged the boys serving the guests to go down on their knees. An American guest receiving for the first time a martini from a kneeling boy with bare torso and a red flower in his hair, was more than mildly surprised. But it was curious how soon they got used to it. The waste of time was appalling, and finally the boys abandoned it, mainly because it left them no time for music between courses. Another performance that delighted visitors began when the hotel staff decided that merely sounding a gong to announce that dinner was ready lacked imagination. A procession around the garden and along the beach would be better, with the leader carrying a lamp and followed by men waving flags, beating xylophones, drums, and cooking pots, or banging homemade lamp reflectors together as cymbals. On special occasions they would let off firecrackers. The Kokes varied an American menu with native-style dishes. They realized that "American coffee, roast suckling pig, and a tropical moon was a sure-fire combination."[6]

Frequently the hotel would bring in dance parties from nearby villages to entertain the guests. I Mario, the outstanding Balinese dancer of the 1930s, was an occasional performer. After dinner, from time to time, Robert Koke would invite his guests to come with him to search for a village festival. There was no need to organize this in advance. The sound of

11. *Little Grass Shacks on the Beach of Bali*

music would be heard for miles across the rice fields; it was just a matter of listening and going in the right direction. Another attraction was much closer. The land leased for the hotel included a small temple, and there were early plans to remove it. It was near the dining room, however, and women coming frequently to make offerings entranced tourists sitting nearby. "Needless to say," said Koke, "the temple was not moved."[7]

After Manx parted with the Kokes and built an exotic hotel of her own nearby, she also did her best to perpetuate the image of "Bali the Paradise." The cottage hotel she established was called Manx's Place and was described by Marian Fairchild, an artist and appraiser, who traveled with her husband, David Fairchild, as being "in a class by itself. With its little thatched houses, its brick patios, its little household temples and its old Gods. It is done as only an artist in love with Bali could do it. The servants are in gay sarong, bare above the waist, and include one small boy and two very little girls who wandered in, one at a time, and just stayed. They work or play as they like. Today they all waited on table, in the solemn way of children, and this afternoon the little girls were busy rearranging the temple offerings; one in purple sarong with orange belt, the other in yellow, and they moved about among the old gray stone statues like gorgeous butterflies."[8]

Both Manx's Place and the Kuta Beach Hotel were clearly of a type described by Bob Koke as a "Little Grass Shack on the Beach of Bali." The Dutch tourist agents snorted their disapproval and described the hotels as a collection of "dirty little huts," but that description seemed to do the hotel more good than harm. Koke's and Manx's hotels were an alternative to the stuffy Bali Hotel, and much to discomfort of KPM, Manx made it her practice to visit the Bali Hotel and lure away their clients with stories of her "paradise." Soon she was turning guests away. The Kuta Beach hotel's primary objective was to create a version of a Hollywood-derived fantasy of Pacific paradise to lure westerners. The two hotels were substantially similar in appearance and standard. The phenomenon of two mirror-image hotels located next to each other, operated by Americans who would not speak to each other, must have seemed bizarre to any guests who crossed the dividing road.

The Kuta Beach hotels attracted not only sex seeking but truly weird visitors who thought Bali was the place to freak out. The Balinese knew about it and had the feeling that the government approved. Tourists ranged from hard-boiled realists who wanted everything proved, to those whose hunger for sensation made them believe everything they were told. There were not many of the second kind—but enough to support racketeers all over the island.

By the summer of 1938, the Kuta Beach Hotel was always full, and many of its guests stayed for months. The Kokes had a steady stream of ranchers from Australia and South Africa, planters from Malaya, British diamond merchants from Bombay and Calcutta, and sometimes a German wool buyer and consul who were "looking around." By that time, some of the Dutch themselves had overcome their fear of an occasional native dish and were staying with the Kokes. In the Kuta Beach Hotel, "a middle-aged American couple with rather tight mouths frowned upon the brown nakedness around them and clearly did not approve of waiters wearing hibiscus blossoms behind the ear and women with no covering from the waist up. On the other hand, an elderly English lady with a kindly face reclaimed loudly and firmly that only the Balinese knew true art. She was a painter and intrigued everyone with her costume—evening clothes as befitted an English lady—even in regions where others might easily let down standards. Another old woman with purple-tinted hair and her face a mask of whitish makeup, with ropes of pearls around her wrinkled neck, and an air of insufferable boredom, amused herself by throwing money to the waiters and house boys, preening herself as Lady Bountiful."

By 1941, the Kuta Beach Hotel was popular and busy, a far cry from its casual beginnings, and Bob Koke and Louise Garrett were established in their career as self-taught hoteliers. People came for days and stayed for weeks. An American journalist described Louise as organizing dances, painting, and presiding graciously over "the most international crowds imaginable." It was too good to last.[9]

Manx was called "a lady of rather doubtful reputation, who liked to present herself as a painter." A friend of the Swiss artist Theo Meier once described her *as ein verdammt begates luder* (a damned cunning witch). Hans van Prag, a Dutch filmmaker, later gave a vivid picture of the Dutch opinion of Manx, describing her by far as the worst and most disliked figure. "She was a horrible woman. Short, ugly, manipulative and very cunning. For many Balinese and westerners alike her behaviour and her red hair made her a real witch. She was absolutely Revolting in Paradise."[10]

Manx was helped by Virgil Tenney, son of a Hawaiian missionary family that owned pineapple plantations in Hawaii. He stayed with the Kokes for a couple of days, drank too much, bought a Buick for two hundred ringgits and drove it like a wild man, and then moved in on Manx. He would go to the local small food stalls with lots of beer, and encourage his Balinese friends to drink with him. After complaints to the Dutch local official, Tenney left Bali and gave the Buick to Manx. He went to Singapore and there boarded a boat to Honolulu. Three days later he disappeared. His absence was discovered too late for the boat to go back and search for him.[11]

By 1939, Manx's hotel was seen as a refuge for aristocratic homosexuals such as author and historian Sir Anthony Weldon. Manx busied herself fighting the homosexual witch-hunt, but things looked grim for the Bohemians, with Manx's Place apparently managing just to survive. It was probably only because Manx was not homosexual and had the support of a number of aristocratic guests that she herself was not jailed or banished from Bali, given the establishment claims that Manx's Place was a brothel. The British consul general in Batavia expressed the views of the establishment when he wrote: "I fear that anyone returning to a place with Bali's present unenviable moral reputation cannot quite escape the moral risk inevitable for those who choose to live near a cesspool."[12]

12
The Last Garden of Eden

During the 1930s, Bali represented an escape for those who no longer felt at home in the Western world, which was threatened by depression and political turmoil. In the mid–1930s, Bali was absolutely "with it." Expensive travel agents sold trips to the little island, and about 30,000 tourists a year visited the island. They loved it, and that was understandable. Bali, with its beautiful, partly animistic Bali-Hindu culture, its lovely rice-fields, its modern comfort of asphalt roads, and its absence of colonial agribusiness was a delight. All the people who really mattered had been there.

Of the transients who lingered in Bali for a week or month or more, some saw and understood the essence of the place and went away with painful hearts, almost as if their eyes suddenly opened and an unimagined vision had come true for them. Some were frankly bored after one *ramé-ramé* (dance for entertainment only) and a day or two of breast hunting with their cameras, and one would see them roaming disconsolately around the streets of Denpasar, wondering how to kill time. They stayed at the luxurious hotel, and a dance would be staged for them in the evening on the lawn of the hotel. The troupe that the hotel generally engaged was an excellent one, but the Balinese music and dancing were obviously meaningless to most westerners the first time.[1]

Joseph Patrick McEvoy, American author and humorist who traveled all over the world and wrote humorous sketches on the foibles of the day, wrote:

> Once in Denpasar, you are in the heart of the tourist belt, or the seat of it, if you look carefully, there is always an opportunity, when your guards are not looking, to escape to the other hotel, which is half as expensive and twice as *gemütlich!* There are a great many lessons to be learned in Bali. One of the most significant is the growing importance of the tourist in the cosmic scheme. There was a time when things just happened and if the tourist came along on schedule, well and good; if not, well and better.

12. The Last Garden of Eden

> Yes, after only a few days in Bali, you realize that the time is coming when all the everything is arranged. You can have kris—sword dance, in which fifty natives try to stab themselves to death for the greater honor and glory of the tourist bureau. Or you can order up a virgin dance with any number of assorted virgins. You merely stop at the hotel desk on your way out and say, "By the way, how about a virgin dance over in the grove tonight?" and the manager salutes smartly and adds twelve guilders to your bill.
>
> Returned travelers are always asked, "Don't the tourist spoil Bali?" The answer is: "No. It's the other way around." In fact, it's a good thing the average tourist is allowed only three days in Bali. Longer that that, his usefulness as a tourist would be gone.[2]

Johan Fabricius was a prolific Dutch adventure novelist who was widely read in both Holland and the English-speaking countries. "We found an island of exquisite beauty," he wrote, "inhabited by a delightful, art-loving people that had known how to express, in stylized, deeply individual forms, its feelings concerning life and death. Art was immanent in everything, not only in the temples with their images and reliefs, their processions and offerings, not only in the *puris*, the princes' palaces, with their gamelan orchestras and *wayang* performances, but also in the rhythmically linked rice fields, the markets with their displays of flowers, even in the humblest of village houses, with its tastefully designed entrance and its elegantly woven fighting cock cages."

The theme that Fabricius chose to develop was that of the incompatibility of East and West as exemplified in Bali by the attempts made, and always in vain, by western artists to live on an equal footing with and among the Balinese, and thus to find a happiness which the over civilized world could no longer give them. The Dutch administrative authorities were not particularly successful in their efforts to put a stop to such over enthusiastic fraternization in which they saw little good, and they provided this tragedy of frustration with a note of comic relief. The district officer of Bangli told Fabricius with a sigh that he had known cases in which an American tourist, charmed by the primitive innocence of Balinese manners, had shown an inclination to adopt the mode of dress of the native women, not realizing that the people of the island would regard the baring of her bosom by a white woman as highly shocking.

> Those Bali tourists...! Here I have in mind not only the day trippers, who swarmed the island every time an Australian or American passenger liner on an East Indian cruise berthed at Buleleng—crowds of holiday-makers in sunglasses, infatuated with a reality surpassing

their wildest dreams, with shamelessly clicking cameras in the presence of which the Balinese girl covered her breasts in instinctive embarrassment. Besides these, Bali had its little international colony of so-called "permanents," visitors who thought they had rediscovered the Garden of Eden and who were well enough off to follow in comfort the example of the more happy-go-lucky painters and settle down for an indefinite period in the new-found paradise.[3]

Cedric Belfrage recorded that apart from Dutch administrators, there seemed to be only about a dozen white people living in Bali. "It was not every escapologist's cup of tea as a tropical island in which to settle. The taxes were high and one had to pay twenty pounds sterling deposit to be allowed to stay more than six months. Unless one was willing to live largely on island produce the cost of living, due to the rate of exchange of the guilder, was heavy as such places went. There was not enough white society for most European's tastes and what there was scattered over great distances. The sea was full of sharks. The natives were charming to look at, but apart from their own impossible language they did not speak a word of Malay. Even when you could speak to those who knew that language they were slow to make friends; the Dutch tax levies and jails and forced road labor did not tend to make them partial to Europeans. But such Europeans who had taken up residence in spite of these factors were firmly rooted in the island. They were agreeable, understanding people who had won the natives' friendship and had their welfare and the maintenance of their fascinating culture at heart."[4]

One of the enthusiasts, Betty Waterman, known as "Tante Betty," was the daughter of Lewis Edson Waterman, who was the inventor of the fountain pen. She held a kind of court on the island in Hollywood style, with a retinue of handsome Balinese youths whom she clad in sarongs with stiff gold thread and trained to drink cocktails; the strains of the gamelan could always be heard coming from her garden in the evening. Another young American woman could be seen drifting, lost in reverie, through the villages with a sarong draped about her hips, attracting lively attention everywhere in her travesty of decent native costume. Her shock of reddish-brown hair, standing out around her head like that of a golliwog, earned her the nickname of "Miss Rangda" among the amused Balinese.

Mr. D., an American millionaire, went to the holy village of Tirta Empul, and out of sheer bravado—"just for the fun of it"—took a dive into the lotus-covered Bath of the Gods; the horrified priests dashed to the scene and submitted a complaint about this sacrilege to the deputy commissioner, whereby Mr. D. generously offered to cover the cost of a banquet to propitiate the fury of the offended deities. The whole affair set him back about twenty dollars, a trifling sum to pay for the pleasure he was going to get out of dishing up the story to his circle of wealthy acquaintances back in New York. He and his friends tore along the peaceful lanes of Bali in their cars in the afternoons, running over dogs and chickens by the dozen in their hurry to hold a noisy get-together in the bar of Mr. D's yacht, at anchor off the coast.[5]

In his Bali novel, *No Return from Bali*, Fabricius amused himself with the crazy doings of the tourists and wealthy would-be artists, which fortunately, left no trace whatsoever on Balinese society—an enchanted world no outsider could penetrate, but which exercised an almost hypnotic power over him.

The expatriates lived a comfortable life in unbelievably cheap Bali. They had numerous servants, owned houses and cars; they commanded theater groups to play for them—the fee was a few dollars. Walter Spies had a small amphitheater in his compound built for a birthday party, and while champagne was flowing, he had two gamelan orchestras playing. The Bali Hotel was the center around which the life of southern Bali's westerners revolved. It was only natural that its directing manager, Jan Edelman, became a prominent figure in the expatriate scene. This was even more true of the omnipresent and indomitable Bram Schotel, the bank representative, who was liked by all who came in contact with him. Faced with a never ending series of problems and odd requests, Edelman and Schotel became the all-important arbitrators between officialdom and all forms of expatriate madness—true guardian angels who changed money, extended visas, and made bookings for boats and planes.

The only English woman who had made a home on Bali, according to Belfrage, was a Mrs. Lettimore. She was the daughter of a clergyman and the widow of a bishop. She lived inland, in the mountainous district. She had rigged up a sort of arena in her garden and the local villagers came sometimes and held *ramé-ramés* there, with Mrs. Lettimore sitting in state like a sort of genial white queen. She was a middle-aged woman of great strength of character who knew her own mind and went after what she wanted. She had been left with a small income. In Bali, she had a full and satisfying life. She knew all her Balinese neighbors, and could talk fluently with them; they had come to regard her as a wise and friendly oracle, and they streamed in and out of her house to ask her advice and help. She was so much in love with the island and its people that she went regularly to their temples to make offerings on the altars. Mrs. Lettimore was also the only European woman in Bali who shared the Balinese passion for the strange durian fruit, which had a pungent and repellent odor, but which those who could learn to care for it declared was the most delicious food in the world.

Belfrage also mentions an American woman, "whose heart overflowed toward Bali," who was distressed, when she visited the island, to see the many dogs running wild in the villages. They barked savagely at her when she went to watch the "simple natives" at play. On returning to America she had put up the money to found a traveling dog hospital and appointed a man to go around the island with it, giving free attention to any canine sufferer. The Balinese thought this an excellent joke.[6]

Theodora Benson, a novelist and travel writer, believed that the reason Bali remained good for tourism and tourism remained not too bad for Bali was chiefly because of the KPM. The finest and most famous Balinese musicians and dancers were engaged by the KPM to perform for the tourists. The proof that these programs were excellent was that they were also watched by a large audience of Balinese. The European and American expatriates who chose to live in Bali painted, wrote, composed, studied, encouraged Balinese art and sold it, ran an aquarium of beautiful fish, and took some medical care of the Balinese, but were far from being a happy family. Benson wrote:

> I was able to make almost everyone's acquaintance early on at the cremation at Tabanan. There almost all of the colony that I ever came to know were gathered together, or, rather, scattered about among the Balinese. A beautiful, cadaverous Polish artist who talked to me about being civilized and about *l'amour*; later he showed me his studio where he had just finished a picture, extremely nervous and fine, of two characteristic Balinese dancers. The German brothers Neuhaus later showed me their aquarium and their *objet d'art* shop. The Houbolts—a German one who ran the lovely antique shop and museum near Den Pasar, and a brand new American brother on a visit, both very amusing; the American couple at Sanur, full of charm and nonsense; they gave me a party. Miss Manx, English and unique; she gave me a party.[7]
>
> I can well see why white people who have no particular job there do choose to settle down and live in Bali. It is much cheaper to live in than Europe. It is beautiful and the climate is good. There are those enchanting performances, something happening at some village almost every night. It has tremendous charm. The people are attractive and friendly and gay. Here is an Eastern people with whom it is comparatively easy for white people to be friends: I do not speak now of toleration or liking or devotion but quite different side of human relationship, the power to communicate.
>
> Under these circumstances you do find that everyone understands the dear Balinese better than everyone else does. People have

12. The Last Garden of Eden

pet artists and pet villages, but they are not boring about it. On the contrary it is big advantage for the visitor when the Europeans who live there are kind and helpful enough to show off their pets. It is only as a settler that one might feel discouraged by the fear that one would never be able to catch up.[8]

Benson had been told, but could not judge the reliability of her sources of information, that no country girl of decent Balinese family will have a liaison with a European. But she had also been told that it was not the difficulty but the danger that should have held the European in check; as much as the Balinese showed no signs of venereal disease, they seemed in the course of time to have become almost immune, but white people very often found them infectious.[9]

Geoffrey Gorer wished to be a playwright but when none of the six plays he wrote was produced, he turned to writing books. Although he earned degrees in the classics and modern languages, he transformed himself into one of the few anthropologists who was never himself an academic. Indeed, in the field of scholarly British anthropology, he was in this way unique. Gorer had gone to Bali as part of his travel to Indo-China and the Dutch East Indies. "In the last ten years this island has been written about, filmed, photographed, and gushed over to an extent which would justify nausea. I went there half-unwillingly, for I had expected an uninteresting piece of ballyhoo picturesque and faked to a Hollywood standard. I left wholly unwillingly, convinced that I had seen the nearest approach to Utopia that I was ever to see."[10]

A reviewer in *The New York Times* found Gorer to be a "clever and impatient" man who traveled "with his head as well as with his legs." He did not pretend to great learning, though he was always ready to offer sweeping pronouncements on life and human nature. Highly intelligent and usually impartial, Gorer had a bias against sexual activity and romantic love, both of which baffled rather than merely puzzled him, and that sometimes obtruded.

Gorer reported that the journey from Surabaya to Bali was, for its distance, probably the most expensive in the world. The KPM had practically gotten the monopoly of the Bali tourist trade; they owned the two hotels in Denpasar, the rest houses, and most of the cars. They issued tickets at an inclusive price for hotel accommodations, cars, guides, and entrance fees to places where they were demanded. For travelers with only a certain time at their disposition, this was very convenient and not unreasonable in price, but people who were making a long stay could probably make much cheaper arrangements. Bali was so small that there was no object in stopping anywhere except Denpasar. Some people found this place too hot and went to stop at the rest house at Kintamani, six-thousand feet up, and surrounded with almost continual mist. It was as good a way as any other of getting pneumonia. The village of Kuta had a shark-free bay where there was excellent bathing. Gorer felt that it was quite impossible to indicate how long a stay was desirable in Bali. One could "do" Bali in two or three days, and one might begin to know something of its riches and its people in two or three months. "You either love or loathe the place," he wrote. Many people who were there at the same time as Gorer, spent all their time grumbling—nothing to do, nowhere to go, no golf, no music, bad food. Without a knowledge of and interest in non–European architecture and art and dancing, he supposed the place seemed dull. There was far more social life in the south of France, or in Singapore.[11]

> The physical beauty of the Balinese has to my mind been greatly exaggerated by people who have written about them. They are well-made and healthy looking; actual ugliness among them is uncommon, but so is outstanding beauty. I know of at least a dozen races in different parts of the world where in an ordinary crowd you will find more satisfying physical types. The reputation of the Balinese is, I believe, founded on two facts: firstly, they photograph extremely well, their brown and even skin, with the contrasting hair and well-marked features being pre-eminently photogenic; and secondly, both sexes habitually go naked except for a sarong.
> Female breasts are considered to be sexually stimulating; those of the Balinese, though often rather broad, are firm and round and well-shaped; if Josephine Baker could be induced to settle in the country you would have a non-stop *revue à grand spectacle*, with a personnel even larger than that of the Folies-Bergère under Lemarchant.
> The outstanding characteristic of the Balinese was their love of art in every form. The Balinese may be described as a nation of artists, professional if you take attitude to their work into account, amateur if you consider their secondary (most especially financial) objectives.
> With the advantages of soil and climate, the work of cultivation was not arduous. After the business of getting a living was done with, the Balinese had sufficient leisure to cultivate whatever arts they favor, either as practitioners or audience. Lest any of my readers should thereby condemn them as "arties," I hasten to add that they kill animals for pleasure and are therefore worthy of all respect as sportsmen.[12]

Vicki Baum was a German-Jewish author who settled in California. The photographs of Bali that she received during the years of World War I made such an impression on her that she coaxed her friend into giving

12. The Last Garden of Eden

them to her. "To these men and animals and landscapes, I turned again and again, whenever the discomforts to which my generation was exposed—war, revolution, inflation, emigration—became unbearable. A strange relationship grew up between these photographs and me: as though I had known those people; as though I had often walked along those village streets and gone in at those temple gates."

In was not until 1935 that Baum could afford to make the voyage to Bali, traveling with her stepbrother Fritz Lindner. Her first visit was the realization of her lifelong wish without a hint of disillusionment. Returning to America full of "sickness of Bali," she was back in Bali a year later for a second and longer visit, which resulted in her book *A Tale from Bali*, a historical novel concerned with the *puputan*. The privilege of seeing the real and unspoiled Bali was due to a letter of introduction to Walter Spies. He took Vicki to remote villages and allowed her to see the real life of the Balinese. Baum based her noel on information received from Walter Spies, although she pretended that she was left notes by "Dr. Fabius," a fictional Bali hand.

Baum's novel about the fall of Badung, first published in 1937 and translated into English as *A Tale from Bali* (the German title was more the more romantic *Love and Death in Bali*), remains the best-known version of the story among Euro-Americans. Baum told the story as it was generally told in the 1930s, in which the demise of the Balinese rulers and the establishment of the colonial administration were peripheral to the lives of the Balinese peasants. Like most other tourists and expatriates, Baum believed that the Dutch had carried out an achievement in colonization that reflected the highest credit on them. "Scarcely anywhere in the world," she wrote, "are natives free to live their own lives under white rule so happily and with so little interference and change as in Bali. The *puputans* impressed upon the Dutch the need of ruling this proud and gentle island people as considerately as they have, and so kept Bali the paradise is it even today."

William Robert Foran, English author and journalist, was a correspondent for various English newspapers, first in the United States, and later in Burma and Singapore. Intending to stay only a few days in Bali, he found so much to fascinate and interest him that he remained on the island for several weeks. There he lived in a modern "Garden of Eden," and decided that he saw things which the average tourist never even knew existed, because those who flocked to the island under the auspices of travel agencies or world cruises were given neither the time nor the opportunity to gain more than a superficial knowledge of the island, its customs, and its delightful inhabitants. Bali fully deserved a longer period of attention, he concluded.

Foran was first attracted to Bali by seeing a small illustrated booklet, *Come to Bali*, in Singapore. He lived to bless the fortunate chance which placed this all-too-modest brochure in his hands. There could be no resisting the appeal it made. Bali was described therein as the "gem of the Dutch East Indies" and "the land for dreams and romance." Both were honest claims, in his opinion. The frontispiece depicted a Balinese girl posing within a most artistic temple. So great was her charm and beauty, so perfect her natural grace and intriguing her *tout ensemble*, that he made up his mind, then and there, to include Bali in his travels. "The reward cannot be measured in mere words. Suffice it is to say, I entertain no particle of regret for having been lured there by this picture of a lovely Balinese belle. I stand confessed. The real bait to Bali was the damsel seen posed in a Hindu temple; and I owe to her picture a delightful memory which the passage of years cannot dim. I went to Bali; saw it; and was enraptured. I have never visited a more picturesque or delightful place. Bali is the superlative *it*."[13]

"There can be no gainsaying that Bali is an artistic wonderland," concluded Foran. "I commend it with the utmost confidence to the most jaded and travel-satisfied spirits, for it cannot fail to fascinate even the most blasé." Foran was one of the travelers who wrote a paean to Bali in verse. As he stood on the deck of the steamer and watched Bali fade, his heart was sad within him:

> The sky is overcast, the rain
> Comes driving up across the plain;
> But yonder on the Bali heights
> There hangs a haze of golden lights.
> Ah! Gleams of gold among the hills,
> I pray that, in the midst of ills
> When life seems desolate and gray,
> I still may see you far away.[14]

Robert Hamilton Bruce Lockhart had been a rubber planter in Malaya for three years in his early twenties until acute malaria brought him home. He then served in the British diplomatic service, and was later editor of *The London Evening Standard*. Lockhart set off on his trip to the Far East on his *recherche du temps perdu*. He found the Bali Hotel to be "a modern building stamped with the hallmark of Dutch cleanliness and Dutch efficiency," but the heat was stifling, for Denpasar was one of the hottest spots not only in Bali, but in the whole archipelago. The modern electric fan provided in his room did not function. The Dutch zeal for economy during difficult times had decreed that the electricity, and therefore the fans, should not operate between the hours of 6 A.M. and 6 P.M.!

12. The Last Garden of Eden

Sitting on the grass terrace separated from the main street only by a low hedge, he had not been there for more than a few moments when he heard a rustle. Looking down he found a Balinese boy kneeling by his chair and offering postcards. Lockhart shook his head. The boy was followed by another and yet another. Finally one came who knew some English: "Like visit pretty Balinese dancer, sir? Very nice—I show you." Lockhart was not even impressed by the Balinese maidens. "I saw several Balinese women with naked breasts, but they looked modest beside an English girl in an almost transparent dress with no back to it."

After dinner, a six-course affair with hot and heavy European foods, he made friends with the Dutch representative of the American Express Company and with Jacob Minas, owner of the island's traveling cinema. Both spoke fluent English. Both were amusing cynics with very definite views on the "cussedness" of the Balinese and on the real nature of the attractions which brought the tourists, or at any rate, the male tourists, to Bali. They had a grudging admiration for the KPM which had acquired almost a monopoly of the tourist traffic. "The KPM were smart. They had made a good business of it. There was not much left for the others."

The dances especially arranged for the tourists were long, and before the end Lockhart found himself yawning. And without a genuine expert to explain things he believed that most Europeans would find it hard to sit through a whole evening's performances, especially in the artificial surroundings of a European hotel.[15]

> During my visit the temple was already being prepared for the feast, and at intervals women climbed the steps and deposited their offerings of fruit and flowers. Several of them brought a kind of fruit which, after it has been blessed, is supposed to have special powers of fecundity. While were talking to the priest, a car drove up. A middle-aged Englishman and a young English girl got out. I could not tell whether they were father and daughter or husband and wife. They were attended by a Chinese guide. The girl was carrying some yellow fruit in her hat. She explained to the guide she wanted it blessed for fecundity. There was an awkward pause. The guide whispered something which the girl did not understand. She walked forward towards the priest. This time the Chinese guide raised his voice: "No, No, missie, these are the wrong fruits. This kind make you pass water six or seven times."[16]

Hugo Bernatzik, Austrian ethnologist and explorer, visited Bali on his way home from a field trip to the Solomon Islands and New Guinea. He wanted to stop in Bali, the "last paradise of the Dutch East Indies before

Europe and all its cares swallowed me up again." He planned to stay eight days, but his stay was extended into many delightful weeks. Bernatzik made his way into the hilly interior of the island on small tough mountain horses, along border paths on foot, over crater lakes in canoes, through dense jungle, past ruined temples and smoking volcanoes. "There, far from the tourists' traffic, I got to know a new world, whose magic completely captivated me."

"What I enjoyed most of all on this glorious island," he wrote, "was the quiet days in the old Bali villages of the mountains. They lay on the shores of the clear Batur Lake, in the shadow of the great cone of Bali's most feared volcano. I was almost in pain to tear myself away, not to let my soul sink in the sweet poison of a blissful and never before known Nirvana, where wishes die. It was a long time after leaving the island before I recovered my balance and became again the sober, thinking man which Europe trains me to be."

"In every situation of life there is a climax, which cannot be passed and after which a decline must inevitably follow. On this expedition I had survived much that was difficult and even dangerous. Now I had been granted the best that can be given to man in life, as in death: to stop at the climax."[17]

Martin Birnbaum, an elegant, persuasive, and knowledgeable art dealer, friend of artists, confidant of the rich and the celebrated, and a friend of American artist Maurice Sterne, wrote:

> Washed by a calm sea, on the surface of which flying fish started silver ripples, Bali's rich green, mountainous shores made an immediate and glamorous appeal, but the waterfront of the town of Boeleleng was painfully ugly. As we approached the wharf in a motorboat, superbly built bathers and fishermen smiled a pleasant welcome, and I discovered a group of half-naked men playing games of chance on the smooth, black volcanic sand, ruled in squares to serve as a gaming board. Dirty-looking, betel-chewing women walked up and down, carrying their possessions on their heads in old oil cans. K.P.M. agents, insistent guides, ubiquitous Chinamen, curio dealers, and greedy chauffeurs surrounded me.
>
> My heart sank, and my spirit of romantic expectancy faded. Disappointed but resigned, I placed myself in the care of a native driver, intending to cross the island at once to Den Pasar on the southerly coast, and mentally decided to return quickly and catch the first available steamer for Java. I had obviously come too late to the isle of dreams which my friend, Maurice Sterne, the American painter, had visited and described to me over twenty years ago, but at least I would see a volcano or two before I sailed away with another dream shattered.

12. The Last Garden of Eden

We sped through Den Pasar's main business street, with its mean buildings, cheap curio dealers, Chinese and Japanese photographers, postcard vendors, and unattractive shops offering the worst European rubbish, and again I asked myself, "Why do I not make more careful inquiries and check my exultant fancy whenever I hear of some remote tropical region?" Suddenly, we turned a corner, to gain the road leading to the temple gate—and I was transported into an incredible world! I had discovered that Sterne's Bali was still in existence, and that there was to be no rest for me on this excited island.

"Excited and mystified," concluded Birnbaum, "I left Bali before the spell was in danger of being broken. Already an erstwhile princess who refused to sacrifice herself on her husband's funeral pyre was persistently trying to sell me cheap tourists' trinkets. Other importunate rascally natives were asking fees for showing salacious reliefs on the walls of a temple. Is it possible that all the beauty I had enjoyed would become a mere legend and a memory? The more I scratched the surface of Balinese life, the more clearly I realized that my allotted time would prove all too short. So I left for Java while the unforgettable island still exercised its powerful fascination. Although a mist enveloped the coast, volcanoes showed their cones above the clouds, and a sunset lighted the clearing sky with an orange flare, only to disappear again as if by magic, leaving me in a twilight which filled the world with sadness. Then night became a fathomless flood of blue, sprinkled with golden stars, and Bali melted in darkness."[18]

Cedric Belfrage, British journalist and self-proclaimed "independent radical" and "escapologist," visited Bali as part of a round-the-world trip.

I had read so much high-powered cockadoodle about Bali that I feared lest my imaginative powers should prove too feeble to make me conscious of its famous fascination. The reality was an agreeable surprise. True, shiploads of Americans and others did arrive from time to time, and on those occasions fleets of perhaps a hundred cars screamed round the island and the air was loud with the snap of kodaks. I had premonitory visions of islanders completely depraved by the commercialization of their culture and chest development, going about in western clothes and hastily undressing and staging a dance at the first sound of an approaching klaxon.

But Bali, a mere speck on the map, was a much larger island than I had imagined. The cruise loads of tourists, from whom as a more leisured traveler one proudly dissociated oneself, rarely stayed more than a day or two. Along their set sightseeing route the natives had become lazy and learned to beg, and many of the girls, tired of having their breasts stared at and photographed, had taken to wearing the ugly *baju* jackets. But the great majority of Balinese came in contact but rarely with tourists, and their lives, being centered almost wholly round the religion with which invaders might not tamper, continued much as they had always done.[19]

Two young Austrian brothers, Hans and Rolf Neuhaus, expert herpetologists who left Austria to travel the world, established on the beach of Sanur a little aquarium of beautiful specimens of tropical fish that they collected, which could be viewed for a fee of fifty cents. They made arrangements with the KPM for groups of tourists to visit the aquarium. When they noticed their visitors' liking for wood carvings and paintings, they started selling these articles in the aquarium, and then opened the first souvenir shop on the beach, Toko Neuhaus. Their prices for the standard tourist souvenir of a carved dancer's head drastically undercut any of their competitors in Denpasar. Their mother created remarkable dolls and assisted her sons in making perfect replicas of reptiles and fish in various media.[20]

The Neuhaus brothers placed the aquarium right across the road from Katharane Mershon's house, so that the tourists and the Balinese vendors who came there turned the place from a private residence, into a regular marketplace. It infuriated Katharane because she felt that there had not been any reason for the Austrians to do this whatsoever, except that they wanted to make money. Katharane later remembered a limerick that was written about that time:

> If you took an X Ray of the Mershons today
> After feeding them a bit of barium,
> You'd find a dull gleam
> At the base of the spleen,
> For their house is too near the aquarium.[21]

Joe B. Kirkwood, American golfer born in Australia, who became one of the best-known trick shot artists in golf, journeyed to Bali to pay a visit to the painter Adrien Le Mayeur. "There's no doubt that I was badly bitten by the Bali 'fever,' for it was here that I decided I had found the paradise that we all long for, but somehow find illusive in the busy commercial world," he recalled. Agreeing to give a show for the Balinese, he arranged to do the performance out on the field which he christened The Ti-Ti Golf Club. He simply sank some tin cans in the ground, fashioned some flags, and cleared several flat spots for tees.[22]

Ruth Masters Rickover, was a student of international law who traveled to Bali with her husband, naval officer Hyman Rickover, who was stationed at the Cavite Navy Yard in the Philippines. Ruth wrote that the

12. The Last Garden of Eden

Dutch were highly resentful when foreigners disregarded their efficient tourist services. The Dutch tourist manager almost lost his good manners when the Rickovers mentioned casually that they did not plan to use the KPM services but intended to set out on their own. Although the representative of the KPM almost succeeded in bundling them into one of KPM cars by sheer willpower, they managed to escape him. "Our worst crime was that we spurned the KPM hotel in Den Pasar," she wrote. She complained about the autocratic behavior of the KPM which used its monopoly to charge exorbitant prices. One of their least endearing capers was to refuse to sell anything but first-class tickets to white persons, allegedly to uphold Dutch prestige but also to increase KPM profits. The Rickovers were very proud of the fact that they never once used the KPM services. "I think the main reason our visit to Bali was successful," she recorded, "was the fact that I knew enough Malay so that we could be independent." Armed with a map, they needed no one's help to get anywhere they pleased.[23]

One of the American travelers who flew to Bali was Frances Norene Ahl, an experienced air traveler who flew a Royal Netherlands Indies Airways (KNILM) Lockheed Electra to the airport at Bukit. "The stationery of the Bali Hotel bore the printed inscription, 'Why don't *you* come and see Bali? It's so unusual and charming!'" Ahl wrote for information, but then decided that Bali was not nearly as enchanting as beautiful Pago Pago.

Every Friday a boat arrived from Surabaya with a new crop of tourists. They were rushed to the hotel in KPM cars. After dinner, as guests of the management, they attended a Balinese musical program and dance in front of the hotel. The following morning the tourists were whisked across the island to Bulelang where they embarked for their next port of call. No doubt they were satisfied that they had seen the paradise of the Netherlands Indies. They were not on the island long enough to realize that tourist travel there was a racket.

Until she had experienced Denpasar for herself, Ahl could not fully appreciate or understand what a British engineer meant when he told her that six days would be altogether too many for her in Bali. And when one of her fellow countrymen exclaimed that he was fed up on travel in the tropics, on poor food and poor hotels, she concluded that he was suffering from dyspepsia, for all that she had ever known had been lavished in poetic splendor on this far away magic isle. But when she inspected her dark, unattractive room, crowded into a corner in such a way that the burning heat of the tropical sun never had a chance to penetrate its musty moldy atmosphere, when cockroaches scuttled in the bathroom before she even had a chance to take one shower, and when she tried in vain to sleep without springs on the thin mattress resting on uneven boards that insisted on sagging in the center, she was loaded with dire uncertainty as to whether this was the famed Eden for the traveler. And the minimum daily rate in that hotel was approximately seven dollars in United States currency.

The Kuta Beach Hotel, however, beautifully located in a grove of palm trees, was a delightfully quiet and restful place. One lounged on the veranda and watched the spray of the breakers as they pounded against the shore. The genial California manager knew how to cater to his guests. As a result, his place so rapidly became a popular rendezvous for American tourists that it was necessary to make reservations well in advance.[24]

Ahl soon discovered that the real beauty of Bali was its handsome, picturesque people, its strangely exotic temples and intense religious fervor, its colorful arts and music, and its luxuriating verdant countryside. Nowhere in the world were the great amphitheaters of rice fields more beautiful than in Bali where the terraces, verdigris green, rose towards the sky.

The commercial spirit of the Western world was fast penetrating the tiny island. That the Balinese were still somewhat inexperienced in modern business methods was evidenced by the fact that they seldom charged more than five or ten cents admission to the various sights, and almost invariably they waited until the tourist was leaving the temple or palace before they came running with a ticket of admission.

Ahl browsed about the dingy shops of Denpasar. Chinese and Japanese photographers on every block displayed numerous pictures of the famous sights of Bali. Curio stores were selling jewelry fashioned from native silver, exquisitely carved pieces of wood, side by side with the hideous and weird souvenirs that always lured the gullible travelers. Beyond the main on the left she reached the native market where block after block was lined with Indian merchants from Bombay and Calcutta selling batik. It was not really batik at all but the inexpensive cotton sarong in flashing colors and gay designs. For as little as seventy-five guilder cents, men and women alike could purchase two and one-half yards of the gaudy material and wrap it tightly around their waists in skirt-like fashion.[25]

Geoffrey Gorer inspired Margaret Mead and Gregory Bateson with an interest in Bali. Jane Belo also spoke of Bali with enthusiasm and piqued Margaret's curiosity. They had seen just enough material in films and still photographs, had heard just enough of the music studied by Colin McPhee, and had read just enough in Jane Belo's careful records. "We had chosen Bali," wrote Mead, "with the knowledge and forethought as the culture we wanted to study next in order to obtain material on one temperamental emphasis we had only hypothesized must exist."[26] Margaret Mead remembered:

12. The Last Garden of Eden

Bali was beautiful with its carefully terraced and planted hills and its roads that were always crowded with people carrying on their heads or shoulders loads under which they trotted lightly and tirelessly. Villages were compactly built and were close together. Bali teemed with expressive ritual. We were never out of the sound of music, if it was only the tinkle of the bells that women fastened to their knives or the flute played by some lonely peasant watching over his crops in a far field. As one drove along the well-kept roads—for the Dutch administrators believed in good roads—one passed from a feast in one temple to a feast in another and met people dressed in glowing colors and carrying offerings, or a whole orchestra on its way to a performance in another village, or dancers in trance, or a bride borne in a palanquin.

The Europeans they met were, many of them, artists and dancers and musicians—people who had come to Bali for months, sometimes for years, to paint or write or simply to delight in the painting and dancing of the Balinese. The food, cooked in the traditional fashion that had been modified over several centuries by Dutch taste, was delicious. It consisted of rice and garnish, accompanied by spicy, pungent condiments, each meal different, and each diminutive chicken or duck cut up and prepared in three or four different ways. Margaret Mead never lost any weight at all in Bali.[27]

Jane Belo had provided Bateson and Mead with introductions to the Bohemian community in Bali. The men appeared to be mainly homosexual, delighting in the Balinese youths, which were attractive and compliant; Mead wrote about the "inverts": "almost everyone in Bali is one, or, if female, is married to one." Walter Spies quickly became their friend, and gave them their first sense of the Balinese scene. Instructed by Jane Belo, he had organized a house, complete with a domestic staff, for Mead and Bateson until they could survey the territory and find a village to suit their purposes. The other artists at first eyed the anthropologists warily. The Batesons were scientists, and scientists were presumed to have an offensively cold, analytic approach. In turn, Mead thought of the artists as "prima donnas" and "Medicis" who might prove to be obnoxious. Europeans transplanted to the tropics, for whatever reason, tended to be difficult and gossipy. But in Bali, the gossip was "all in artistic terms," which made a refreshing change. Bateson and Mead's research methods brought them into some conflict with their artists hosts. Beryl de Zoete, who had an acid tongue and a gift for destructive criticism, effectively satirized this conflict between science and art, and Mead identified Beryl with the witch, a prevailing Balinese figure.[28]

The contrasts in Bali immediately fascinated Margaret. She and Bateson arrived in Bali to extol the island, but got things very wrong in their studies of Balinese children. Their basic assumptions were inherently flawed, and their study presented an inaccurate and misleading characterization of the Balinese. The Balinese resented Margaret Mead. They realized that her information about Bali was very inaccurate. The Balinese saw that what she was doing was a very superficial probe. They were very perceptive and saw through her very quickly. They were not about to be taken by something like that. Margaret would have long lists of questions that she would give to her secretary to ask the Balinese, for example: "Which gives you the most pleasure, defecation or fornication?" When the Balinese got hold of questions like that, Katharane's son, Murda, said to her: "Oh, mother, but we are going to have fun with this!" So they took the questions to the village and they asked the people in the village, and, "Oh, mother, did the people in the village have fun with that!" The Balinese had a tremendous sense of humor, and this struck them as being just one to howl over. Mead and Bateson's research methods were satirized in a series of photographs entitled "Anthropology in Bali," photographed by Walter Spies, but staged by the Balinese. The photographs featured a clock, an assistant with a notebook, a tripod, a carving and a tape measure. In one picture, a china lavatory bowl was present, poking fun at studies of potty training and mocking the austere conditions that the anthropologists imposed on themselves.[29]

After two months, Mead and Bateson left their fellow westerners and settled in the remote mountain village of Bayung Gede, near Kintamani in the district of Bangli. Mead's account of Bayung Gede demonstrated her close attention to detail. She also demonstrated the strongly opinionated approach that was chosen because the village was seen as isolated, radically different from the lowland villages where she and Bateson had worked, and therefore, a truer guide to the "Balinese character" they wished to map out. It "represented the lowest and dourest stratum" of the island's culture. They paid two dollars a month for the house, from which they deducted the cost of anything stolen from the house or any money begged from them. They paid separately for rituals, which they ordered like meals. Margaret put her medical kit to good effect, although with surprising equanimity she avoided interfering with native medicine when she wished to study its customary aspects.

Life in Bayung Gede was hard, dirty, and relatively unhealthy. There were no electric lights, no toilets, and no running water; the streets were dusty and mud was everywhere in the rainy season. Travel was very laborious. Bateson and Mead braved a physically taxing environment, especially

12. The Last Garden of Eden

"Anthropology in Bali." Margaret Mead and Gregory Bateson's research methods satirized by the Balinese. Courtesy of The Horniman Museum and Gardens, London.

for foreigners, and withstood the physically and emotionally draining effects of a bout of malaria contracted in New Guinea. They treated these hardships not at all or only casually in their writings. Even their critics were impressed with their pioneering spirit. Made Kaler, their Balinese assistant and secretary during the two years of study, spoke later with lasting amazement and admiration about their energy and their long hours of daily work on observation and data.

Kaler also stated that the villagers of Bayung Gede were afraid of Mead because to them she looked somewhat like Rangda, the evil witch with which they were so familiar. This was because of her light skin, light hair, eyes, and strange appearance (to them). The villagers regarded Bateson and Mead as Europeans, like the Dutch, of whom they were generally afraid and whom they believed to be persons of ultimate power and superiority. Mead attempted to make the villagers accept her as far as possible, and the villagers obviously liked her but she remained a curiosity.

"Only those who have worked in societies where money has not power to persuade people who do not, at the moment, feel like doing something," wrote Margaret, "can realize what a paradise Bali was for us. Ceremonies every day—if not in this village, then in another only a short distance away. Informants, scribes, secretaries were ready to be trained for the asking. Household help, too, and when we came home at midnight, dinner would be waiting, hot and delicious, when we were ready."[30]

In Bali there was no such thing as a quiet moment alone. Bali was in no way a quiet place. "A hundred dogs yapped at their ankles and vituperated from every doorway, with the nerve-racking impersonal hatred which is characteristic of the thin, badly fed, unloved and untalked-to Balinese dogs."[31]

Bateson and Mead photographed manifestations of village organization, rites of passage, calendrical ceremonies, the gestures in dance, daily life, cockfighting, wood carving, painting, death and marriage rituals, but most of all, they focused on parent-child and sibling interaction. Bateson did the photography and cinematography. He planned to take two thousand photographs; he took twenty-five thousand, as well as twenty-two thousand feet of 16 mm film.

Bateson was disappointed. "The Bali show was a great success—as far as anthropology was concerned, but they left us and we left them without either side very much attached. It's like trying to make friends with beautiful gazelles. They are beautiful and move beautifully. And they are gay in a light gentle way. But human personal contact with them ends there, and their contact with each other ends there. And the landscape rather in the same way. I think it is physically the most lovely place I have been in—but, somewhat, what of it?" If the beauty of the island pleased Bateson, the people evidently did not. He found the Balinese formally uncomfortable and too reminiscent of England. "The most striking thing about these people," he felt after two months among them, "is their nervousness—always expecting that something is going to bite them when they are in any sort of uncultured situation (i.e. in their contact with us). This leads to the appearance of impenetrable dullness."[32]

When Margaret Mead and Gregory Bateson left Bali after two years, they were completely exhausted, and Margaret had been suffering spells of toothaches, malaria, and stomach complaints.

13
Belated Gauguins

> *It was a paradise above all for painters. Several Dutch painters who had come there for inspiration had found it in inexhaustible profusion and were unable to tear themselves away. The standard of work done by the white artists was on the whole elementary compared with that of the Balinese themselves, but the artists had good life and were happy.*
>
> Cedric Belfrage[1]

Bali's expatriate community boasted a lively and dynamic art scene, filled with many painters who, like belated Gauguins, had gone there in search of their own island of paradise, and had sometimes even found it. The 1930s were a good period for the development of the rich potential of Dutch East Indies painters, who produced art works of admirable quality. The term "Dutch East Indies artist" was used to specify foreign artists who worked in Bali during this period. They originated from Austria, Belgium, Switzerland, France, Poland, Mexico, the United States, and other countries, besides Holland. This group was cynically defined later under the term *Mooi Indie* (Beautiful Indies). They painted honestly, by observation, feeling, or with their hearts, but unlike Walter Spies and Rudolf Bonnet, they had no influence on Balinese art.

When Harold Acton visited Bali in 1932, "the few foreigners conspicuous in Bali were arty folk in Basque berets and sandals, mouthing sentences in Malay as if they were singing '*Vissi d'arte*,' and picking up bits of batik for their studios. They had drifted here from Greenwich Village or Montparnasse. But all islands attract the same tribe of self-conscious international 'arties,' who invariably assume proprietary and patronizing airs. They were sufficiently sparse in Bali not to spoil, but one could foresee that their colony would increase, with detriment to the pastoral innocence of the native population, and that the tourists would breed the usual type of shark."[2]

While there was much interaction between the artists, rivalry, intrigue, and jealously was rife among the painters of paradise when staking their exclusive claims to their muse. Many artists who were passing through set foot in Bali out of curiosity and ended up staying far longer than they had intended. The island had a cultural atmosphere that was quite unique because its resident artists had settled there, purely and simply, to work.[3]

By the 1930s, the image of Bali as the new South Seas paradise on earth for an eager Western public was created, to a large part, by the artists. In Bali, Western artists discovered the exotic world of their dreams, but to keep reality within the limits they had fixed to it, they had to overlook things or to observe them with squinted eyes. They painted on the spot or made sketches they worked up into larger pieces in their studio's peace and quiet. Their works may have been dream-like, realistic, or symbolical, but they rarely emanated this culture's true spirit. To some of them, Bali represented the dream come true so totally that the artists tried to penetrate its peoples' very soul.

That was certainly true for the Belgian painter Adrien Jean Le Mayeur de Merpes. An eccentric member of the Belgian royal family, Le Mayeur rejected his heritage and sought to follow in the footsteps of Gauguin by sailing to French Polynesia to become a painter in Tahiti.

He lived on the shore in a little thatched house, which he had built along with all its furnishings. He had a large windowless studio open to the sea, and a bedroom, kitchen quarters built separately behind, and a stable with a pony and cart in it. When one went to his house there were never less than two or three lovely Balinese female models about the place. As well as modeling, the girls cooked, waited on the table, and tended the little shrines they had placed in the front garden. To lunch there was a pleasure; there was no "if she could only cook" about these stately golden-brown divinities, whom to watch moving in and out and around the table was a delight in itself; the native-style rice and curry dishes, the liquors distilled from rice and coco-palms, and the mangosteens and other fruits they brought to the table were delicious. Le Mayeur planted a mass of bougainvillea and hibiscus, and all around the cottage he put groups of intertwining plants. He built little temples, completely made of white coral, and dug little ponds in which the reflections of all the gods of Hindu mythology could be seen among the sacred lotus flowers. The two temples were surrounded by approximately two hundred of these little sculptures, which had integrated with the flowers and whose silhouettes were drawn on the purple and pink tropic skies. His energetic efforts to render his surroundings as beautiful as possible were conducive to inspiration. "I've evidently made all things serviceable to my art," he wrote. "All my actions have but one purpose: facilitating my work. And my urge to set to and render expression to all those things enchanting me never left me for even a single instant during all those years."[4]

Le Mayeur stopped in Bali late in 1929 on his way from Tahiti to India, but went back to Bali three years later. He settled in Kelandis, a little village near Denpasar. He asked two legong dancers to be his models, paying them one rupiah a day, always a month in advance. After four months in Kelandis, he moved to a rented cottage at Sanur.

In a post-war interview he stated: "I am an impressionist. There are three things in life that I love. Beauty, sunlight, and silence. Now could you tell me where to find these in a more perfect state than in Bali?" In 1935, he married Ni Pollok, one of his models. "I noticed she was crying a lot and I couldn't bear it. Then it turned out she had made a vow of marriage but in the end she couldn't face the idea. So I set that right financially and married her myself."

After their marriage, they built their own cottage on Sanur Beach, far away from other people, especially Europeans. He employed five house servants for Pollok: a coachman, a gardener, two kitchen maids, and a chambermaid. "Of course I'd pick them myself and they were very beautiful girls in the first place. I didn't want them to be primarily servants. I wanted to have friends around us who took pleasure in their jobs. I forbade them to work in the later afternoon, during those hours I wanted them to sit around in their beautiful sarongs, weaving fine fabrics." And when one saw those beautiful girls, dressed in their finest silk sarongs, with flowers in their hair, and carrying themselves like princesses it was difficult to imagine that they were actually a cook and a chamber girl. In those colorful surroundings full of palms, hibiscus and bougainvillea, Le Mayeur clearly felt immensely happy. Every day he was swimming and riding his little horse Gypsy through the waves.[5]

Belfrage described Le Mayeur as "a real Gauguin character," except that he seemed to have found the peace that Gauguin sought in vain in the South Seas. He wore only the native *kain* and his body was very brown. The sharks did not bother him at all and he went swimming, keeping fairly close inshore, whenever he felt hot. He had found the kind of escape he wanted.[6]

Le Mayeur was not only a talented painter but also a clever businessman who aptly used his connections, his wife's talents, and the myth of Bali to further his sales. In 1939, his financial successes in Singapore evoked the admiration and envy of every artist on the island. While the lovely Ni Pollok danced and created a sensation, Le Mayeur adroitly sold his colorful canvasses, in which she was prominently featured, for large sums. Le Mayeur's impressionist, colorful, easily accessible style attracted many tourists to Sanur Beach. An excursion to Le Mayeur's house was even included in a tour offered by the KPM to its patrons at the Bali Hotel. Guests would be treated to a copious dinner and a dance performance by Ni Pollok, and were "entitled" to purchase the artist's works. Numerous other tourists, just off the round-the-world cruise boats, would visit Le Mayeur to be served drinks and snacks by his gracious topless wife and her pretty servants.

The Dutch senior official in Denpasar, "a small fish magnified by a small puddle," did not like foreigners, even his own countrymen. He visited Le Mayeur one day to check his permit to live in the Dutch East Indies, and found the artist in his front yard, dressed in a sarong with no shirt, painting a Balinese girl who, like him, wore a sarong with no top. The official examined the permit and left. A few days later he notified Le Mayeur that he objected to a European wearing native dress—and also to a European painting what he termed "nude women." Le Mayeur promptly cabled his cousin, the king of the Belgians, who cabled his friend, the queen of Holland, who cabled the governor general of the Dutch East Indies, who cabled the Resident of Bali and Lombok, who instructed the senior official in Denpasar to be nice to Le Mayeur.[7]

Willem and Maria Hofker came to the Dutch East Indies to deliver a portrait of Queen Wilhelmina that Willem was commissioned by the Amsterdam director of KPM to paint for the KPM headquarters in Batavia. After the delivery they were allowed to travel freely on KPM ships throughout the Indies in order to enable Willem to create fifty drawings or paintings on any Indonesian subject of his choice. These were then reproduced in a small portfolio and distributed in KPM ships throughout the world to promote the growing tourist trade in Java and Bali, in which the KPM had a great interest. Soon after their arrival in Java, the Hofkers met the archaeologist Willem Stutterheim and his companion, the American Claire Holt. Both told them of the wonders of Bali and its colorful expatriate community. The Hofkers traveled to Bali, arranging to share a compound opposite the main temple in Klandis between Denpasar and Sanur, but later moved to Ubud. Contrary to most members of the international circle, the Hofkers preferred a rather withdrawn existence, as they did not like to be distracted from their work. Both Willem and Maria got completely under the spell of Bali. For Willem, the most important thing was to be able to work. In particular, it was the stature and beauty of the proud Balinese women that fascinated him, as it did many of the other artists who visited Bali at the time.[8]

Denpasar, in those days, was the only town of any importance in all of southern Bali. Once a week, Maria would go to the Chinese-operated

Toko Betwai, southern Bali's main sundries store. Only here could one purchase such simple luxuries as soap and other basic requirements of civilization. The little bars of perfumed soap that Maria bought there became an important trade item. Looking through the incredible range of items, while the proprietors and their families were seated around a large table playing mahjong or having dinner, Maria would sometimes turn up small treasures. Before returning home she would also visit the photo studio, operated by a Japanese photographer (who was also a Japanese spy), where she would buy a few of his many beautiful postcards.

The Swiss painter Theo Meier also sought inspiration by traveling like Gauguin to Tahiti, and he also failed to achieve his South Seas dream until he arrived in Bali. Tahiti turned out to be a grave disappointment. The days of Gauguin were long gone and far away. He left in a dejected state of mind, and when he was told about Bali, he decided to try again. "Then the delirium laid hold of me which even today has not subsided," he wrote. First settling in Sanur, he later renovated Spies's house in Isdeh in east Bali. All that he found in Bali corresponded to his inner desires and his inner vision. "I had no need to invent settings for my compositions," he wrote. "I saw them continually before me, in the temples and in daily life." The style he developed was reminiscent of that of his great idol Paul Gauguin. He married a Balinese girl, but the marriage was dissolved after five years, and he became involved in mysticism and the Balinese way of life. Meier took great pride in his reputation as an unpredictable eccentric and spent much time and energy promoting it. Louise Garrett described Meier as "an enthusiastic drinker" with an open eye for female beauty, not disinclined to make some extra money by selling (at excessive prices) pieces of batik or wood carvings. Another of Meier's chief sources of income was the export of Balinese handicrafts to the Basel Ethnographic Museum.

Willem Dooijewaard returned to Bali and so did Roland Strasser, who built a studio in Kintamani, just above Lake Batur, and lived there some ten years. Strasser so disliked visitors that he built a secret door in the back of his studio, through which he could escape when not in the mood to meet with tourists in search of artists. Strasser recalled: "What I found in Bali was of quite a different character—the soothing inducement of a delightful language and charming people. Here the lights were ablaze with distant stars and always full of the syncopated music of the gamelans that accompanied dance and drama. The love of the Balinese for elaborate religious ceremonies is universal. The people were shy and unaccustomed to being painted as they engaged in cock fighting, ritual dancing, or their professional ceremonials. It was truly fascinating to work and live among such graceful wealth of everyday life."

The Dutch artist Charles Sayers went to Bali and decided to stay as he considered this region his prime inspirational source. The mystical aspects of Balinese culture especially appealed to him. Then there were the Dutch painters Auke Sonnega, the Swiss Willy Quidrot, the Polish Czeslaw Mystkowski, the Dutch sculptor Louis Simon Willem van der Noordaa, the Slovakian sculptor Arthur Fleischmann, and the Italians Romualdo Locatelli and Emilio Ambron.

Arthur Fleischmann was trained first as a doctor before studying sculpture. He used his medical training to join the Viennese ice hockey team as team doctor and went with them to South Africa. In 1938 he moved to Bali "out of a sense of adventure—a time which was one of the happiest of his life and a tremendous source of inspiration for his work," but he left for Australia in 1939 on the last KLM flight out.[9]

Romualdo Locatelli was perhaps the most successful artist of his era to visit Bali and certainly the most expensive. Patronized by the rich and powerful in Italy, including the Pope and Mussolini, Locatelli was invited to the Dutch East Indies by the governor general. Having a speech impediment, Locatelli rarely spoke where he went, even though he was the guest of the highest echelons of society. In Bali, he and his wife, moved into Colin McPhee's house in Sayan, where life was most pleasant.[10]

Emilio Ambron came to Bali after seeing Gregor Krause's photo book and the exhibition of Balinese art in Paris. He was accompanied by his sister, Gilda Ambron, who was also an artist. When he decided to stay in Bali, Ambron wrote in a letter: "Bali is invaded by tourists, who pack into boisterous groups into automobiles. A shady European colony, a little like Capri, resides here. Yet, day after day, I am more and more attracted by the beautiful and genuine population. Finally I am beginning to understand why Bali is called the last paradise."[11]

Carl Shreve, American traveler, journalist, author and painter traveled through Bali, when he was ordered by KPM to visualize "the Lure of the East." His book, *Romance Calling*, published by the KPM, was illustrated with numerous reproductions after Indonesian oil paintings and sketches by his hand. His realistic style tended toward expressionism due to its flamboyant tropical coloring and abundant use of paint. Shreve learned that the most interesting part of the island lay to the south of the great mountain wall that ran from east to west, rising sharply from the north coast and sloping gently down to the south. The coast was rugged and wild, with few roads. Here was the unspoiled Bali, living a simple, carefree existence in the huge shadow of the great peak of Bali. It was the ideal spot for a beachcomber in search of romance and color. Descending the ridge, the coconut palms appeared in dense jungles, overhanging the road like a

13. Belated Gauguins

"Morning Market, Bali." Painting by George W. Parker. Courtesy of the Peter A. Juley & Son Collection, Smithsonian American Art Museum, Washington, D.C.

triumphal archway. At each village his approach was heralded by a host of mangy pariah dogs. A white man on foot was a great rarity.[12]

In 1934, the painter George W. Parker began a series of classes in his studio in New York, and during the summers these were conducted in various interesting localities. One cold winter day, a group of students decided it would be pleasant to be painting in Bali or some other tropical country. Several weeks later they sailed from New York for an art adventure to last six months with Bali as their objective. They made their home in the village of Bangli. "Surrounding us on all sides was the most beautiful landscape, new forms, new color, new light," wrote Parker, "here, was a race of handsome people; new characters, a different philosophy, a strange culture and religion; here too, was native art practiced by all, exquisite music played constantly by the gamelan orchestras, fanciful dances, and architecture and sculpture strange to Western eyes; painting, too, so very primitive and decorative. Despite it all, we did work from dawn to dusk, inspired more perhaps than ever before in our lives."

On his trip, Parker met Lanning McFarland, a Chicago banker, and later sold him the painting *Morning Market, Bali*, "in exchange for four cows (Hereford), passionate, not over five years old (regardless of sex)." Based on the current price of beef, the five cows were worth about twelve hundred dollars. A writer for the *New York World-Telegram*, began his report on this sell: "American art strode bravely forward this week when a Nantucket painter became owner of four cows in Montana, and a Chicago banker proudly shouldered a canvas of dawn in Bali and three seminude women."[13]

Carl Newland Werntz, painter and educator, founded the Chicago Academy of Fine Arts, teaching the commercial aspects of creative art. After thirty years, he turned the school over to his brother-in-law to travel and resumed his creative painting where he left it off. He intended to be gone for a year, but didn't show up again in Chicago for six years. He wandered across strange islands along the equator for sketch material, visiting Bali on the way. "Joseph Conrad could have made an enthralling tale of Carl Werntz, who has been wandering in strange islands and mainlands along the equator." There was a flavor of a new Gauguin in it all, except that Werntz's wife, Milicent, was his companion on all his travels.[14]

Martha Sawyers, an illustrator from Cuero, Texas, lived and painted in Bali and later exhibited her Bali paintings in New York City. "This is an enchanted land of an indulgent caste system, easy living, make-believe," she wrote, "and many strange customs. A Balinese, for example, pulls the hair from his face with two coins. Fingernails as long as four inches—even on just one hand—are signs of distinction, and young girls wear five-inch solid gold nail protectors. They file their teeth even, polish some white with ashes, and blacken others. Food is considered *nyam-nyam* (uneatable) without the violent flavoring of crushed pungent spices, aromatic roots and leaves, nuts, onions, garlic, fermented fish paste, lemon juice, grated coconut, and burning red peppers! In Bali, a person eating should not be spoken to. They take their meals according to the position of the sun in the sky, which is their way of telling time."[15]

Bali's Bohemians, however, all remained dependent on the Western economy, mostly the Western tourists who were guests in their hotels or bought their paintings. While their lives were often unconventional by Dutch colonial standards, they were regularized, to great extent, by the necessities of their tourist-oriented businesses. They were probably less unconventional by the standards of European and American societies that provided most of their customers. They only rejected some aspects of Western society, but they firmly remained part of the Western colonial economy

13. Belated Gauguins

and international transatlantic culture. But the year 1940 brought an interruption to life on Bali. Holland was occupied, and the authority of the colonial power was greatly inhibited. For many of the European painters, the dream of a rich, inspired artist's life, was shattered.

14
The Dark Side of Paradise

The "traditional" Bali, so admired by travelers and scholars alike was a historical fiction, a product of political calculation and conservative political objectives. The popular image of "traditional" Bali as a "Last Paradise" was perpetuated and exploited by the Dutch government and the tourist industry. The photographs of bare-breasted Balinese women, reinforcing the image of Bali as an erotic paradise, helped to obscure the political and economic realities of Dutch colonial rule. The experts who came to work in Bali also developed an elaborate and respectable portrait of the island as a sort of "Last Paradise," even when they saw evidence to the contrary.

The image of a harmonious, exotic, and apolitical Bali gained wide acceptance when Dutch colonial power in Bali was at its height and the restoration of Balinese "tradition" had become a central feature of a conservative Dutch colonial strategy of indirect rule. The military conquest of Bali was the first step in the complex process of the Dutch colonial control of the island. The twin Dutch colonial objectives of maintaining political order and maximizing tax revenues were justified by reference to Balinese "tradition." The Dutch sent their bureaucratic "managers" to survey the island they wanted to control, describe it, and then see where it was amenable to change. The Dutch then defined and categorized Balinese "caste," "religion," and "society" in their own terms, and made their hypothetical models binding on those who had never believed in them. Dutch interpretations of "traditional" duties involved forcing the Balinese to perform slave labor, which was exacted by public authorities usually in lieu of taxes for the construction and repair of roads, bridges, and canals. Resistance to slavery and to unrealistic caste categorizations was met with force and bureaucratic regulations. The Balinese were expected to suffer in silence, to fit the colonial image of docile natives. The Balinese got the reputation of being a submissive people because the Dutch police state was very effective.

In their writings, Bali-struck foreigners always conveniently ignored the poverty, disease, and injustice that made the colonial era a time of continuous hardship and fear for many Balinese; the fact that with the dance performances for tourists came forced labor.

The Balinese reaction, however, came out sometimes in song. *Janger*, a traditional-looking dance, in traditional costumes, was performed in a square created by rows of male and female choruses. The songs of these choruses were a mixture of Malay, Balinese, and sometimes Javanese. One of the more poignant songs from this form was written by one of Colin McPhee's house "boys,"

> Were I rich I would take you to the Bali Hotel.
> There the beds are covered with fine silk
> We would lie down
> And when we had made love we would leave
> In a fine Chevrolet
> Blowing our horn loudly along the way.[1]

This song, along with paintings for tourists and other new artistic forms, came out of a colonial context where tourism was turning Bali into a paradise for Europeans. This love song speaks of a luxury unobtainable for virtually all Balinese. Even if they could afford it, they would not have been allowed into this hotel. The people who came to Bali, who represented it to the rest of the world, and to whom Balinese represented Bali, were Europeans and Americans. The Balinese tended to see all white people as Dutch and all Dutch as civil servants. And they were very afraid of civil servants. The Balinese never told the Dutchmen what they really thought, and foreigners were treated the same way.

Many white residents were self-chosen exiles who came to Bali for its "easy" sex, its beauty, its music, its art, and not for its problems. Many lived for years in Bali and easily misunderstood it. They accepted the colonial views on the history and sociology of Bali. They had not the faintest idea that Bali, like the rest of the Dutch Indies, was a police state. The Balinese knew that they had to keep silent about it, that they could not be frank with westerners, even their own employers, because to be open with them was dangerous.

The apparent "peace and order" during the Dutch rule masked serious conflicts over caste, as well as political and economic issues, but the community of westerners formed a collective myth that the Balinese were a gentle people. The westerners accepted the view that Bali was an earthly paradise, whose artistic and deeply religious people lived in harmony with nature and with one another. Jane Belo wrote that the "people of Bali, during the years that I was privileged to live among them, were at peace with the outer world and prosperous." During those years, there was also plenty of rice grown in the wet rice paddies.²

Willard Hanna, a well-known professor of Asian studies, described life in Bali in the 1930s as "agreeable not only for the affluent foreigners but also for the Balinese. The foreigner could and did live very comfortably on an income of about $150 per month, which was the average for the official and the expatriate. It was quite sufficient to allow for a home and a car, a staff of half a dozen household servants, and a bountiful table. The large and numerous Balinese royal families were wealthy and privileged, enjoying every Balinese amenity and imported luxuries as well. The ordinary people had on the whole plenty of rice and relatively few complaints."³

Paul Cravath, a well-known lawyer who visited Bali in 1931, described similar conditions: "The people of Bali's ambitions and demands upon life are modest and easily satisfied; perhaps that is why they are happy. They are not troubled with political or social ambitions and cares; they leave that to the Dutch civil servants. They are not troubled with the cares of business; they leave them to the Chinese shopkeepers and the Arab money lenders. They have no incentive to become rich as their only need to accumulate money is to provide for their cremations. Their physical wants are easily satisfied; they raise their own food which consists principally of rice and fruit with a little pork now and then. In the mild equatorial climate of Bali they need very few clothes and such as they need they make themselves. They have not as yet learned to care for imported luxuries. The Balinese escape the curse of social unrest because the wealth of the island is very evenly distributed, and the economic gap between prince and peasant is not wide. There is no extreme poverty or great wealth."⁴

Gregory Bateson even remarked that the Balinese were not hungry or poverty-stricken and that they were wasteful of food. However, those who got to know intimately the living conditions of the common people in Bali discovered just how gray and poverty-stricken it was. The majority of the people lived in abject poverty, and the conditions deteriorated steadily.

While "suffering" was not a concept frequently associated with Bali in the 1930s, the economic crisis caused widespread poverty and despair among ordinary Balinese. The generation of revenue was a central concern of the Dutch administration in Bali, and the island was no economic paradise for the ordinary Balinese peasant or tenant farmer. The chief source of the problem was the tax system of the colonial administration. The heavy burden imposed on Bali's rural population, through both taxation and forced labor, contributed to serious poverty and increasing landlessness and pauperization. Bali became by far the most heavily taxed area in the

Netherlands Indies. The Balinese were subjected to a bewildering array of taxes, including lax tax, slaughter tax, an income tax, a personal wealth tax, export and import taxes, street-light tax, bicycle tax, and the corveé labor exemption fee, to say nothing of the local taxes, fines, and religious obligations. In 1935, a government report noted that Bali's small holders "could scarcely make ends meet" and that the general state of health on the island was poor, with high levels of malnutrition, tuberculosis, and venereal disease.[5]

The Balinese made little out of the tourist traffic. They were the magnet that attracted it, but the Dutch took the profits. Western travelers could live in Bali for next to nothing, but for the Balinese peasants and share croppers life was quite different.

Even before the Great Depression had brought economic problems to a head, the Balinese already suffered under one of the heaviest tax burdens in the Netherlands Indies and were still required to perform an average of twenty-five days per year of forced labor for the government or the local rulers. Bruce Lockhart recorded coming across scores of Balinese in loincloths, who were busily engaged in road-mending. Obviously they were working for the government. He asked what rate of pay they received, and was told none. Those were the Balinese who could not pay their taxes, and the government took it out of them in forced labor. The Dutch told him that the Balinese preferred this work to paying taxes.[6]

Covarrubias reported that in 1933 the Dutch gold currency had gone up, and prices had crashed to bottom levels. Only twenty-five cents could be obtained for one of the great sheaves of rice that before brought ten times as much; a cow could be bought for five guilders, and a pig for one. The Balinese were unable to obtain cash to pay back taxes, and their lands were being sold at auction.

Social conditions in Bali changed under colonization and not to their advantage. In the mid-1930s, part of the nobility were up to their ears in debt. They were not content to raise money from the bank until they could not pay interest any more; their subjects, poor devils who, day in, day out, worked like bees in the rice fields, suffered too. They, who still as in olden times hanged with affection on the princely families, were induced to take mortgages on their fields when their lord was short of money. "Can anything be more gratifying for a poor coolie than to do his lord a service?" As a rule he paid for it with the loss of his land, which the bank ruthlessly put up to auction later on. The noble lords could then do what they liked again for a while: buy whisky, motor cars and cotton, perhaps there was even enough money to repair the splendid old temple; corrugated iron was easily good enough for that. It came cheaper than the old roofs of sugar-palm fiber.[7]

Writing in 1932, before the full effects of the depression were evident, the Dutch scholar Victor Emanuel Korn stated what few wanted to hear: "Whoever gets to know more fully the living conditions of the ordinary man in Bali quickly discovers what a gray and impoverished mass of humanity populates this beautiful island. The people live for the most part in bitter poverty and this poverty is growing worse." When the effects of the depression began to be fully felt, poverty, hunger, and landlessness became acute. There were parts of the island where people lived off sweet potatoes and maize. The housing of the poor was appalling.[8]

Despite the appearance of being an unusually healthy race, the Balinese were victims of many serious afflictions for which they knew no cure. Worst among these were the widespread venereal diseases including syphilis and gonorrhea. The violent rainy seasons brought epidemics of tropical fevers, and malaria took many lives, especially of children.

Economic development, stimulated by the Dutch, had not been wholly beneficial. Bali, once prosperous, suffered like other countries from economic depression. Copra were going badly. The price of beef had fallen from twenty-six cents to six a kilo. Pig prices had declined similarly. Government wages had been reduced. There was also a depression in the tourist trade. The American slump had cut the supply of rich Englishmen and Americans. And so, in the 1930s, when the people of Bali were told that the reason fewer tourists were coming to Bali than previously was that there was a world depression, they responded by holding an elaborate purification and propitiation ceremony at Besakih, the head temple on the slopes of the volcanic Great Mountain (Gunung Agung), in order to bring the world depression to an end. The situation proved hopeless.

The beautiful appearance of Bali and the well-established image of a carefully isolated traditional society did the island a disservice. Luxuriant nature and colorful rituals created the impression that life in Bali was one long feast. The Western image of Bali as paradise had endured against all odds and in spite of reality. Many westerners advocated the view that every Balinese was an artist, and they overlooked the fact that during the misery of the 1930s many Balinese were very eager to enter this field because the relatively wealthy Westerners were willing to pay for it in hard currency. While Western travelers and expatriates thought of Bali as a well-balanced artistic culture or an exotic paradise, to the greater part of the Balinese, the 1930s were dark and dismal years.

In 1940, Philip Hanson Hiss described the situation of the Balinese:

> Now, though they export no more, they are importing many things: corrugated iron roofs are, in some places, being substituted for thatch;

cheap cotton cloth is taking the place of many of the native cloths; bicycles are being bought and European shirts are appearing, as well as gasoline pressure lamps, and other unnecessary innovations. In a few years the Balinese are likely to become pauperized. Those Balinese who have become chauffeurs and have contact with Europeans, the servants in European households, the tourists, and many of the resident foreigners, have all done their part, consciously or unconsciously, to undermine Balinese life. The few understanding Europeans have been in the minority and have been able to do little to counteract the bad effects of others. Tourists have been introduced to the various arts of the island, and the artists now cater to people without experience in Balinese art, who are consequently unable to discriminate between the good and the bad. The missionaries have again taken up their work, and are sowing the seeds of disharmony among the people.[9]

15
Witch Hunt

The Dutch looked at the expatriate community of Western artists in Bali with mixed feelings. On one hand, Spies and his friends were good at advertising Bali as a fancy tourist resort. On the other hand, however, there was also the image of Bali as a sexual permissive society, a paradise for homosexuals. That, eventually, was not tolerated by the Dutch. When senior Dutch officials suddenly initiated a witch hunt in 1938 against homosexuals all over the Netherlands Indies, most members of the Bali set were also targets. The Dutch police clamped down on homosexuals and threw some of them into jail for good measure. Westerners in Bali did not have an easy time, as accusations of homosexuality had been flung at many. Colonial conservatism and modern artists were not made for each other.[1]

Concerns about these allegedly deviant sexual practices among men reached a fever pitch in late 1938, when they spilled over into an obsessive crackdown. Newly promoted Dutch officials seeking clout shifted toward right wing policies of law, order, and conformity. The last governor general of the Netherlands Indies, a man of strict, orthodox principles, revived long-lapsed laws against suspect behavior including homosexuality and ordered a general clampdown on the many homosexuals in the Dutch Indies, intending to stop the ever-growing practice of homosexual prostitution of young boys. With judgment clouded by apprehension about the Axis Powers' threat, the Dutch ruling minority began to look for scapegoats. Relationships that had been tolerated for years were suddenly seen as a threat to law and order. Officials well disposed toward Walter Spies were replaced. Conservative and suspicious Dutch administrators ordered Spies to be taken into custody on criminal charges of moral turpitude. He was caught in a dragnet and was confined.

Suddenly, a veritable "witch-hunt against homosexuals," as Margaret Mead called it, was started. The Dutch state had gone haywire. Against the backdrop of a press smear campaign, search warrants were issued and police inquiries intensified. Accusations of homosexuality were leveled at a wide range of distinguished European men—arresting, among many others, such luminaries as Walter Spies and Roelof Goris, in Bali. Other expatriates, of both Dutch and other nationalities, hurriedly left the island. In the space of a few months, over one hundred suspects were arrested and hundreds more lived in fear that the same could happen to them. A series of suicides, dismissals, broken marriages, and ruined careers was the result. The painter Rudolf Bonnet was in deep despair about the humiliation and anguish heaped upon many of his close friends. He reported that the Dutch police had also treated the Balinese, who did not understand any of this, in an unduly harsh manner. The Balinese looked like frail, frightened birds because homosexual relationships were nothing special to them.[2]

Jane Belo was also harassed. She wrote to her mother in February, 1939 that the official who was the head of the south Bali district had "got a bee in his bonnet" and was trying to oust all the foreigners throughout the country, that is, those living not immediately in Denpasar, where he could keep an eye on their doings. The Batesons, however, were not to be bullied, and since their arrival, the westerners had been less pestered by the snooping police, although the police were in and out of their houses as part of the clean up the government had been conducting regarding "certain misdemeanors to which residents of these parts were prone." The method was to arrest and put in jail all suspects, pending investigation of their cases. Jane Belo wrote: "All of us who lived in a pleasant way have been investigated—police in and out of our houses, all our servants arrested and questioned. Of the thirty-four dancing girls in my village, all were questioned on my habits, down to a three-year old. Thank heaven I had a free conscience and could stand up in a haughty manner and demand an explanation for such bandying of my good name. At least half of the westerners living in Bali have been asked to leave, or have left of their own records, one dares not wonder why. Thank heaven for the Batesons and their firm scientific reputations to back us up." Since Colin had kept their divorce secret, Jane had difficulty convincing the authorities that she was "an individual, with a name, a passport, and a soul of my own." Finally, after several days of questioning, she was allowed to live in the Sayan house again. Jane was among the lucky ones.[3]

Walter Spies refused to acknowledge the threat, and became one of the victims of this persecution. He was arrested for immoral conduct and was detained for almost a year. Spies was arrested on several counts, especially for turning his house in Ubud into "a rendezvous for homosexuals" and for having sexual relations with minors, but his arrest was also based on a smear campaign against him by some jealous colonial officials. Belo wrote that the Balinese thought that the "whole white caste" had gone stark raving mad. The Balinese were shocked and dismayed at losing their best friend and helper. Spies had been a good friend, with much sympathy for Balinese culture. In the evenings, his favorite gamelan gathered beneath the prison walls in Denpasar to express their solidarity with a serenade. Throughout the time of his absence, fresh offerings were laid every day on the household shrine at Campuan and prayers were offered for his early and safe return.[4]

In her final months in Bali, Jane Belo was involved in getting Walter Spies released. She was devoted to Spies, and together with Mead, Bateson, and Katharane Mershon, she found him a lawyer and worked on his behalf. In her letters, Jane was circumspect in describing the charges against Spies, primarily because the mail was being censored. Another supporter of Walter Spies was one of his most dedicated admirers, Marianne van Wessen, a wealthy Dutch woman who arrived in Bali in 1939, where she had taken the position as curator of the Bali Museum in Denpasar and as secretary to the *Pita Maha*. Like several other women before her, she had fallen in love with Walter despite the obvious impracticality of such a sentiment. She went to extraordinary lengths to support him morally and financially. She occupied Campuan as caretaker lessee. She would do anything within her power to make life for Walter more bearable, sending him books and painting materials. She even discussed a nominal marriage with Spies for his protection, which Spies declined. She then attempted, unsuccessfully, to help him evade arrest.[5]

Meanwhile, the Balinese population looked on in astonishment, unable to understand what had possessed the Dutch to behave in this way. The Balinese were baffled. Homosexuality was not a crime to them. The whole affair could be explained only in terms of the neurotic hysteria of the times, the pressures generated in Batavia, and the petty-minded vengefulness of certain Dutch officials. But the expatriate community was decimated. The days of joy for westerners in Bali were temporarily over.

16

Paradise Lost

For those fortunate enough to experience Bali during the "golden age," Bali became the embodiment of paradise on earth, and was all the more scintillating as the clouds of war grew darker. Tourist numbers continued to climb. By 1940, Bali averaged about two hundred and fifty tourists a month, with a small proportion arriving by air. But as war drew nearer, tourists became fewer and only a few guests lingered until 1941.

Steven Runciman, fellow at Trinity College, at Cambridge University and university lecturer, arrived in Bali in January 1939 and stayed there a week. He recalled that it was a bad moment for arriving at Bali:

> During the last previous years numbers of people, Europeans and Americans, men and women, had settled in Bali and had almost all of them become rather too intimate with the natives. The government in Java had at last become aware of these shocking activities; and, barely a week before our arrival, sudden action was taken. Nearly all the male settlers had been taken off to be tried and gaoled in Java, while the women settlers were ordered to leave the country. I had come armed with a letter of introduction to Mr. Walter Spies, the now elderly German whose writings had brought Balinese art and, in particular, Balinese dancing to the notice of the Western world. Being interested in all forms of ballet I was eager to talk to him. But when I asked how to find him a stern Dutchman looked at me strangely and advised me to destroy the letter. It was only when we met a French artist who had actually married a Balinese girl and was therefore considered to be respectable, that the awful story was explained to me. The atmosphere was therefore somewhat muted. No Balinese now ventured to talk to a foreigner; though, when it was reported that a tourist ship was arriving, the maidens all hastened to bear their bosoms, knowing that that was what visitors liked, dressing respectably again as soon as the tourists departed. Nevertheless we were able to see Balinese dancing and to hear Balinese music and to witness a great Balinese funeral ceremony; and we drove all over the island, which, however, I did not think as lovely as several other islands that we had visited. I have never been

able to feel the enthusiasm for Bali that most later travelers seem to have enjoyed.[1]

The English author Marjorie Appleton visited Bali just before World War II. "I was prepared to be disappointed," she wrote, "the glamour attaching to the very name of 'Bali' was, I suspected, of travel agents' manufacture. Too much has been said of its beauty and the charms of an unspoiled people, and so it was quite astonishing to find a delicious island inhabited by lovely people—even although those people are not all lovely, although some of them are, in fact, exceedingly ugly, with blackened teeth, distorted mouths and protruding lips stained by the chewing of betel-nut. There was not cause for disappointment with the island itself. It seemed to me all loveliness, having the natural beauty of dramatic wild scenery, and the added richness of age-long cultivation.

The Dutch authorities were encouraging what might be called controlled tourist traffic. They wished, and rightly, to save Bali from spoliation; visitors were urged to keep the country free from beggars by refraining from giving money to children or offering tips at temples. The Balinese must be greatly influenced by the arrival of people now and then in large vessels which anchor not far from the shore, who whirl in fine cars along their roads, buy their wood carving and hand-loom weaving and beaten silver ware, and watch, as a spectacle, the dances and plays which for the Balinese themselves have profound religious significance. I used to wonder why it is that so many people come back from Bali with an urge to write a book about so tiny a country. Being there, I understood. Time has given Bali a fourth dimension."[2]

The actress Ruth Draper was a professional monologist, performing various character sketches, which she wrote herself. She arrived in Bali as part of a tour. Later Spies reported to his mother that Ruth Draper, the famous performing artist, stayed several days at his house. Spies found her terribly funny and her performance delightful and incredible. In a letter she sent from Bali, Draper wrote:

> This place is idyllic—really so—but fiendishly hot. As I write a lovely breeze blows over me so I shouldn't complain! I flew here from Java yesterday—over a blue sea, and this Island of rich forests and mountains, rice fields in perfectly curved terraces under water, so they look like a lovely design in greens reflecting clouds and sky. The natives have enormous charm, sweet smiles, gentle ways, graceful and beautiful; to watch them passing with their baskets of fruits and vegetables is endless pleasure. I saw wonderful dancing last night ... all rather slow,

studied and perfect—*completely* satisfying and tho' one cannot understand, one knows it is high art, come down through ages of sincere and intense devotion; and I love the music! The young boys and girls are incredibly mature in their mastery of gesture, poise, and expression, and become almost rapt in the intensity of the smallest movement; yet they do not seem tired, or breathless or bored, and each motion has a freshness and significance that leaves one moved and admiring.

In another letter, written after she left Bali, Draper called Bali "the last real Paradise," declaring she had never seen such beautiful country or such a beautiful people and such unspoiled, untroubled lives. "It was moving, and thought provoking, and one trembles to think it will not last if tourists and merchants and missionaries are allowed to come in too great numbers!"[3]

Michael Lerner was a successful businessman who turned an early and avid interest in hunting and fishing into a mature scientific avocation. As a trustee of the American Museum of Natural History, he led expeditions to collect ethnographic objects and zoological specimens from all over the world. He made a side trip to Bali with his wife and photographer James Barnes Shackelford and made there two films, *Bali*, a color film portraying the life and customs of the Balinese, and *Bali, the Lost Paradise*. Included in the first one were scenes of Balinese engaged in everyday activities, growing and cultivating rice of hillside terraces, cockfighting, a funeral procession and cremation of a member of the Brahman caste, as well as four Balinese dances, showing the costumes and the gamelan orchestra instruments.

Mrs. Anne Archbold was a wealthy sportswoman, explorer, and world traveler. Her father was an independent oil producer and the president of Standard Oil of New Jersey. In 1939, she went to Hong Kong and built a Chinese junk, the *Cheng Ho*, an authentic copy of a fifteenth-century vessel. The first Archbold expedition of the *Cheng Ho* was headed by Dr. David Fairchild, an American agricultural explorer and plant collector, to gather tropical plants. Fairchild wrote that he found it impossible to generalize about the world of the Balinese, to make comparisons, and pass judgments. This "gay, imaginative, but deeply 'religious' people; its picturesque dances; its amazing pageants; its night concerts given by the light of flickering torches and marked by the cadences of the great gongs and the rhythm of the 'gamelan'; its walled-in kampongs with their decorated doorways; its temple services, with streams of women bearing votive offerings; its bamboo poles with their streams of fresh coconut leaves; its paddy fields covered with water that reflects the sunshine, and dotted with little shrines; its bits of forest; its gray beaches of volcanic sand on which the long rollers come tumbling in; and its three volcanoes, six thousand, seven thousand, and nine thousand feet high—these are things that make any adequate description of ten days spent there almost impossible."

> How easily one forms a prejudice, and how often it is utterly unwarranted! Many of the books about Bali are filled with pictures of women dressed to the waist only, just as the Miami papers are filled with photographs of bathing beauties dressed even more scantily. In consequence I had the feeling that I could get along without seeing Bali. I found that I had judged too hastily, and that what I took as representative of the Balinese was no more so than the bathing beauties of our beaches are representatives of our American culture as a whole.

Fairchild concluded: "A special place in the world should somehow be made for the gay, lovable, musical, artistic, imaginative people of this little island. It would be so easy to exploit them and snuff out their charming civilization forever."[4]

Maynard Owen Williams, staff correspondent for *National Geographic Magazine*, wrote in an article in that magazine: "How's Bali. Some call it a paradise. Rich volcanic soil, a friendly climate, and control of water make misery uncommon and famine unknown. Leisure leavens soil; artistic skill is widely shared and generally appreciated, and there is a subtle harmony between the people and their island home. The gods are ever-present friends. Escape from the numerous evil spirits is a familiar, exciting routine. Amusements, founded in the mythology of the people, are free to all, even to those babes in arms who stay out most of the night, drinking in the Hindu classics with their mothers' milk. Not the least of Bali's charm is that it enables one to gaze on beauty with detachment. Balinese temples, brown bodies, grotesque idols, lush-green paddy, humming-bird fluttering of fingers and fan, fighting cocks in wicker-baskets—all were there, not as made-to-order local color but as phases of normal existence. Everyday life rather than superficial glitter gives character this amazing little island. Although its culture is old, Bali is not a ruin, rising above an alienated countryside."[5]

Mona Gardner, an American author who lived in Japan for twelve years and was later a newspaper correspondent in Shanghai, stopped at Bali on her slow journey home. "Except for narrow strips where tourists whirl by," Gardner wrote, "the rest of Bali is steeped in the culture of a thousand years ago. This is true of other neighboring islands in the Java

Sea, but Bali's pattern of living is more esthetic to our notion, more civilized and more comfortable, and so the word *Bali* has become a synonym for escape with us."

> But, alas, it is regimented escape now. Unless you go there speaking Dutch and Malay and stay for several months at some rest house in an out-of-the-way mountain village, you become a part of the carefully, deliberately regimented, Dutch system of selling escape by the day or the week. You are bowled through forests and rice-fields on a circular paved track, you are housed at a Dutch hotel complete with *stoep*, you view natives—whom the hotel pays to perform for tourists—dancing in the hotel courtyard or at a village, and you sit in a seat the hotel buys for you at a cockfight. It is much like looking at a well-made, carefully edited screen play. The difference is that all eight reels are in Technicolor, that it is three-dimensional, and that you have to take four shower-baths a day to keep yourself in condition to do the watching.[6]

Philip Hanson Hiss, architectural designer and professional photographer, left his business and sailed to the Dutch East Indies on an expedition, under the auspices of the Riverside Museum and the government of the Netherlands Indies, to be gone a year. He did not realize that he would spend most of his time in Bali, but a week after he had stepped ashore in Bali he knew it, although his arrival coincided with the beginning of the war in Europe. He worked for eight months, photographing by day and by night. He had probably seen more of Bali than any other American, having driven his car over seven thousand miles of its area. Its inhabitants provided plenty of subject matter, as did the superb tropical scenery. But Hiss's trip to Bali was terminated by Hitler's march into the Netherlands.

Hiss was concerned that certain special conditions, upon which the achievements of Balinese civilization had been largely dependent, were gradually being destroyed. It seemed to him that it was unlikely that the Balinese could long survive in their present state. However, Hiss concluded: "It is remarkable that such a place as Bali should exist. To have lived there is to have looked at life with other eyes. It is an inspiration to know that man can live at peace and in harmony with man. If it has been done once, it can be done again!"[7] Introducing later an exhibition of his photographs at the Baltimore Museum of Art, Hiss wrote that "Bali, that halcyon island in the East Indies, has always been a synonym for 'heaven on earth' to escapists—which include nearly all of us who have indulged in the usual amount of day dreaming."

Serge Lifar, the colorful, internationally known dancer and choreographer, and ballet master of the Paris Opera Ballet, stopped for several days in Bali on his way back from a tour of Australia. He was breathless at the beauty of the mountains and volcanoes. Ever since he had seen the Balinese dancers at the Colonial Exhibition in Paris, he had longed to come to the island. Remembering the gestures of those dancers, he mimicked the difficult jerks of the head and sidelong eye movements that were especially characteristic. Louise Garrett said to him: "You must be the only European who can do that." Bob Koke took Lifar to Luk-Luk, where they found I Mario, who gave Lifar a lesson. Then Lifar showed the Balinese audience some ballet steps, performing his celebrated *entre-chat*, a jump during which his feet change position with regard to one another ten times. The Balinese, being taken aback by this seeming miracle, burst out laughing. Lifar then did it again and it dawned on them that they were witnessing something remarkable; this time there was a deep silence as they gazed at him. Lifar said that, with the exception of Nijinsky and Pavlova, I Mario was the greatest dancer he had seen. Lifar remembered a somewhat different experience:

"One day," Lifar wrote, "after I had danced together with the sacred dancers, I wanted to show them, in my turn, some Western dancing. First of all I danced *L'Apres Midi d'un Faune* to the music of a record. Then I wanted to dance *L'Oiseau Bleu* accompanied by their orchestra. But they did not know what we call *danse d'élévation*. When I leapt and bounded they took me for a demon and ran after me wanting to kill me. I owed my escape to the prompt action of a few friends."[8]

Silvia Baker, an illustrator from Manchester, began to travel after her husband died. Ever since she read *The Last Paradise*, she had wanted to go to Bali. She had to sell jewelry, borrow money, and half starve herself to pay for the ticket, but it was worth it. "Bali is like Capri in many ways, for both these islands are fantastic, but it resembles Venice in one thing—it doesn't disappoint you. Whatever they may have said in praise of the island, on arriving there, you say with the Queen of Sheba: 'And the half was not told me.'"

She took the ferry to Gilimanuk and then the bus, which was tied together with hairpins and string, to Denpasar, she stayed at the Kuta Beach Hotel for ten months. She described Bob and Louise Koke as so friendly and gay and efficient, that their small hotel prospered and grew and became famous in the East, but in the Spring of 1940 there were very few guests in the hotel because of the *Pirang besar* (the great war). According to Baker, there were, however, drawbacks to the enchanted island. "For instance, when one had toothache at Kuta in Bali, one had to drive two hundred miles across the island in a Balinese bus. One then crossed, in a tiny boat, an appallingly rough stretch of sea, where two oceans meet. The waves are so enormous that one was crazy with fear, unless one drank Dutch gin, which tasted of turpentine, and gave one courage. Then as a consolation prize there was a very charming fair-haired Dutch dentist at one's journey's end."

When Sylvia Baker arrived, the few original wattle huts had increased in size, splendor, and numbers, and the servants were relatively highly-trained.[9] "When I lived at Kuta beach," Sylvia wrote, "I slept in a wattle hut on the edge of the shore. There was superb American plumbing in the bathroom, and one had only to walk a few steps to the main Hotel building. There was a gecko in the roof, a toad under my bed, while rats, land-crabs and beige-colored flying-beetles, together with enormous ants, dragon-flies, grasshoppers (which the Balinese eat fried), and scorpions were not infrequent visitors. Fishermen and burglars also drifted in and out of this room, where there was hardly a dull moment." She tried to cultivate the Buddha heart towards insects, but all the same she said; "Thank Heaven for Flit."

The English and Americans in Bali were apt to fall prey to what the Dutch disapprovingly called "The Bali sickness." Those who became a victim of this disease had usually been seriously disturbed psychologically. Some of the "Bali-owners" gave the people medical aid (still further enraging the Dutch officials). They learned Balinese, a most difficult language, in addition to the Bazaar Malay that was customary. They wore sarongs, walked about Denpasar lovingly entwined with a couple of Balinese, and even went so far as to flirt with the Balinese religion by making offerings and encouraging priests to come and ring bells in their kampongs. "The Balinese like it," they said. Actually, the Balinese knew which side their bread was buttered, and were artists in soft-soap, as in everything else. But, although the "Bali-owners" could become rather boring by reason of their mania, they showered kindness on the people of the island.[10]

From the social point of view, life in Kuta was surprising. One lived for months on end in this ultimate island, seeing only a few people on account of the war and the scarcity of tourists, and then suddenly one was in the midst of an influx of travelers from New York, Shanghai, Hong Kong, and San Francisco. Bali seemed all at once to have become the very hub of civilization. Often there was the typical American butter-and-eggs man to be found at the long dinner table, who looked at temples and said; "Just another heap of stones to me," and after seeing the elaborate ritual of cremation he said; "Seems to me like a lot of natives getting silly." A Mrs. Banks, another American, who was staying in Bali to find shells for her collection, had to get up earlier and earlier each morning to hunt for them. The boys from the village were on the beach before she got there, and they picked up the best shells and sold them to her. Captain and Mrs. Irving

Johnson came to Bali on their schooner *Yankee,* and were on their way around the world for the third time. They had fifteen American boys as crew, and their two babies were on board. A Russian painter who had lived in Bali for ten years told stories about the island, but he was bored with Bali. He spoke of it with something like hatred. Places, Baker supposed, were like people, in one way. It was when one had loved them a great deal, and was tired of them, that one hated them most.[11]

Donald Oenslager, an American theatrical stage designer, was known for his artistic originality and adaptability and his stage designs were described as "delightful fantasies." He visited Bali in the summer of 1940 and reported, soon after his return, that "War or no war, Bali dances on." Life in Bali continued along as placidly as it had for generations, and every incident was literally a part of the Balinese theatre. "All this life stream of the theatre I observed and delighted in on a trip." The roads of Bali unfolded in a continuous procession of scenic spectaculars. Theatre was essential to life. The throbbing music of the gamelan players was ever present, close by or far away in a village kampong or temple court or by the seaside. It generated the rhythm of dance for pleasure, dance for seasonal festivities, or dance for solemn ceremonies, for opera, comedy, or tragedy. Theatre was ever in the air—twenty-four hours a day. All this strange ubiquitous theatre they discovered fascinated them. The Oenslagers wanted to remain in Bali indefinitely. Again and again Oenslager thought, "If the Balinese only needed a little scenery we might have a possible excuse to stay longer." But they needed no scenery, and fortunately for their theatre he hoped it would never need any. He carried away a lasting impression of an extraordinary kind of theatrical vitality, which the drama-loving Balinese had everywhere generously shared with him. A small book, *Theatre of Bali,* which he wrote after his return, became a collector's item.

Lili Kraus established herself as a highly respected concert pianist and became one of the most popular recitalists and symphony orchestra soloists in England and in continental Europe during the 1930s. Kraus, her husband, Otto Mandl, a noted philosopher, and their two children went to the Dutch East Indies in March 1940 for a four-month concert tour, but their stay kept being extended. In the fall of 1941 they moved to Sayan in Bali. There they rented a thatched-roof house nestled beside a big river, and thick and lusty green rain forests encircled them on all side. A huge covered porch furnished with rattan furniture surrounded the house, and a guest cottage was nearby. Kraus had a piano trucked in over rough roads. She practiced during the days. In the evenings, the family socialized, often sitting outside listening to gamelan orchestras and watching people dance. They quickly adjusted to the local cuisine of rice and sambal. Life in Bali was well suited to Kraus's decidedly open and sensual style. Things physical played a critical and central role in her life. People who knew Kraus then remember her enjoyment of Bali, recalling her daringly liberated personality there, punctuated by sexual energy and overtones.

The Western image of Bali as paradise has endured against all odds and, increasingly, in spite of reality. But in early 1942 the fragility of the paradise the Dutch had created in Bali for westerners became obvious as the nemesis of European colonialism, the Japanese military, began to move towards the Malay archipelago. But at Kuta Beach the parties continued. Sometime around mid-November 1941, aristocratic tourism had its last hurrah in Bali. Duff Cooper, Britain's minister of state for the Far East and his glamorous wife, Diana, the British actress, flew in from Singapore, en route to Australia. They were determined to see Manx's Place. The Coopers' frantic overnight stay on Kuta Beach was to be Manx's last encounter with transatlantic "high society," of which she so longed to be part. Even as the international catastrophe loomed, Diana Cooper was smitten by Bali's utopian romance. She described Kuta Beach as precisely the innocent "earthly paradise" she expected—"Nothing lovelier could there be."

"In the jungle garden there were three or four little grass houses with a fresh cool native bath apiece, a grass bar and a terrace to eat on overlooking the sea. The women are naked to the waist, not of course all Milos but all with the serene face. After dinner the dancing—that I couldn't describe if I wanted to—the beauty, the strangeness, the fantastic music." So the Western dream of Bali remained intact. K'tut Tantri wrote that "it was my hour of triumph." Sadly, however, Diana Cooper made it clear that, however pleasant that had been, "old girl Manx" remained, despite her ambitions, only an amusing and slightly odd outsider.[12]

By this time, most Americans had already left Bali, or were planning to leave. The Balinese told Katharane Mershon that she must leave because the Japanese were going to come to Bali and they would take her. Because the Balinese loved her, she knew they would fight and they would get killed. Since there was no need to have all this killing, she went away. The Kokes boarded the ferry that plied between Bali and Java on the last day of 1941. "Behind us," wrote Bob, "was the most peaceful and innocent place that man had permitted to remain on the face of the earth—with tank obstacles set up on its roads and barbed wire on its beaches." K'tut Tantri chose not to evacuate with the Dutch and other westerners but stayed in Bali, enduring privation, torture, and hardship during the Japanese occupation. After the Japanese surrendered, she joined the Indonesian revolution to fight for independence, broadcasting from clandestine Indonesian radio stations as "Surabaya Sue."[13]

Chapter Notes

Introduction
1. Quoted in Hugh Mabbett, *The Balinese* (Wellington, N.Z.: January Books, 1985), 20

Chapter 1
1. Miguel Covarrubias, *Island of Bali* (New York: Knopf, 1937), 32–37; R. H. Bruce Lockhart, *Return to Malaya* (New York: Putnam, 1936), 326–328; Willard A. Hanna, *Bali Profile: People, Events, Circumstances* (1001–1976) (New York: American Universities Field Staff, 1976), 72–75; Gregor Krause, *Bali 1912*, translated by W. H. Mabbett (Wellington, N.Z.: January Books, 1988), 83–87.
2. Geoffrey Robinson, *The Dark Side of Paradise: Political Violence in Bali* (Ithaca, N.Y.: Cornell University Press, 1995), 41.
3. Michel Picard, *Bali: Cultural Tourism and Touristic Culture* (Singapore: Archipelago, 1996), 22–23.
4. Covarrubias, *Island of Bali*, 399.
5. Lockhart, *Return to Malaya*, 325; Ruth Masters Rickover, *Pepper, Rice, and Elephants: A Southeast Asian Journey from Celebes to Siam* (Annapolis, Md.: Naval Institute Press, 1975), 4.
6. Hanna, *Bali Profile*, 98–99.

Chapter 2
1. Harry Salpeter, "Sterne, the Maestro in Art," *Esquire* 15 (February 1941): 78.
2. Jane Belo, ed., *Traditional Balinese Culture; Essays* (New York: Columbia University Press, 1970), xvi.
3. Maurice Sterne, *Shadow and Light: The Life, Friends and Opinions of Maurice Sterne*, edited by Charlotte Leon Mayerson (New York: Harcourt, Brace & World, 1965), 96.
4. Sterne, *Shadow and Light*, 97–98.
5. Sterne, *Shadow and Light*, 105–106.
6. Bruce Carpenter, *W. O. J. Nieuwenkamp: First European Artist in Bali* (Singapore: Periplus Editions, 1997), 45.
7. Krause, *Bali 1912*, 8.
8. Krause, *Bali 1912*, 8–9.
9. Vicki Baum, *A Tale from Bali*, translated by Basil Creighton (Garden City, N.Y.: Doubleday, Doran, 1937), vii.
10. Krause, *Bali 1912*, 87
11. *Illustrated Tourist Guide to East Java, Bali and Lombok* (Batavia: Weltevreden Official Tourist Bureau, 1914).

Chapter 3
1. Cedric Belfrage, *Away from It All; An Escapologist's Notebook* (New York: Simon and Schuster, 1937), 205–206.
2. Michael Hitchcock and Lucy Norris, *Bali, the Imaginary Museum: The Photographs of Walter Spies and Beryl de Zoete* (Kuala Lumpur: Oxford University Press, 1995), 24.
3. Carpenter, *W. O. J. Nieuwenkamp*, 10.
4. Bruce Carpenter and Maria Hofker-Reuter. *Willem Hofker, 1902–1981: Schilder van/Painter of Bali* (Wijk en Aalburg: Pictures Publishers, 1993), 49–50.
5. Debbie Guthrie et al., eds., *Bali*,

revised edition, (New York: Alfred Knopf, 2001), 39.
6. Wim Bakker, *Bali Verbleed* (Delft: Volkenkundig Museum Nusantara, 1985), 30
7. *Inter-Ocean* 10 (January-February 1929): 12.
8. Adrian Vickers, "Thilly Weissenborn: The Romance of the Indies," In *Toward Independence: A Century of Indonesia Photographed*, edited by Jane Levy Reed (San Francisco: Friends of Photography, 1991), 79–81; Adrian Vickers, *Bali: A Paradise Created* (Berkeley: Periplus Editions, 1989), 103.
9. Gabrielle Ferrand, "In a Hindu Paradise: A Rhapsody about the Isle of Bali," *The Trans-Pacific* 13 (22 May 1926): 6.
10. Janice Lovoos, "Roland Strasser: Painter of the Far East," *American Artist* 24 (November 1960): 33–34.
11. Violet Clifton, *Islands of Queen Wilhelmina* (London: Constable, 1927), 134; Frank Clune, *Isles of Spice* (New York: Dutton, 1942), 310.
12. Myron Zobel, "Life in a Pasanggrahan," *Inter-Ocean* 8 (January 1927): 15.
13. Oswald Hering, *Down the World; Random Tales of a Traveler* (New York: Robert M. McBride, 1932), 42–43.
14. Templeton Crocker, *The Cruise of the Zaca* (New York: Harper & Brothers, 1933), 175.
15. E. Alexander Powell, *Where the Strange Trails Go Down* (New York: Scribner, 1921), 157–158.
16. Hering, *Down the World*, 43; Louis Couperus, *Eastward*, translated by J. Menzies-Wilson and C. C. Crispin (New York: George H. Doran, 1924), 246.
17. Jan Poortenaar, *An Artist in Java and Other Islands of Indonesia*, translated by Horace Shipp (Singapore: Oxford University Press, 1989), 126–127.
18. Poortenaar, *An Artist in Java*, 120.
19. Poortenaar, *An Artist in Java*, 133, 145.
20. Helen Eva Yates, *Bali: Enchanted Isle; a Travel Book* (Boston: Houghton Mifflin, 1933), 71; Couperus, *Eastward*, 251, Elinor Mordaunt, *The Further Venture Book* (New York: Century Co., 1927), 261.
21. Mordaunt, *The Further Venture Book*, 272–273.
22. Hermann Norden, "Unspoiled Bali," *Asia* 26 (December 1926): 1102–1103.
23. Carl Shreve, *Romance Calling: Java, Bali, Sumatra, Nias, Siam, Indo-China* (Australia: J. Sands, 1939), 119.
24. Covarrubias, *Island of Bali*, xviii.
25. Hassoldt Davis, *Islands Under the Wind* (London: Longmans, Green, 1933), 193.
26. Hassoldt Davis, *World Without a Roof: An Autobiography* (New York: Duell, Sloan and Pearce, 1957), 62.
27. Renée Roosevelt Denis, *To Live in Paradise* (Fort Bragg, Calif.: Lost Coast Press, 1996), 11–14; Hickman Powell, *Bali; The Last Paradise* (London: Jonathan Cape, 1930), 40–41.
28. Denis, *To Live in Paradise*, 12–13.
29. Denis, *To Live in Paradise*, 34.
30. Denis, *To Live in Paradise*, 37.
31. Davis, *Islands Under the Wind*, 231–232.
32. Armand Denis, *On Safari; The Story of My Life* (New York: Dutton, 1963), 40.
33. Denis, *On Safari*, 41.
34. Denis, *On Safari*, 46–47
35. André Roosevelt, "Introduction," in Hickman Powell, *Bali: The Last Paradise* (London: Jonathan Cape, 1930), xii, xvii.
36. Powell, *The Last Paradise*, 143–145.
37. Powell, *The Last Paradise*, 162.
38. Lucian Swift Kirtland, *Finding the Worth While in the Orient* (New York: Robert M. McBride, 1926), 308–313.

Chapter 4

1. Inez Baranay, *The Edge of Bali* (Pymble, NSW, Australia: Angus & Robertson, 1992), 98.
2. Rickover, *Pepper, Rice, and Elephants*, 9.

3. Colin McPhee, *A House in Bali* (New York: John Day, 1946), 14–15.
4. Belfrage, *Away from It All*, 227–228.
5. Robinson, *The Dark Side of Paradise*, 27, n. 31.
6. Covarrubias, *Island of Bali*, 145.
7. Hugo Adolf Bernatzik, *South Seas*, translated by Vivian Ogilvie (New York: Henry Holt, 1935), 156.
8. Powell, *Where the Strange Trails Go Down*, 152.
9. Powell, *The Last Paradise*, 150–151.
10. Geoffrey Gorer, *Bali and Angkor, or Looking at Life and Death* (London: Michael Joseph, 1936), 68.
11. Richard Halliburton, *The Royal Road to Romance* (Indianapolis: Bobbs-Merrill, 1925), 308–309, 313–314, 326.
12. Grace Gallatin Seton, *Poison Arrows: A Strange Journey with an Opium Dreamer Through Annam, Cambodia, Siam, and the Lotus Island of Bali* (London: J. Gifford, 1938), 252.
13. Seton, *Poison Arrows*, 299.
14. Erik Barnouw, "Robert Flaherty (Barnouw's File)," *Film Culture* no. 53/55 (Spring 1972): 161–185.
15. Hendrik De Leeuw, *Crossroads of the Java Sea* (New York: Jonathan Cape, 1931), 276.
16. Davis, *Islands Under the Wind*, 189.
17. Davis, *Islands Under the Wind*, 193.
18. Davis, *World Without a Roof*, 64–65.
19. Norden, "Unspoiled Bali": 1100.
20. Norden, "Unspoiled Bali": 1140.
21. William Douglas Burden, *Dragon Lizards of Komodo: An Expedition to the Lost World of the Dutch East Indies* (New York: Putnam, 1927): 61–64.
22. Helen Churchill Candee, *New Journeys in Old Asia: Indo-China, Siam, Java, Bali* (New York: Frederick A. Stokes, 1927), 235–237.
23. Franklin Price Knott, "Artist Adventures on the Island of Bali," *National Geographic* 53 (March 1928): 326–328.
24. Knott, "Artist Adventures on the Island of Bali": 346–347.
25. Hering, *Down the World*, 41.
26. Hering, *Down the World*, 45.
27. Hering, *Down the World*, 47–48.
28. E-mail from Anne Holliday, 29 August 2000.
29. Malvina Hoffman, *Heads and Tales* (New York: Scribner, 936), 262.
30. John Charles Van Dyke, *In Java and the Neighboring Islands of the Dutch East Indies* (New York: Scribner, 1929), 161, 169.
31. Ruth Page, *Page by Page*, edited by Andrew Mark Wentink (Brooklyn, N.Y.: Dance Horizons, 1978), 34.
32. Powell, *The Last Paradise*, 3–4.
33. Powell, *The Last Paradise*, 6.
34. Yates, *Bali: Enchanted Isle; a Travel Book*, 177–178.

Chapter 5

1. Baranay, *The Edge of Bali*, 96.
2. Hans Rhodius, ed., *Schonheit und Reichtum des Lebens: Walter Spies, Maler und Musiker auf Bali, 1895–1942; eine Autobiographie in Briefen* (The Hague: L. J. C. Boucher, 1964), 392.
3. Louise G. Koke, *Our Hotel on Bali: How Two Young Americans Made a Dream Come True: A Story of the 1930s* (Wellington, N.Z.: January Books, 1987), 49–50.
4. Martin Birnbaum, "Balinese Panorama," In *Vanishing Eden: Wanderings in the Tropics* (New York: William E. Rudge's Sons, 1942), 125–126.
5. Rhodius, *Schonheit und Reichtum des Lebens*, 313.
6. Johan Fabricius, *A Dutchman at Large: Memoirs*, translated by Roy Edwards (London: Heinemann, 1952), 175.
7. Covarrubias, *Island of Bali*, xxii.
8. Margaret Mead, *Letters from the Field 1925–1975* (New York: Harper & Row, 1977), 160.
9. Timothy Lindsey, *The Romance of K'tut Tantri and Indonesia: Text and Scripts, History and Identity* (Kuala Lumpur: Oxford University Press, 1997), 86–88.

10. Carpenter, W. O. J. Nieuwenkamp, 10.
11. Tjokorda Gde Agung Sukawati, *Reminiscences of a Balinese Prince*, as dictated to Rosemary Hilbery (Honolulu: Southeast Asian Studies, University of Hawaii, 1979), 16.
12. Powell, *The Last Paradise*, 157–158.

Chapter 6

1. Quoted in Tessel Pollman, "Margaret Mead's Balinese: The Fitting Symbols of the American Dream," *Indonesia* 49 (April 1990): 12.
2. Margaret Mead," "The Arts in Bali," in Belo, *Traditional Balinese Culture*, 332–333.
3. Paul Drennan Cravath, *Letters Home from the Far East and Russia, 1931* (Garden City, N.Y.: The Country Life Press, 1931), 38.
4. Cravath, *Letters Home from the Far East*, 53.
5. Cravath, *Letters Home from the Far East*, 28.
6. Paul Morand, "Bali, or Paradise Regained," *Vanity Fair* 38 (May 1932): 40.
7. G. H. von Faber, *The Land of a Thousand Temples: Bali, a Guide and Souvenir*, translated by Leonard Arndt (Sourabaya: H. van Ingen, 1932), 83, 91.
8. Julius Fleischmann, *Footsteps in the Sea* (New York: Putnam, 1935), 165–166, 179.
9. Harold Peters, "The Pilgrim Sails the Seven Seas," *National Geographic* 72 (August 1937): 251; Donald C. Starr, *The Schooner Pilgrim's Progress: A Voyage Around the World 1932-1934* (Salem, Mass.: Peabody Essex Museum, 1996), 253, 262–263.
10. Crocker, *The Cruise of the Zaca*, 186–188, 213–214; e-mail from Anne Holliday, 29 August 2000.
11. C. David Heymann, *Poor Little Rich Girl: The Life and Legend of Barbara Hutton* (New York: Random House, 1983), 69.
12. Pony Duke and Jason Thomas, *Too Rich: The Family Secrets of Doris Duke* (New York: HarperCollins, 1996), 89.
13. Rhodius, *Schonheit und Reichtum des Lebens*, 338–340.
14. Harold Acton, *Memoirs of an Aesthete* (London: Methuen, 1948), 307–308.
15. Rhodius, *Schonheit und Reichtum des Lebens*, 376.
16. Moss Hart, "My Trip Around the World." Moss Hart and Kitty Carlisle Papers, 1922–1962. State Historical Society of Wisconsin Archives, Madison, Wisconsin, 40–41, 45.
17. Cole Lesley, *The Life of Noel Coward* (London: Jonathan Cape, 1976), 174.
18. Isabel Anderson, *In Eastern Seas: With a Visit to Insulinde and the Golden Chersonese* (Boston: Bruce Humphries, 1934), 194–195, 200, 205–206, 212.
19. James Saxon Childers, *From Siam to Suez* (New York: Appleton, 1932), 106–107, 138.
20. Alan John Villiers, "Salt in My Eyes—and a Look at Bali," *Scribner's Magazine* 8 (December 1935): 323–324; Alan John Villiers, *Cruise of the Conrad* (London: Hodder & Stoughton, 1940), 87–88.
21. Villiers, *Cruise of the Conrad*, 89–92, 95.
22. Villiers, *Cruise of the Conrad*, 92–93.
23. Villiers, *Cruise of the Conrad*, 95.
24. Philip Hanson Hiss, *Bali* (New York: Duell, Sloan and Pearce, 1941), 64.
25. Lockhart, *Return to Malaya*, 324.

Chapter 7

1. Belfrage, *Away from It All*, 227.
2. Belfrage, *Away from It All*, 228.
3. Patricia King Hanson and Alan Gevinson, eds., *American Film Institute Catalog of Motion Pictures Produced in the United States: Feature Films 1931-1940*, (Berkeley: University of California Press, 1993), 813.
4. *The New York Times*, 20 September 1932.

5. *Variety*, 27 September 1932.
6. Hanson, *Feature Films 1931-1940*, 1043.
7. *New York Times*, 21 July 1932.
8. "Bali: The Blessed Isle," *Literary Digest* 114 (3 September 1932): 18.
9. Hanson, *Feature Films 1931-1940*, 2338; *Variety Bulletin*, 14 October 1932.
10. *Variety*, 13December 1932.
11. Hanson, *Feature Films 1931-1940*, 1601; *Variety*, 20 December, 1932.
12. Covarrubias, *Island of Bali*, 12.
13. Denis, *On Safari*, 54.
14. Hanson, *Feature Films 1931-1940*, 1176; *Variety*, 9 October 1935.
15. Hanson, *Feature Films 1931-1940*, 322; *The Hollywood Reporter*, 12 July, 1938.

Chapter 8

1. Carpenter, *Willem Hofker*, 11.
2. *Sumatra, Java, Bali: Tours by Rotterdam Lloyd Royal Mail Line* (Rotterdam: Rotterdamsche Lloyd, 1932), 37–38.
3. Roelof Goris, *The Island of Bali; Its Religion and Ceremonies* (Batavia: Royal Packet Navigation Co., 1931), unpaged.
4. Covarrubias, *Island of Bali*, xviii.
5. Covarrubias, *Island of Bali*, 187.
6. Goris, *The Island of Bali*, unpaged.
7. G. H. von Faber, *The Land of a Thousand Temples*, 84–85.
8. Bernatzik, *South Seas*, 154.
9. Covarrubias, *Island of Bali*, 41–42.
10. Covarrubias, *Island of Bali*, 63.
11. Covarrubias, *Island of Bali*, 371.
12. Covarrubias, *Island of Bali*, 103
13. John Beauford, "The Other Al Hirschfeld," *The Christian Science Monitor*, 31 August 1983; Stefan Kanfer, "The World According to Al," *Connoisseur* 216 (July 1986): 70–75.
14. Charlie Chaplin, "Comedian Sees the World," *Women's Home Companion* 61(January 1934): 21.
15. Chaplin, "Comedian Sees the World," 21.
16. Chaplin, "Comedian Sees the World," 21.
17. Chaplin, "Comedian Sees the World," 23.

Chapter 9

1. Rhodius, *Schonheit und Reichtum des Lebens*, 213.
2. Carol J. Oja, *Colin McPhee, Composer in Two Worlds* (Washington: Smithsonian Institution Press, 1990), 66.
3. McPhee, *A House in Bali*, 16–17.
4. McPhee, *A House in Bali*, 21–22.
5. Bernatzik, *South Seas*, 157–158.
6. Oja, *Colin McPhee, Composer in Two Worlds*, 142.
7. "Uncensored Joys of Happy Balinese," *Literary Digest* 122 (25 July, 1936): 20.
8. Katharane Edson Mershon and Charles F. Edson, "Katherine Philips Edson Remembered: Oral History." Oral History Program, University of California, Los Angeles, 93.
9. Belo, *Traditional Balinese Culture*, 226.
10. Belfrage, *Away from It All*, 226.
11. Katharane Edson Mershon, *Seven Plus Seven: Mysterious Life-Rituals in Bali* (New York: Vantage Press, 1971), 262.
12. Mershon, "Katherine Philips Edson Remembered," 78.
13. Margaret Mead, *Blackberry Winter: My Earlier Years* (New York: William Morrow, 1972), 231.
14. Beryl De Zoete and Walter Spies, *Dance and Drama in Bali* (London: Faber and Faber, 1938), 2–3.

Chapter 10

1. The verse was originally published in Clune, *Isles of Spice*. p. 317. Clune stated that it was written by Noël Coward, but that does not seem likely. For one thing, Noël Coward did not stay at the Bali Hotel where the poem was supposedly written, but with Walter Spies (see Rhodius, *Schonheit und Reichtum des Lebens*, p. 345). Clune and those who followed him (the poem was reprinted sev-

eral times in various versions) also stated that Coward wrote the verse for Charlie Chaplin. Chaplin, however, was in Bali three years before Coward.

One version of the poem may be found on http://home.att.net/~jaoloma/muci/Coward.htm/.

2. Clune, *Isles of Spice*, 318–320.
3. Theodora Benson, *In the East My Pleasure Lies*, (London: W. Heinemann, 1938), 168–170.
4. Belfrage, *Away from It All*, 228.
5. Gorer, *Bali and Angkor*, 61.

Chapter 11

1. K'tut Tantri, *Revolt in Paradise* (New York: Harper & Brothers, 1960), 15–16.
2. K'tut Tantri, *Revolt in Paradise*, 18–20.
3. Erminia Locatelli Rogers, *Romualdo Locatelli: The Ultimate Voyage of an Italian Artist in the Far East* (Jakarta: Darga Fine Arts, 1993), 48–49; Belfrage, *Away from It All*, 228; Bruce W. Carpenter, *Emilio Ambron: An Italian Artist in Bali* (Singapore: Archipelago Press, 2001), 50.
4. Robert Koke, "Blackout in Bali," *Fortune* 32 (May 1942): 32.
5. Rickover, *Pepper, Rice, and Elephants*, 19.
6. Koke, "Blackout in Bali": 32.
7. Koke, "Blackout in Bali": 32.
8. David Fairchild, *Garden Islands of the Great East* (New York: Scribner, 1943), 146.
9. Koke, "Blackout in Bali": 32, 46.
10. Lindsey, *The Romance of K'tut Tantri and Indonesia*, 44.
11. Lindsey, *The Romance of K'tut Tantri and Indonesia*, 46–47.
12. Lindsey, *The Romance of K'tut Tantri and Indonesia*, 91–92.

Chapter 12

1. Belfrage, *Away from It All*, 227.
2. Joseph Patrick McEvoy, "Just an Old Balinese Custome," *The Saturday Evening Post* 208 (23 November, 1935): 64.

3. Fabricius, *A Dutchman at Large*, 173–174.
4. Belfrage, *Away from It All*, 223–224.
5. Fabricius, *A Dutchman at Large*, 174.
6. Belfrage, *Away from It All*, 226–227.
7. Benson, *In the East My Pleasure Lies*, 166–167.
8. Benson, *In the East My Pleasure Lies*, 192.
9. Benson, *In the East My Pleasure Lies*, 170–171.
10. Gorer, *Bali and Angkor*, 52.
11. Gorer, *Bali and Angkor*, 238–239.
12. Gorer, *Bali and Angkor*, 61, 63.
13. W. Robert Foran, *Malayan Symphony* (London: Hutchinson, 1935), 234–235.
14. Orient Touring Company, *Travel Through the Mystic Isles of Java, Sumatra and Bali*, (G. Kolff, 1925), 14.
15. Lockhart, *Return to Malaya*, 321–323.
16. Bernatzik, *South Seas*, 332.
17. Bernatzik, *South Seas*, 159, 162, 167.
18. Birnbaum, "Balinese Panorama": 119–122, 144.
19. Belfrage, *Away from It All*, 213–214.
20. Rickover, *Pepper, Rice, and Elephants*, 31.
21. Mershon, "Katherine Philips Edson Remembered," 141–142. Katharane Mershon thought that Noël Coward wrote this limerick, but this seems impossible since Coward was in Bali several years before the Neuhaus brothers arrived and built the aquarium.
22. Joe Kirkwood, *Links of Life*, as told to Barbara Fey (Oklahoma City, 1973), 83–85.
23. Rickover, *Pepper, Rice, and Elephants*, 15.
24. Frances Norene Ahl, *Let's Fly* (Boston: Christopher Publishing House, 1940), 152–154.
25. Ahl, *Let's Fly*, 156, 164, 167.
26. Gorer, *Bali and Angkor*, 224.

27. Mead, *Blackberry Winter*, 227–230.
28. Jane Howard, *Margaret Mead, a Life* (New York: Simon and Schuster, 1984), 191.
29. Mershon, "Katherine Philips Edson Remembered," 103–104; Hitchcock, *Bali; The Imaginary Museum*, 63–64.
30. Gordon D. Jensen and Luh Ketut Suryani. *The Balinese People: A Reinvestigation of Character* (Singapore: Oxford University Press, 1992), 47–48; Mead, *Blackberry Winter*, 230–232; Margaret Mead, "Men and Gods of a Bali Village," *The New York Times Magazine*, 16 July 1939, 13.
31. David Lipset, *Gregory Bateson: The Legacy of a Scientist* (Englewood Cliffs, N.J.: Prentice-Hall, 1980), 152.
32. Lipset, *Gregory Bateson*, 152.

Chapter 13

1. Belfrage, *Away from It All*, 224.
2. Acton, *Memoirs of an Aesthete*, 310.
3. Jeannette ten Kate, "Painting in a Garden of Eden: European Artists in Bali During the First Half of the Twentieth Century," In Marie-Odette Scalliet et al., *Pictures from the Tropics: Paintings by Western Artists During the Dutch Colonial Period in Indonesia*, translated by Karn Beks (Wijk en Aalburg: Pictures Publishers, 1999), 129.
4. Jop Ubbens and Cathinka Huizing, *Adrien Jean Le Mayeur de Merpes, 1880-1958: Painter-Traveller/Schilder-Reizinger*, translated by Karin Beks and Gillian Stuart-Lyon (Wijk en Aalburg: Pictures Publishers, 1995), 119–120.
5. Ubbens, *Adrien Jean Le Mayeur de Merpes*, 101–105, 119, 123.
6. Belfrage, *Away from It All*, 224–225.
7. Koke, "Blackout in Bali": 52.
8. Carpenter, *Willem Hofker*, 35.
9. http://news.bbc.co.uk/hi/english/entertainment/arts/newsid_1731000/1731799,stm
10. Locatelli Rogers, *Romualdo Locatelli*, 43.
11. Carpenter, *Emilio Ambron*, 39.
12. Carl Shreve, *Distant Horizons* (London: Herbert Jenkins, 1940), 119–120, 122.
13. George Waller Parker, *The Paintings of George Parker* (New York: The Art Digest, 1940), 10; *New York World Telegram*, 2 July, 1941.
14. *Carl Newland Werntz 1874-1944: Memorial Exhibition* (Chicago: Chicago Academy of Fine Arts, 1945), unpaged.
15. Martha Sawyers and William Reusswig, *India and Southeast Asia* (New York: Grossett & Dunlap, 1964), 127.

Chapter 14

1. McPhee, *A House in Bali*, 91.
2. Belo, *Traditional Balinese Culture*, xi–xii.
3. Hanna, *Bali Profile*, 106–107.
4. Cravath, *Letters Home from the Far East and Russia*, 51–52
5. Henk Schulte Nordholt, "The Making of Traditional Bali: Colonial Ethnography and Bureaucratic Reproduction," In *Colonial Subjects: Essays on the Practical History of Anthropology*, edited by Peter Pels and Oscar Salemink (Ann Arbor: University of Michigan Press, 1999), 272–273; Robinson, *The Dark Side of Paradise*, 55.
6. Lockhart, *Return to Malaya*, 319–320.
7. Robinson, *The Dark Side of Paradise*, 52–53; Bernatzik, *South Seas*, 155.
8. Quoted in Robinson, *The Dark Side of Paradise*, 53.
9. Hiss, *Bali*, 103.

Chapter 15

1. Schulte Nordholt, "The Making of Traditional Bali": 267.
2. Oja, *Colin McPhee*, 143.
3. Oja, *Colin McPhee*, 145.
4. Oja, *Colin McPhee*, 145–146.
5. Rhodius, *Schonheit und Reichtum des Lebens*, 398–406.

Chapter 16

1. Steven Runciman, *A Traveller's Alphabet: Partial Memoirs* (London: Thames and Hudson, 1991), 159.

2. Marjorie Appleton, *East of Singapore* (London: Hurst & Blackett, 1942), 80–82, 90.

3. Ruth Draper, *The Letters of Ruth Draper: 1920–1956, A Self-Portrait of a Great Actress*, edited by Neilla Warren (New York: Scribner, 1979), 198, 200.

4. Fairchild, *Garden Islands of the Great East*, 141–142, 157.

5. Maynard Owen Williams, "Bali and Points East," *National Geographic* 75 (March 1939): 313.

6. Mona Gardner, *The Menacing Sun* (New York: Harcourt, Brace, 1939), 254–255, 103–104.

7. Gardner, *The Menacing Sun*, 103–104.

8. Serge Lifar, *Ma Vie from Kiev to Kiev: An Autobiography*, translated by James Holman Mason (New York: World, 1970), 159; Silvia Baker, *Alone and Loitering: Pages from an Artist's Travel-Diary* (London: P. Davies, 1946), 64–65.

9. Baker, *Alone and Loitering*, 14–16.

10. Baker, *Alone and Loitering*, 34–35.

11. Baker, *Alone and Loitering*, 43–45.

12. Diana Cooper, *Trumpets from the Steep* (London: Century, 1960), 123–124; Lindsey, *The Romance of K'tut Tantri and Indonesia*, 98–100.

13. Mershon, "Katherine Philips Edson Remembered," 86; Koke, "Blackout in Bali": 32.

Bibliography

Acton, Harold. *Memoirs of an Aesthete*. London: Methuen, 1948.
Agung, Ide Anak Agung Gde. *Bali in the 19th Century*. Jakarta: Yayasan Obor Indonesia, 1991.
Agung Rai Gallery of Fine Art. *Selected Paintings from the Collection of the Agung Rai Fine Art Gallery*, edited by Abby C. Ruddick. Peliatan, Ubud, Bali: Agung Rai Fine Art Gallery, 1992.
Ahl, Frances Norene. *Let's Fly*. Boston: Christopher Publishing House, 1940.
Anderson, Benedict. "In Memoriam Claire Holt." *Indonesia* no. 10 (October 1970): 191–193.
Anderson, Isabel. *In Eastern Seas: With a Visit to Insulinde and the Golden Chersonese*. Boston: Bruce Humphries, 1934.
Appleton, Marjorie. *East of Singapore*. London: Hurst & Blackett, 1942.
Baker, Silvia. *Alone and Loitering: Pages from an Artist's Travel-Diary*. London: P. Davies, 1946.
Bakker, Wim. *Bali Verbeeld*. Delft: Volkenkundig Museum Nusantara, 1985.
Bali. Batavia: Officieele Vereeniging voor Toeristenverkeer in Nederlandsche-Indie, 1930.
Bali. Batavia: Travellers' Official Information Bureau for Netherlands India, 1939.
"Bali: The Blessed Isle." *Literary Digest* 114 (3 September 1932): 18.
Baranay, Inez. *The Edge of Bali*. Pymble, NSW, Australia: Angus & Robertson, 1992.
Barnouw, Adriaan Jacob. *A Trip Through the Dutch East Indies*, n.p., 1924.
Barnouw, Erik. "Robert Flaherty (Barnouw's File)." *Film Culture* no. 53/55 (Spring 1972): 161–185.
Baum Vicki. *It Was All Quite Different; The Memoirs of Vicki Baum*. New York: Funk & Wagnalls, 1964.
_____. *A Tale from Bali*, translated by Basil Creighton. Garden City, N.Y.: Doubleday, Doran, 1937.
Beauford, John. "The Other Al Hirschfeld." *The Christian Science Monitor*, 31 August, 1983.
Belfrage, Cedric. *Away from It All; An Escapologist's Notebook*. New York: Simon and Schuster, 1937.
Belo, Jane, ed. *Traditional Balinese Culture; Essays*. New York: Columbia University Press, 1970.
Benson, Stella. "Tourists in Bali." *London Mercury* 31 (January 1935): 261–268.
Benson, Theodora. *In the East My Pleasure Lies*. London: W. Heinemann, 1938.

Bernatzik, Hugo Adolf. *South Seas*, translated by Vivian Ogilvie. New York: Henry Holt, 1935.
Birnbaum, Martin. "Balinese Panorama," In *Vanishing Eden: Wanderings in the Tropics*. New York: William E. Rudge's Sons, 1942, 119–144.
_____. "Sojourn in Bali." *Natural History* 47 (March 1941): 156–169
Boon, James A. "Between-the-Wars Bali: Rereading the Relics." In *Malinowski, Rivers, Benedict, and Others: Essays on Culture and Personality*, edited by George W. Stocking, Jr. Madison: University of Wisconsin Press, 1986: 218–247.
Burden, William Douglas. *Dragon Lizards of Komodo: An Expedition to the Lost World of the Dutch East Indies*. New York: Putnam, 1927.
Burman-Hall, Linda. "The Fahnestock South Sea Expedition: Excursions in Madurese Music." In *Across Madura Strait: The Dynamics of an Insular Society*, edited by Kees van Dijk, Huub de Jonge, and Elly Touwen-Bouwsma. Leiden: KITLV, 1995: 135–156.
Burton, Deena Elise "Sitting at the Feet of Gurus: The Life and Ethnography of Claire Holt." Ph.D. dissertation, New York University 2000.
Butler, Frank Hedges. *Round the World*. New York: F. A. Stokes Co., 1925.
Camegy, Patrick. "The Gauguin of Bali," *Apollo* 94 (July 1971): 60–63.
Candee, Helen Churchill. *New Journeys in Old Asia: Indo-Chin, Siam, Java, Bali*. New York: Frederick A. Stokes, 1927.
Carpenter, Bruce W. *Emilio Ambron: An Italian Artist in Bali*. Singapore: Archipelago Press, 2001
_____. *W. O. J. Nieuwenkamp: First European Artist in Bali*. Singapore: Periplus Editions, 1997.
_____, and Maria Hofker-Reuter. *Willem Hofker 1902–1981: Schilder van Painter of Bali*. Wijk en Aalburg: Pictures Publishers, 1993.
Chaplin, Charlie. "Comedian Sees the World." *Women's Home Companion* 61 (January 1934): 21–23.
_____. *My Autobiography*. New York: Simon and Schuster, 1964.
Childers, James Saxon. *From Siam to Suez*. New York: Appleton, 1932.
Clifton, Violet. *Islands of Queen Wilhelmina*. London: Constable, 1927.
Clune, Frank. *Isles of Spice*. New York: Dutton, 1942.
"Converting Bali: Dutch Colonial Policy Frowns on Missionary Activity." *Literary Digest* 123 (10 April 1937): 30–31.
Cooper, Diana. *Trumpets from the Steep*. London: Century, 1960.
Couperus, Louis. *Eastward*, translated by J. Menzies-Wilson and C. C. Crispin. New York: George H. Doran, 1924.
Couteau, Jean. *Museum Puri Lukistan*. Ubud, Bali: Yayasan Rathna Warta, 1999.
Covarrubias, Miguel. *Island of Bali*. New York: Knopf, 1937.
Craft, Robert. "Bali H'ai." *New York Review of Books* 38 (24 October 1991): 56–60.
Cravath, Paul Drennan. *Letters Home from the Far East and Russia, 1931*. Garden City, N.Y.: The Country Life Press, 1931.
_____. *Letters Home from the South Sea Islands, China and Japan, 1934*. Garden City, N.Y.: The Country Life Press, 1934.
Crocker, Templeton. *The Cruise of the Zaca*. New York: Harper & Brothers, 1933.
Daniel, Oliver. *Stokowski: A Counterpoint of View*. New York: Dodd, Mead, 1982.
Davies-Moore, Dan. "The Girls of Bali." *Inter-Ocean* 9 (September 1928): 485–489.
Davis, Hassoldt. *Islands Under the Wind*. London: Longmans, Green, 1933.

_____. *World Without a Roof: An Autobiography*. New York: Duell, Sloan and Pearce, 1957.
Decoteau, Pamela Hibbs. "Malvina Hoffman and the Races of Man." *Woman's Art Journal* 10 (Fall/Winter 1989-1990): 7-12.
Defries, Amelia Dorothy. "Maurice Sterne at Bali." *International Studio* 61, no. 2 (April 1917): liii-lvi.
Delbruck, Elisabet. "Bali Through an Artist's Eyes." *Inter-Ocean* 8 (July 1927): 414-415.
De Leeuw, Adele. *Island Adventure, a Novel for Girls*. New York: Macmillan, 1934.
De Leeuw, Hendrik. *Crossroads of the Java Sea*. New York: Jonathan Cape, 1931.
Denis, Armand. *On Safari; The Story of My Life*. New York: Dutton, 1963.
Denis, Renée Roosevelt. *To Live in Paradise*. Fort Bragg, Calif.: Lost Coast Press, 1996.
De Zoete, Beryl and Walter Spies. *Dance and Drama in Bali*. London: Faber and Faber, 1938.
Dominik, Janet. "Artist, William Ritschel, N.A." *Art of California* 1 (February-March 1989): 21-27.
Draper, Ruth. *The Letters of Ruth Draper: 1920-1956, A Self-Portrait of a Great Actress*. Edited by Neilla Warren. New York: Scribner, 1979.
Dreesen, Walter, and Fritz Lindner. *Hundert Tag auf Bali, Beschrieben und Gezeichnet*. Hamburg: Broschek, 1937.
Duke, Pony, and Jason Thomas. *Too Rich: The Family Secrets of Doris Duke*. New York: HarperCollins, 1996.
Faber, G. H. von. *The Land of a Thousand Temples: Bali, a Guide and Souvenir*. Translated by Leonard Arndt. Sourabaya: H. van Ingen, 1932.
Fabrès, Oscar. *Aux Indes Néerlandaises*. Amsterdam: P. N. van Kampen & Zoon, 1934.
Fabricius, Johan. *A Dutchman at Large: Memoirs*. Translated by Roy Edwards. London: Heinemann. 1952.
Fairchild, David. *Garden Islands of the Great East*. New York: Scribner, 1943.
Ferrand, Gabrielle. "In a Hindu Paradise: A Rhapsody about the Isle of Bali." *The Trans-Pacific* 13 (22 May, 1926): 6.
Fleischmann, Julius. *Footsteps in the Sea*. New York: Putnam, 1935.
Foran, W. Robert. *Malayan Symphony*. London: Hutchinson ., 1935.
"Foreign Artists in Bali 1904-1967." http://baliwww.com/bali/arts/foreign.htm
Gardner, Mona. *The Menacing Sun*. New York: Harcourt, Brace, 1939.
Geertz, Hildred. *Images of Power: Balinese Paintings Made for Gregory Bateson and Margaret Mead*. Honolulu: University of Hawaii Press, 1994.
Gorer, Geoffrey. *Bali and Angkor, or Looking at Life and Death*. London: Michael Joseph, 1936.
Goris, Roelof. *The Island Bali; Its Religion and Ceremonies*. Batavia: Royal Packet Navigation Co., 1931.
Gouda, Frances. *Dutch Culture Overseas: Colonial Practice in the Netherlands Indies, 1900-1942*. Amsterdam: Amsterdam University Press, 1995
Grant, Stephen, ed. *Former Points of View: Postcards & Literary Passages from Pre-Independence Indonesia*. Jakarta, Indonesia: Lontar, 1995.
Guthrie, Debbie, et al., eds. *Bali*. Revised ed. New York: Alfred Knopf, 2001.
Haks, Leo, and Guus Maris. *Haks & Maris Lexicon of Foreign Artists Who Visualized Indonesia (1600-1950): Surveying Painters, Watercolourists, Draughtsmen, Sculptors,*

Illustrators, Graphic and Industrial Artists. Utrecht, Netherlands: Gert Jan Bestebreurtje, 1995.
Halliburton, Richard. *The Royal Road to Romance.* Indianapolis: Bobbs-Merrill, 1925.
Hamel, Didier, ed. *Emil Rizek, 1901-1988: An Austrian Artist in Indonesia.* Jakarta: Duta Fine Arts Foundation, 1996.
Hanna, Willard A. *Bali Profile: People, Events, Circumstances (1001-1976).* New York: American Universities Field Staff, 1976.
Hanson, Patricia King and Alan Gevinson., eds. *American Film Institute Catalog of Motion Pictures Produced in the United States: Feature Films 1931-1940.* Berkeley: University of California Press, 1993.
Hart, Moss. "My Trip Around the World." Moss Hart and Kitty Carlisle Papers, 1922-1962. State Historical Society of Wisconsin Archives, Madison, Wisconsin.
Hering, Oswald. *Down the World; Random Tales of a Traveler.* New York: Robert M. McBride, 1932.
Heymann, C. David. *Poor Little Rich Girl: The Life and Legend of Barbara Hutton.* New York: Random House, 1983.
Hirschfeld, Al. *Hirschfeld.* New York: Dodd. Mead, 1979.
_____. *Hirschfeld: Art and Recollections from Eight Decades.* New York: Scribner, 1991.
_____. *Hirschfeld On Line.* New York: Applause, 1998.
_____. *Hirschfeld's World.* New York: Harry N. Abrams, 1981.
Hiss, Philip Hanson. *Bali.* New York: Duell, Sloan and Pearce, 1941.
Hitchcock, Michael, and Lucy Norris. *Bali, the Imaginary Museum: The Photographs of Walter Spies and Beryl de Zoete.* Kuala Lumpur; New York Oxford University Press, 1995.
Hoffman, Malvina. *Heads and Tales.* New York: Scribner, 1936.
Holleman, Frida. *Frida Holleman: Memories of Indonesia, 1937-1945.* Amsterdam: Haks & Maris, 1992.
Hoppe, Emil Otto. "Bali: An Artist's Pardise." *London Studio* 4 (December 1932): 344-347.
_____. *Round the World with a Camera.* London: Hutchinson, 1934.
Howard, Jane. *Margaret Mead, a Life.* New York: Simon and Schuster, 1984.
Huss, Dolores M. *The Henry Eichheim Collection of Oriental Instruments: A Western Musician Discovers a New World of Sound.* Santa Barbara: University Art Museum, 1984.
Illustrated Tourist Guide to East Java, Bali and Lombok. Batavia: Weltevreden Official Tourist Bureau, 1914.
Jacknis, Ira. "Margaret Mead and Gregory Bateson in Bali: Their Use of Photography and Film." *Cultural Anthropology* 3 (May 1988): 160-177.
James, Jamie. "Ubud, the Heart of Bali." *The Atlantic Monthly* 284 (August 1999): 26-30.
Japan Department of Railways. *An Official Guide to Eastern Asia: Transcontinental Connections between Europe and Asia. Vol. V: East Indies, including Philippine Islands, French Indo-China, Siam, Malay Peninsula, and Dutch East Indies.* Tokyo: Imperial Government Railways of Japan, 1917.
Jensen, Gordon D., and Luh Ketut Suryani. *The Balinese People: A Reinvestigation of Character.* Singapore: Oxford University Press, 1992.
Kam, Garrett. *Perceptions of Paradise: Images of Bali in the Arts.* Ubud: Yayasan Dharma Seni Museum Neka, 1993.

Kanfer, Stefan. "The World According to Al." *Connoisseur* 216 (July 1986): 70–75.
Kate, Jeannette ten, "Painting in a Garden of Eden: European Artists in Bali During the First Half of the Twentieth Century." In Marie-Odette Scalliet, et al., *Pictures from the Tropics: Paintings by Western Artists During the Dutch Colonial Period in Indonesia*, translated by Karin Beks. Wijk en Aalburg: Pictures Publishers, 1999: 129–140.
Kempers, A. J. Bernet. *Monumental Bali: Introduction to Balinese Archaeology & Guide to the Monuments*. Berkeley, Calif.: Periplus Editions, 1991.
Kilmer, Joyce. "Interview with Maurice Sterne." *The New York Times*, (21 March 1915).
Kirkwood, Joe. *Links of Life*. As told to Barbara Fey. Oklahoma City, 1973.
Kirtland, Lucian Swift. *Finding the Worth While in the Orient*. New York: Robert M. McBride, 1926.
Knott, Franklin Price. "Artist Adventures on the Island of Bali." *National Geographic* 53 (March 1928): 326–347.
Koke, Louise G. *Our Hotel in Bali: How Two Young Americans Made a Dream Come True: A Story of the 1930s*. Wellington, N.Z.: January Books, 1987.
Koke, Robert. "Blackout in Bali." *Fortune* 32 (May 1942): 32, 46, 48.
Krause, Gregor. *Bali 1912*. Translated by W. H. Mabbett. Wellington, N.Z.: January Books, 1988.
———, and Karl With. *Bali: People and Art*. Translated by Walter E. J. Tips. Bangkok, Thailand: White Lotus Press, 2000.
Lapsley, Hilary. *Margaret Mead and Ruth Benedict: The Kinship of Women*. Amherst: University of Massachusetts Press, 1999.
Leake, Grace. "Lucille Sinclair Douglass, Artist-Archaeologist." *Holland's: The Magazine of the South* (August 1933): 7, 23.
Lesley, Cole. *The Life of Noel Coward*. London: Jonathan Cape, 1976.
Lifar, Serge. *Ma Vie from Kiev to Kiev: An Autobiography*. Translated by James Holman Mason. New York: World, 1970.
Lindsey, Timothy. *The Romance of K'tut Tantri and Indonesia: Text and Scripts, History and Identity*. Kuala Lumpur; New York: Oxford University Press, 1997.
Lipset, David. *Gregory Bateson: The Legacy of a Scientist*. Englewood Cliffs, N.J.: Prentice-Hall, 1980.
Locatelli Rogers, Erminia. *Romualdo Locatelli: The Ultimate Voyage of an Italian Artist in the Far East*. Jakarta: Darga Fine Arts, 1993.
Lockhart, R. H. Bruce. *Return to Malaya*. New York: Putnam, 1936.
Lovoos, Janice. "Roland Strasser: Painter of the Far East." *American Artist* 24 (November 1960); 30–35, 68–70.
Mabbett, Hugh. *The Balinese*. Wellington, N. Z.: January Books, 1985.
———. *In Praise of Kuta: From Slave Port to Fishing Village to the Most Popular Resort in Bali* Wellington, N.Z.: January Books, 1987.
McBrien, William. *Cole Porter: A Biography*. New York: Alfred A. Knopf, 1998.
McEvoy, Joseph Patrick. "Just an Old Balinese Costume." *The Saturday Evening Post* 208 (23 November, 1935): 12–13, 64, 68
McPhee, Colin. *A House in Bali*. New York: John Day, 1946.
McWilliams, Tennant S. "James Saxon Childers and Southern Liberalism in the 1930s," In James Saxon Childers, *A Novel about a White Man and a Black Man in the Deep South*. Tuscaloosa: University of Alabama Press, 1988: ix–xxiii.

Mead, Margaret. *Blackberry Winter: My Earlier Years.* New York: William Morrow 1972.
―――. *Letters from the Field 1925-1975.* New York: Harper & Row, 1977.
―――. "Men and Gods of a Bali Village." *The New York Times Magazine,* 16 July 1939: 12-13, 23.
Mershon, Katharane Edson. *Seven Plus Seven: Mysterious Life-Rituals in Bali.* New York: Vantage Press, 1971.
―――, and Charles F. Edson, "Katherine Philips Edson Remembered: Oral History." Oral History Program, University of California, Los Angeles.
Morand, Paul. "Bali, or Paradise Regained." *Vanity Fair* 38 (May 1932): 40-41, 68.
Mordaunt, Elinor. *The Further Venture Book.* New York: Century Co., 1927.
Morris, Joe Alex. *Nelson Rockefeller: A Biography.* New York: Harper, 1960.
Nieuwenkamp, W.O. J. "Bali, the Tropical Wonderland." *Studio* 94 (September 1927): 182-188; 95 (January 1928): 33-38; 95 (April 1928): 246-251.
Nochlin, Linda. "Malvina Hoffman: A Life in Sculpture." *Arts Magazine* 59 (November 1984): 106-110
Norden, Hermann. *Byways of the Tropic Seas, Wanderings Among the Solomons and in the Malay Archipelago.* Philadelphia: Macrae Smith, 1926.
―――. "Unspoiled Bali." *Asia* 26 (December 1926); 1100-1104, 1137-1140.
Oenslager, Donald. *The Theatre of Donald Oenslager.* Middletown, Conn.: Wesleyan University Press, 1978.
―――. "War or No War, Bali Dances On." *The New York Times Magazine,* 20 October, 1940.
Oja, Carol J. *Colin McPhee, Composer in Two Worlds.* Washington: Smithsonian Institution Press, 1990.
Orient Touring Company. *Travel Through the Mystic Isles of Java, Sumatra and Bali.* n.p.: G. Kolff, 1925.
Page, Ruth. *Page by Page.* edited by Andrew Mark Wentink. Brooklyn, N.Y.: Dance Horizons, 1978.
Parker, George, *The Paintings of George Parker.* New York: The Art Digest, 1940.
Peters, Harold. "The Pilgrim Sails the Seven Seas." *National Geographic* 72 (August 1937): 223-262.
Picard, Michel. *Bali: Cultural Tourism and Touristic Culture.* Singapore: Archipelago, 1996.
―――. "Cultural Tourism' in Bali: Cultural Performance as Tourist Attraction," *Indonesia* 49 (April 1990): 37-74.
Pijbes, Wim. "W. O. J. Nieuwenkamp: First European Artist on Bali." *Arts of Asia* 28 (January-February 1998): 128-135.
Pollman, Tessel. "Margaret Mead's Balinese: The Fitting Symbols of the American Dream." *Indonesia* 49 (April 1990): 1-35.
Ponder, H. W. "By Ferry to Bali." *Blackwood's Magazine* 237 (April 1935): 551-558.
―――. *In Javanese Waters; Some Sidelights on a few of the Countless Lovely, Little Known Islands Scattered Over the Bands Sea & Some Glimpses of Their Strange & Stormy History.* London: Seeley, Service, 1944.
Poortenaar, Jan. *An Artist in Java and Other Islands of Indonesia,* translated by Horace Shipp. Singapore: Oxford University Press, 1989.
Powell, E. Alexander. *Where the Strange Trails Go Down.* New York: Scribner, 1921.
Powell, Hickman. *Bali: The Last Paradise.* London: Jonathan Cape, 1930.
Reitsma, S. A. "Bali, the Blessed Isle." *Inter-Ocean* 10 (June 1929): 237-242.

_____. "Sunlight and Shadows in Bali." *Inter-Ocean* 8 (July 1927): 384–391.

_____. *Van Stockum's Travellers' Handbook for the Dutch East Indies.* The Hague: W. P. Van Stockum & Son, 1930.

Rhodius, Hans, ed. *Schonheit und Reichtum des Lebens: Walter Spies, Maler und Musiker auf Bali, 1895–1942, eine Autobiographie in Briefen.* The Hague: L. J. C. Boucher, 1964.

_____, and John Darling. *Walter Spies and Balinese Art.* Zutphen: Terra, 1980.

Rickover, Ruth Masters. *Pepper, Rice, and Elephants: A Southeast Asian Journey from Celebes to Siam.* Annapolis, Md.: Naval Institute Press, 1975.

Robinson, Geoffrey. *The Dark Side of Paradise: Political Violence in Bali.* Ithaca, N.Y.: Cornell University Press, 1995

Robertson, Steve. *Lili Kraus: Hungarian Pianist, Texas Teacher, and Personality Extraordinaire.* Fort Worth, Tex.: TCU Press, 2000.

Roever-Bonnet, H. de. *Rudolf Bonnet: Een Zondagskind: Zijn Leven en Zijn Werk.* Wijk en Aalburg, Netherlands: Pictures Publishers, 1993.

Rofe, Husein. "Bali and the Foreigners." *Eastern Horizon* 20, no. 1 (1981): 15–18.

Rubinstein, Rachelle and Linda H. Connor, eds. *Staying Local in the Global Village: Bali in the Twentieth Century.* Honolulu: University of Hawaii Press, 1999.

Runciman, Steven. *A Traveller's Alphabet: Partial Memoirs.* London: Thames and Hudson, 1991.

Rusman, E. *Wings Across Continents (The K.L.M. Amsterdam-Batavia Line).* Amsterdam: Andries Blitz, 1935.

Salpeter, Harry. "Sterne, The Maestro in Art." *Esquire* 15 (February 1941): 78–79, 123–124.

Savarese, Nicola. "Antonin Artaud Sees Balinese Theatre at the Paris Colonial Exposition." *TDR: The Drama Review* 45 (Fall 2001): 51–77.

Sawyers, Martha, and William Reusswig. *India and Southeast Asia.* New York: Grosset & Dunlap, 1964.

Schulte Nordholt, Henk. "The Making of Traditional Bali: Colonial Ethnography and Bureaucratic Reproduction." In *Colonial Subjects: Essays on the Practical History of Anthropology,* edited by Peter Pels and Oscar Salemink. Ann Arbor: University of Michigan Press, 1999: 241–281.

Schwartz, David M. "On the Royal Road to Adventures with 'Daring Dick'." *Smithsonian* 19 (March 1989): 159–178.

Seton, Grace Gallatin. *Poison Arrows: A Strange Journey with an Opium Dreamer Through Annam, Cambodia, Siam, and the Lotus Island of Bali.* London: J. Gifford, 1938.

Shreve, Carl. *Distant Horizons.* London: Herbert Jenkins, 1940.

_____. *Romance Calling: Java, Bali, Sumatra, Nias, Siam, Indo-China.* Australia: J. Sands, 1939.

Sowell, John. "Walter Spies: The Artist as Photographer." In *Toward Independence: A Century of Indonesia Photographed,* edited by Jane Levy Reed. San Francisco: Friends of Photography, 1991: 97–99.

Sowerby, Arthur de C. "Touring Netherlands India". *The China Journal* 13 (October 1930): 193–206.

Spruit, Ruud. *Artists on Bali.* Amsterdam: The Pepin Press, 1997.

_____. *Indonesische Impressies: Oosterse Thema's in de Westerse Schilderkunst/Indonesian Impressions: Oriental Themes in Western Painting.* Wijk en Aalburg: Picture Publishers, 1992.

Starr, Donald C. *The Schooner Pilgrim's Progress: A Voyage Around the World 1932-1934*. Salem, Mass.: Peabody Essex Museum, 1996.
Stephenson, Nina Kay. "Becoming Bali: Photography and the Fabrication of an Island Paradise." M.A. thesis, University of New Mexico, Albuquerque, 1998.
Sterne, Maurice. *Maurice Sterne Drawings*. Edited by Martin S. Ackerman and Diane L. Ackerman. New York: Arco, 1974.
_____. *Maurice Sterne: Retrospective Exhibition 1902-1932: Paintings, Sculpture, Drawings*. New York: The Museum of Modem Art, 1933.
_____. *Shadow and Light: The Life, Friends and Opinions of Maurice Sterne*, edited by Charlotte Leon Mayerson. New York: Harcourt, Brace & World, 1965.
Stowitts, Hubert. "Letters." Stowitts Museum and Library, Pacific Grove, California.
Stuart-Fox, David J. *Bibliography of Bali: Publications from 1920 to 1990*. Leiden: KITLV Press, 1992.
Sukawati, Tjokorda Gde Agung. *Reminiscences of a Balinese Prince*. Dictated to Rosemary Hilbery. Honolulu: Southeast Asian Studies, University of Hawaii, 1979.
Sullivan, Gerald. *Margaret Mead, Gregory Bateson, and Highland Bali: Fieldwork Photographs of Bayung Gede. 1936-1939*. Chicago: University of Chicago Press, 1999.
Sumatra, Java, Bali: Tours by Rotterdam Lloyd Royal Mail Line. Rotterdam: Rotterdamsche Lloyd, 1932.
Tantri, K'tut. *Revolt in Paradise*. New York: Harper & Brothers, 1960.
Telling, Elisabeth. "Papers, 1902-1965." Sophia Smith Collection, Smith College, Northampton, Mass.
Tenzer, Michael. *Balinese Music*. Berkeley, Calif.: Periplus Editions, 1991.
Tomlinson, Henry Major. *Tidemarks: Some Records of a Journey to the Beaches of the Moluccas and the Forest of Malaya in 1923*. London: Cassell, 1924.
Tropical Holland, the Archipelago of Eternal Summer: Information for Travellers to the Dutch East Indies. Amsterdam: Koninklijke Paketvaart Maatschappij, 1927.
Ubbens, Jop, and Cathinka Huizing. *Adrien Jean Le Mayeur de Merpes, 1880-1958: Painter-Traveller/Schilder-Reizinger*. Translated by Karin Beks and Gillian Stuart-Lyon. Wijk en Aalburg: Pictures Publishers, 1995.
"Uncensored Joys of Happy Balinese." *Literary Digest* 122 (25 July, 1936): 20.
Ury, Miriam. "Some Notes Towards a Life of Beryl de Zoete." *Journal of the Rutgers University Libraries* 48 (1986): 1-54.
Van Dyke, John Charles. *The Autobiography of John C. Van Dyke: A Personal Narrative of American Life 1861-1931*. Edited by Peter Wild. Salt Lake City: University of Utah Press, 1993.
_____. *In Java and the Neighboring Islands of the Dutch East Indies*. New York: Scribner, 1929.
Vickers, Adrian. *Bali: A Paradise Created*. Berkeley: Periplus Editions, 1989.
_____, ed. *Being Modern in Bali: Image and Change*. New Haven: Yale University Southeast Asia Studies, 1996.
_____. "Thilly Weissenborn: The Romance of the Indies." In *Toward Independence: A Century of Indonesia Photographed*, edited by Jane Levy Reed. San Francisco: Friends of Photography, 1991, 79-81.
Villiers, Alan John. *Cruise of the Conrad*. London: Hodder & Stoughton, 1940.
_____. "Salt in My Eyes—and a Look at Bali." *Scribner's Magazine* 8 (December 1935): 321-325.

Wadia, Ardaser Sorabjee N. *The Belle of Bali*. London: J. M. Dent and Sons, 1936.
Waley, Alison. *A Half of Two Lives*. London: Weidenfeld and Nicolson, 1982.
Warren, Dorothy. *The World of Ruth Draper: A Portrait of an Actress*. Carbondale: Southern Illinois University Press, 1999.
Watson, Ernest W. "Martha Sawyers, Illustrator of Oriental Lore." *American Artist* 8 (April 1944): 22–23, 30.
Webb, Norton. "Charles Sayres—Painter of the Dutch East Indies." *Apollo* 16 (May 1932): 31–33.
Wenk, Klaus, and Theo Meier. *Theo Meier: Bilder aus den Tropen/Pictures from the Tropics*. Dietikon-Zurich: Stocker-Schmid, 1980.
Werntz, Carl Newland. *Carl Newland Werntz 1874–1944: Memorial Exhibition*. Chicago: Chicago Academy of Fine Arts, 1945.
Wiener, Margaret J. *Visible and Invisible Realms: Power, Magic, and Colonial Conquest in Bali*. Chicago: University of Chicago Press, 1995.
Wild, Peter. "Curmudgeon or Campus Ornament? Focusing the Images of John C. Van Dyke, Librarian and Professor." *New Jersey History* 108 (1990): 31–34.
Williams, Maynard Owen. "Bali and Points East." *National Geographic* 75 (March 1939): 313–344.
Yates, Helen Eva. *Bali: Enchanted Isle; A Travel Book*. Boston; New York: Houghton Mifflin, 1933.
Zobel, Myron. "The Enchanted Camera." *Inter-Ocean* 8 (February 1927): 77–79.
_____. "Feathered Gladiators of Bali." *Travel* 49 (May 1927): 23–24.
_____. "Fires of the Dead." *Inter-Ocean* 7 (December 1926): 705–710, 714.
_____. "Life in a Pasanggrahan." *Inter-Ocean* 8 (January 1927): 15–19.
_____. "The National Sport of Bali." *Inter-Ocean* 8 (March 1927): 156–157.
_____. "Trampled Alters." *Inter-Ocean* 7 (October 1926): 630–636.

Index

Acton, Harold 90, 165
Ahl, Frances Norene 159–160
Ambron, Emilio 138, 170
Anak Agung Ngurah 137
Anderson, Isabel and Larz 92–93
Appleton, Marjori 184
Archbold, Anne 185
Archipenko, Angelica Schmitz 68
art in the image of Bali 81, 98–99, 110

Baker, Silvia 188–189
Bali: Enchanted Isle (book) 71–72
Bali Hotel 50–51, 53, 97
Bali Museum 182
Barnouw, Adriaan Jacob 58
Bateson, Gregory 160–164, 176, 182
Baum, Vick 8, 20, 105, 152–153
Beatty, Lord and Lady 90
Belfrage, Cedric 22, 55, 128, 148–150, 157–158
Belo, Jane 79, 101, 121–125, 129, 161, 80–182
Benson, Theodora 77–78, 133–134, 150–151
Bernatzik, Hugo Adolf 56, 110, 124, 155–156
Birnbaum, Martin 75, 77, 99, 156–157
Bonnet, Rudolf 80–81
Burden, William Douglas 61
Butler, Frank Hedges 29

Caldwell, George Walter 133
Candee, Helen Churchill 62
Chaplin, Charlie 114–118
Chaplin, Sydney 115, 118
Childers, James Saxon 93–94

Clemenceau, Georges 29
Clifton, Talbot 30–31
Clifton, Violet 29–30
Clune, Frank 31, 132–133
Cokorda Gde Raka Sukawati 138
Colbert, Claudette 108
Colonial Exposition in Paris 1931, 85, 101, 103
colonial rule 174–176
Corrigan, Laura May 89
Couperus, Louis 32–33, 35
Covarrubias, Miguel 11, 20, 56, 77–78, 99, 108–114, 177
Covarrubias, Rosa 78, 108, 110–113
Coward, Noel 92
Cravath, Paul Drennan 84, 176
Crocker, Templeton 32, 86–87, 99

dance in the image of Bali 97, 99–100, 155
dancing girls in the image of Bali 25–26, 28
Davis, Hassoldt 59–60
Delamere, Lady Mary 90
Delbruck, Elisabet 67–68
De Leeuw, Adele 59
De Leeuw, Hendrick 59
Denis, Armand 41–44
De Zoete, Beryl *see* Zoete, Beryl de
Dickason, Deane H. 104–105
Dodge, Geoffrey 86
Dooijewaard, Willem 29–30, 169
Douglass, Lucille Sinclair 61–62
Draper, Ruth 184–185
Dreesen, Walter 79
Duke, Doris 88–89
Dunbar, Bill 140

economy of Bali 176–178
Eichheim, Henry 68
Eyres-Monsell, Sir Bolton Meredith 90

Faber, G. H. von 85, 109–110
Fabrès, Oscar 30, 33, 68, 88
Fabricius, Johan 147–149
Fairchild, David 185–186
Fairchild, Marian 143
Falaise de la Coudraye, Marquis Henri de la 106, 134
Ferrand, Gabrielle 29
Flaherty, Robert 58–59
Fleischmann, Arthur 169
Fleischmann, Julius 85–86
Foran, W. Robert 153–154
Ford, John 108–109
Foster, Norman 108
Fuller, Horace W. 86

Gardner, Mona 186–187
Garrett, Louise see Koke, Louise Garrett
Goona-Goona (film) 41–43, 79, 102, 104–105
Gordon, Hilda May 29
Gorer, Geoffrey 57, 151–152, 160
Goris, Roelof 56, 109, 180

Haliburton, Richard 57–58
Hanna, Willard 176
Hart, Moss 91–92
Hering Oswald 31–32, 64–65, 67
Hirschfeld, Al 113–116
Hiss, Philip Hanson 99, 178–179, 187
Hoffman, Malvina 67
Hofker, Maria 168–169
Hofker, Willem 168–169
Holt, Claire 119–12, 168
homosexuality in images of Bali 55–56
House in Bali (book) 120
Huntington, Grace Goodhue 106
Hutton, Barbara 87–88

I Mario 142
Island of Bali (book),11 20, 113
Island of the Demons (film) 79, 81, 102–104
Isle of Paradise (film) 104

Kennerly, Jean 87–88
Kennerly, Morley 87

King, Alexander 63, 71, 96
Kirkwood, Joe 158
Kirtland, Lucian Swift 46–48
Kleen, Froken Tyra de 29
KNILM 51, 159
Knott, Franklin Price 62, 64
Koke, Louise Garrett 74, 138–140, 191
Koke, Robert 24, 138–140, 142, 191
Koninklije Nederlandsh-Indische Luchtvaart see KNILM
Koninklijk Pakestvaart Maatschappij see KPM
Korn, Victor Emanuel 178
KPM 11, 24–25, 27, 31, 35, 40, 49–51, 94–95, 97, 99, 150–151, 168
Kraus, Lili 190191
Krause, Gregor 18–21, 57
The Kriss see Goona-Goona
K'tut Tantri see Tantri, K'tut
Kuta Beach Hotel 139–142, 144, 160

La Rochefoucauld, Vicomte de 89
Last Paradise (book) 71
Lattimore, Mrs. 149–150
Le Mayeur de Merpes, Adrien Jea 166–168
Lerner, Michael 185
Lifar, Serge 187–188
Lindner, Fritz 79, 153
Locatelli, Romualdo 170
Lockhart, Robert Hamilton Bruce 99–100, 154–155, 177

Manx, Mrs. see Tantri, K'tut
Manx's Place 143–145
Maugham, Somerset 29
McEvoy, Joseph Patrick 146–147
McPhee, Colin 54–55, 68, 101–102, 120–126, 175
Mead, Margaret 57, 74, 78, 83–84, 120, 130, 160–164, 180, 182
Meier, Theo 169
Mershon, Jack 127
Mershon, Katharane Edson 127–129, 158, 182, 191
Minas, Jacob 35–36
Mogilevsky, Alexander 68
Moojen, Pieter Adriaan Jacobus 30
Morand, Paul 84–85
Mordaunt, Elinor 35, 37
Mountbatten, Lord and Lady Edwina 90

Murda 128, 162
Murnau, Frederick Wilhelm 58–59, 73–74
Music, Balinese
Mystkowski, Czeslaw 169

Netherlands East Indies Government 7–9, 11–12
Neuhaus, Hans and Rolf 158
Ni Pollok 167
Nicolson, Harold 90
Nieuwenkamp, Wijnand Otto Jan 16–18
No Return from Bali (book) 149
Norden, Hermann 60–61

Oenslager, Donald 190
Official Tourist Bureau 21, 26–27, 31, 49–50
opium 11–12

Page, Ruth 69
Parker, George Walker 171–172
Patimah, Mah 35, 37–38
Peters Harold 86
"Pig Express" 27
Pita Maha 182
Plessen, Baron Victor von 79, 81–82
Plunkett, Lord and Lady 90
Pond, Dana 68
Poortenaar, Jan 33–34
Poputan 5–7
Porter, Cole 91–92
Pos, Mary 83
Powell, E. Alexander 32, 45–46, 56–57
Powell, Hickman 57, 69–71

Quidrot, Willy 169

Ravensdale, Lady 90
Rickover, Hyman 158
Rickover, Ruth Masters 11, 140, 158–159
Ritschel, William Frederick 29
Rizek, Emil 68
Roosevelt, André 35–36, 38–41, 44, 58, 64, 71, 79, 98–99
Roosevelt, Leila 41
Rotterdam Lloyd's Royal Mail 108
Rouffaer, Gerrit Pieter 8
Royal Netherlands Indies Airways *see* KNILM
Royal Packet Navigation Company *see* KPM
Runciman, Steven 183–184

Sampih 125
Satrya Hotel 51–52
Sawyers, Martha 172
Sayers, Charles 169
Seton, Grace Gallatin 58
sexuality in the image of Bali 55–57
Shreve, Carl 170–171
Sonnega, Auke 169
Spies, Walter 20, 56, 73–82, 88–91, 117, 128, 130, 180, 182
Starr, Donald C. 86
Sten, John 29
Sterne, Maurice 14–16, 156
Stokowski, Leopold 68, 78
Stowitts, Hubert 67,
Strasser, Roland 29–30, 169
Stutterheim, Willem 91, 99, 168
Sukawati, Princess Gilberte 138
Sutherland, Duke and Duchess 90

Tagore, Rabindranath 29
Tales from Bali (book) 8, 153
Talleyrand de Perigord, Marquis 89
Tantri, K'tut 135–140, 142–145, 191
Telling, Elisabeth 68
Tenney, Virgil 144
Tredegar, Viscount Evan Frederic Morgan 90
Trego, Charles Tillyer 104

Vanderbilt, William K. 105
Van der Noordaa, Louis Simon Willem 169
Van Dyke, John Charles 68–69
Villiers, Alan John 94–95, 97–98
Virgins of Bali (film) 104–105

Walker, Muriel Stuart *see* Tantri, K'tut
Waterman, Betty 148
Weissenborn, Thilly 25
Weldon, Sir Anthony 145
Wells, Herbert George 29
Werntz, Carl Newland 172
Wessen, Marianne van 182
Williams, Maynard Owen 186
Wooley, Monty 91

Yates, Helen Eva 35, 71–72

Zobel, Myron 27, 31
Zoete, Beryl de 101, 129–131, 161

www.ingramcontent.com/pod-product-compliance
Lightning Source LLC
Chambersburg PA
CBHW032055300426
44116CB00007B/744